OXFORD READINGS IN PHILOSOPHY

LEIBNIZ:
METAPHYSICS AND PHILOSOPHY OF SCIENCE

Also published in this series

The Philosophy of Law, edited by Ronald M. Dworkin
Moral Concepts, edited by Joel Feinberg
Theories of Ethics, edited by Philippa Foot
The Philosophy of History, edited by Patrick Gardiner
Knowledge and Belief, edited by A. Phillips Griffiths
Philosophy and Economic Theory, edited by Frank Hahn and Martin Hollis
Divine Commands and Morality, edited by Paul Helm
Reference and Modality, edited by Leonard Linsky
The Philosophy of Religion, edited by Basil Mitchell
The Philosophy of Science, edited by P. H. Nidditch
Aesthetics, edited by Harold Osborne
The Theory of Meaning, edited by G. H. R. Parkinson
The Philosophy of Education, edited by R. S. Peters
Political Philosophy, edited by Anthony Quinton
Practical Reasoning, edited by Joseph Raz
The Philosophy of Social Explanation, edited by Alan Ryan
The Philosophy of Language, edited by J. R. Searle
Semantic Syntax, edited by Pieter A. M. Seuren
Causation and Conditionals, edited by Ernest Sosa
Philosophical Logic, edited by P. F. Strawson
The Justification of Induction, edited by Richard Swinburne
Locke on Human Understanding, edited by I. C. Tipton
The Philosophy of Perception, edited by G. J. Warnock
The Philosophy of Action, edited by Alan R. White

Other volumes are in preparation

LEIBNIZ: METAPHYSICS AND PHILOSOPHY OF SCIENCE

EDITED BY
R. S. WOOLHOUSE

OXFORD UNIVERSITY PRESS
1981

Oxford University Press, Walton Street, Oxford OX2 6DP

London Glasgow New York Toronto
Delhi Bombay Calcutta Madras Karachi
Kuala Lumpur Singapore Hong Kong Tokyo
Nairobi Dar es Salaam Cape Town
Melbourne Auckland

and associate companies in
Beirut Berlin Ibadan Mexico City

Published in the United States by
Oxford University Press, New York

British Library Cataloguing in Publication Data

Leibniz: metaphysics and philosophy of science–
(Oxford readings in philosophy)
1. Leibniz, Gottfried Wilhelm von–
Criticism and interpretation
I. Woolhouse, R. S.

ISBN 0-19-875050-1

Set in IBM Press Roman by
Graphic Services, Oxford, England.
Printed in the United States of America

CONTENTS

ABBREVIATIONS

For convenience all references employ the abbreviations of the list below. Thus '*Rescher* 71' refers to page 71 of Nicholas Rescher's *The Philosophy of Leibniz*, and 'GP iv.504: L 809/498' refers to page 504 of vol. iv of C. I. Gerhardt's edition of Leibniz's philosophical writings and to the English translations at page 809/498 of the first/second edition of L. E. Loemker's *Leibniz: Philosophical Papers and Letters.* So far as is possible there are references both to original texts and to English translations. Usually these last are now to the very useful and easily available Loemker's *Leibniz: Philosophical Papers* [L] and G. H. R. Parkinson's and Mary Morris's *Leibniz: Philosophical Writings* [PM]; but this has meant that translations sometimes come from sources different from those initially used. If a translation differs from that of the first English source cited then it is (at least partly) the author's own.

A	*Leibniz-Clarke Correspondence*, ed. H. G. Alexander (Manchester, 1956).
AT	*Oeuvres de Descartes*, ed. C. Adam and P. Tannery (Paris, 1897–1910).
B	*G. W. Leibniz's General Investigations concerning the Analysis of Concepts and Truths, etc.*, ed. and trans. Walter H. O'Briant (Athens, Georgia, 1968).
C	*Opuscules et Fragments inèdits de Leibniz*, ed. L. Couturat (Paris, 1903).
FC	*Nouvelles Lettres et Opuscules inèdits de Leibniz*, ed. Foucher de Careil (Paris, 1857).
Frankfurt	*Leibniz: A Collection of Critical Essays*, ed. Harry G. Frankfurt (New York, 1972).
G	*G. W. Leibniz: Textes inèdits*, ed. G. Grua (Paris, 1948).
GM	*Leibnizens mathematische Schriften*, 7 vols., ed. C. I. Gerhardt (Berlin and Halle, 1849–63).
GP	*Die philosophischen Schriften von Gottfried Wilhelm Leibniz*, 7 vols., ed. C. I. Gerhardt (Berlin, 1875–90).
GU	*Leibnitz's Deutsche Schriften*, 2 vols., ed. G. E. Guhrauer (Berlin, 1838–40).
H	*G. W. Leibniz: Theodicy*, ed. and trans. E. M. Huggard (London, 1952).
HR	*The Philosophical Works of Descartes*, trans. E. S. Haldane and G. R. T. Ross (Cambridge, 1967; 1st ed. 1911).

Ishiguro	Hidé Ishiguro, *Leibniz's Philosophy of Logic and Language* (London, 1972).
L	*Leibniz: Philosophical Papers and Letters*, ed. and trans. L. E. Loemker (1st ed. Chicago, 1956/ 2nd ed. Amsterdam, 1970).
La	*New Essays Concerning Human Understanding by G. W. Leibniz*, ed. and trans. A. G. Langley (La Salle, Ill., 1916).
LG	*G. W. Leibniz: Discourse on Metaphysics*, ed. and trans. P. Lucas and L. Grint (Manchester, 1953).
MP	*Leibniz-Arnauld Correspondence*, ed. and trans. H. T. Mason, introd. G. H. R. Parkinson (Manchester, 1967).
P	*Leibniz: Logical Papers*, ed. and trans. G. H. R. Parkinson (Oxford, 1966).
Parkinson	G. H. R. Parkinson, *Logic and Reality in Leibniz's Metaphysics* (Oxford, 1965).
PM	*Leibniz: Philosophical Writings*, ed. and trans. G. H. R. Parkinson and Mary Morris (London, 1973).
Rescher	Nicholas Rescher, *The Philosophy of Leibniz* (Englewood Cliffs, N.J., 1967).
Russell	Bertrand Russell, *The Philosophy of Leibniz* (2nd ed. London, 1937).
S	*Gottfried Wilhelm Leibniz: Fragmente zur Logik*, ed. F. Schmidt (Berlin, 1960).
W	*Leibniz: Selections*, ed. and trans. P. P. Wiener (New York, 1951).

INTRODUCTION

LEIBNIZ'S extant philosophical thought is embodied in a mass of writing much of which is still in manuscript, much not available in English translation. Not all of this material has the same status, for some of it consists of private memoranda or notes, some of occasional pieces and letters sent to correspondents (sometimes directly, sometimes via others), some of anonymously published reviews, some of articles in learned journals published under Leibniz's own name, and some (but relatively little) of lengthier published work. One does not have to agree with Bertrand Russell that Leibniz had a 'bad' philosophy ('published with a view to fame and money') and a 'good' philosophy ('kept to himself') to accept that a systematic account of his thought should not treat these different kinds of writing, produced for different audiences, in a uniform way [*Russell* vi]. Furthermore, there is a temporal dimension to this material in that its date of composition ranges from 1663 when Leibniz was 17, to 1716 when he died at 70. So not only is there no great and significant public landmark, no *magnum opus* like Kant's *Critique of Pure Reason* or Locke's *Essay concerning Human Understanding*, on which the student of Leibniz can take his bearings, but also there is no such thing as the static, atemporal Leibnizian system which Russell claimed to be uncovering [*Russell* xii].

Yet in spite of these difficulties there is a point from which one can take one's departure and work outwards, and this is the 'mature philosophy' which Leibniz is commonly agreed to have had, having come to it in about 1685–6 [*Parkinson* 4; *Rescher* 6; *Russell* 7]. To this period there belong, most notably, his *Discourse on Metaphysics* and his *Correspondence with Arnauld*. The first of these is a shortish work written in the winter of 1685–6 when Leibniz was 39. He never published it and does not seem to have thought of doing so; but he did send a summary of it (consisting of the headings to each section) to Antoine Arnauld, and this occasioned and formed the basis of their somewhat lengthier *Correspondence* of 1686–7. At various times up to as late as 1708 Leibniz thought of publishing their letters, but in fact he never did [MP xiii]. In both cases publication was not till the nineteenth century.

The general idea that one should first make contact with Leibniz around 1685-6 has support from his own report, to Thomas Burnet in 1697, that he has been satisified with his views only over the previous twelve years [GP ii.205]. The idea that one should begin in particular with the *Discourse* and the *Arnauld Correspondence* has support from the reference to them and to Arnauld in the opening sentence of the first published account of the mature system, the article *A New System* of 1695: 'It is some years ago that I conceived this system and began communicating with learned men about it, especially with one of the greatest theologians and philosophers of our time, who had been told about certain of my opinions . . . and had found them very paradoxical' [GP iv.477: L 740/453].

It should not be supposed, though, that Leibniz's ideas in these years were completely new, nor that from then on they never changed. For example, on the one hand much of the thought of the *Discourse* can be traced back through earlier years [MP xxxix ff.]; and, on the other, the very things for which Leibniz is popularly famous, his 'monads', though prefigured in the *Discourse*, do not clearly make their appearance till at least ten years later. But despite this it nevertheless remains true that much of the earlier work is best seen in perspective from the work of this period rather than vice versa; and as for the later work, Russell bears eloquent witness to the relevance to it of the years around 1685. He relates how in preparing a course of lectures in 1899 he felt 'as many others have felt—that the *Monadology* (1714) was a kind of fantastic fairy tale, coherent perhaps, but wholly arbitrary'; 'at this point', he continues, 'I read the *Discours de Métaphysique* and the letters to Arnauld. Suddenly a flood of light was thrown on all the inmost recesses of Leibniz's philosophical edifice' [*Russell* xiii-xiv].

It is, then, the *Discourse on Metaphysics* and the *Correspondence with Arnauld* which form the best introduction to Leibniz's philosophical thought.[1] So the articles reprinted in this volume were selected because, taken together, they had something to say by the various ways of exegesis, explanation, and criticism about most of the central ideas and lines of thought of these related works. In the remainder of the space available I shall identify some of these ideas and relate them not only to the articles

[1] The *Discourse* is partially available in G. H. R. Parkinson and Mary Morris's excellent paperback collection, *Leibniz: Philosophical Writings*, and fully so in L. E. Loemker's classic, *Leibniz: Philosophical Papers and Letters* (and it is to these, i.e. PM and L, that reference is mainly made in this collection). It is also conveniently available in P. Lucas and L. Grint's *G. W. Leibniz: Discourse on Metaphysics* [LG]. The H. T. Mason and G. H. R. Parkinson edition of *The Leibniz-Arnauld Correspondence* [MP] is especially recommended. The *Correspondence* is partially printed in L and PM, and completely so (along with the *Discourse*) in G. R. Montgomery's older *Leibniz: Discourse on Metaphysics* (Chicago, 1902).

which follow but also to those listed in the 'Bibliography of Further Reading' at the end of this book. Someone wanting a survey of Leibniz's philosophy over the whole of his life could do little better than consult the bibliographical items (4), chapter 10, and (57), or the *Encyclopaedia Britannica* articles on Leibniz by M. Kneale [1971 ed.] or W. R. Sorley [11th ed., 1910-11]. Item (56) in the 'Bibliography of Further Reading' gives a concise and very readable account of Leibniz's mature philosophy.

Arnauld's reaction to the summary of the *Discourse* which Leibniz had sent him was rather strong, for he found in it 'many things that frighten me'. But, because it seemed to have the worrying consequence that everything that happens does so 'through a more than fatal necessity', he picked for particular mention the epitome of section 13 according to which 'the individual concept of each person contains once for all everything that will ever happen to him' [GP ii.15: MP 9]. It would not have been clear from the summary that this idea simply follows on from what is said in section 8 of the full *Discourse* about 'individual substance', but it is here that one should begin.

Leibniz himself said that 'the consideration of substance is one of the most important and fruitful points of philosophy' [GP v.137: La 154]; and he said of his own account of it that it is 'so fruitful that there follow from it primary truths, even about God and minds and the nature of bodies—truths heretofore known in part though hardly demonstrated, and unknown in part, but of the greatest utility for the future in the other sciences' [GP iv.469: L 709/433]. The idea of substance must perhaps always take its place along with others at the foundation of metaphysical thought in general, but Leibniz's estimate of its place within his own philosophy is perfectly judged. Certainly most of what is contained in the following articles connects, directly or indirectly, with it. The bibliographical items (36) and (46) provide a good historical introduction to the idea, and against their background it can be seen that what is distinctive about substances for Leibniz is the stress that he lays on their having 'complete concepts' or 'complete natures'. At least to begin with and somewhat roughly, one could think of a substance as an individual thing such as (to use Leibniz's own examples) Julius Caesar, or the stone sphere on Alexander the Great's tomb. These, says Leibniz,

> have a concept so complete that it is sufficient to make us understand and deduce from it all the predicates of the subject to which the concept is attributed. [GP iv.433: L 471–2/307]

Now there is no single straightforward thing that is meant by a substance's having a complete concept or nature, for Leibniz can be found placing different interpretations and glosses on the idea, now focussing on and polishing one of its many facets, now another. But, not too surprisingly, these different aspects of Leibnizian substances often correspond to the different lines of thought that traditionally have contributed to the idea of substance. Thus, as it first appears in the *Discourse*, the just-quoted definition of substance arises out of the traditional idea of substances as bearers of properties. For one could, Leibniz says at this point, characterize a substance as a subject to which several predicates are attributable and which is not itself attributable to anything else as a predicate. But this characterization—which in fact has its source in Aristotle's *Categories* [2a11 ff.]—is inadequate, he thinks, for it leaves unexplained what it is for a predicate truly to be attributable to a subject. But when this is explained, the old idea of a substance as the bearer of properties is transformed into the Leibnizian idea of substance as something with a complete concept.

This route to Leibnizian substances is 'the logical argument' of the title of John W. Nason's article, the first of this collection [see also (10) sect. 2, (41) sect. 1]. It is clear that the important staging post on it is the account of true predication, the claim that true propositions which attribute a predicate to a subject are such that 'the subject term must always include the predicate term in such a way that anyone who understands perfectly the concept of the subject will also know that the predicate pertains to it' [GP iv.433: L 471-2/307]; and this account forms the focus of some debate [see Nason, pp. 12 ff., and (10) sect. 1, (34)]. Leibniz says that if it is not a matter of conceptual containment then 'I do not know what truth is' [GP ii.56: MP 63]. But is this, as he claims, simply a piece of traditional Aristotelianism? It is hard to accept that it *is* quite as uncontentious as he likes to think, especially given the surprising conclusions he goes on to derive from it, and the difficulties which (we shall see) he himself finds with it.

In the second article reprinted here Wilfrid Sellars traces and discusses some further routes towards the idea of substances as having complete concepts which include reference to everything that is true of them. One of these (sect. VII ff.) relates the more recent idea of the sense of a proper name to that of an individual substance's complete concept: so that the latter becomes the sense or meaning that the substance's name has for God, who knows everything [see also (44) sects. 2 and 3]. Another (sect. VI) brings into play the idea of there being timeless facts about what happens to substances at different times and relates this to their complete concepts [see also (8) sects. 1–4].

For my own part I am doubtful that these lines of thought—the first of which supposes him anachronistically to have more of an interest in modern philosophical logic than in traditional metaphysics—really were followed to any great extent by Leibniz. But even if at times they were, Bertrand Russell is quite wrong to afford the second the importance he does when he says that my having a complete concept 'amounts to little more than [that] . . . [w]hatever my future action may be, it must be true now that they will be such as they will be' [*Russell* 46]. For there is no doubt whatsoever about the importance for Leibniz of another idea which Sellars discusses (sects. I–V) and with which the one stressed by Russell may be illuminatingly contrasted.

This further idea connects, significantly, with a feature of the traditional idea of substance. For besides being thought of simply as the bearers of properties substances have often been seen as the substratum of changes in those properties, as having 'natures' which explain or account for at least many of these properties and changes. Now so far I have used the term 'nature' interchangeably with 'concept', but it would be more exact to think of an individual *concept* as something which needs to be embodied in, or instantiated in, an individual substance in order to be a *nature*. Thus, for a substance to have a *complete* concept is for it to have a *nature* which gives rise to *all* its properties, changes and activities, and hence for it to be constituted as completely self-explaining.[2] This idea of complete concepts as detailed 'life-plans' (to use Sellars' highly illuminating phrase) does far more justice to the excitement of the Leibnizian metaphor, used in connection with substances, to the effect that 'the present is big with the future' [GP v.48: La 48], than does the limp idea of them as collections of timeless facts [see here (41) sect. 2, (69), (70)].

Earlier I mentioned Arnauld's worry that Leibniz's account of substances, to the effect that their concepts contain 'once for all everything that will ever happen to them' appeared to lead to a kind of determinism, to a closed and fixed future. In fact in the *Discourse* itself Leibniz was already sensitive to and tried to rebut the apparent implication 'that it will leave no place for human liberty' [GP iv.437: L476/310], that if it was part of Arnauld's concept, or nature, to be celibate, then he had no choice about not marrying. But Arnauld's questions on the matter forced him to develop his position, which also is discussed in Nason's article (pp. 22–4).[3]

This problem about there not being room for human free will within

[2] Hidé Ishiguro, in her paper in this collection and elsewhere [(32) 112f., (33)], is a noteworthy dissenter from this common view that a substance's nature is sufficient *by itself* to give rise to and explain *all* that is specified in its complete concept.

[3] See also (15), (35), and (47), the first and last of which also discuss Leibniz's views on human freedom as they appear outside of the *Discourse* and the *Correspondence*.

what Leibniz says about individual substances is, of course, simply a particular aspect of a more general problem which arises directly out of his account of truth. Leibniz is quite clear that the predicate is contained in the subject of true contingent as well as true necessary propositions; so unless he can find a mark of contingent truth besides what otherwise might have seemed to be the obvious one of the predicate *not* being contained in the subject, he does seem faced with the disappearance of contingency altogether. Indeed he recognizes himself that it may seem that what he says 'will destroy the difference between contingent and necessary truths' [GP iv.436: L 476/310].

This problem, Leibniz reports, 'had me perplexed for a long time; for I did not understand how a predicate could be in a subject, and yet the proposition would not be a necessary one' [C 18: PM 97]; and his strugglings with it are complex and many-sided. The articles by John W. Nason and Margaret Wilson contribute to an understanding of this issue as they go along, but those by Dennis Fried and Hidé Ishiguro are specifically devoted to it [see also (1), (2), (3), (14), (18), (24), (43), (44) sect. 7, (50), (67)].

Something that is discussed in these last two (directly in the first, in passing in the second) is the question of the connection between the contingency of, say, Caesar's crossing the Rubicon, and the contingency, on which Leibniz insists, of Caesar's having been created at all. This introduces the idea of 'possibles which neither do exist, nor will exist, nor have existed' [FC 178: L 404–5/263], for if Caesar had not been created, had not been an actual individual substance, he would still have been possible. The idea plays an important part in the Arnauld Correspondence [e.g. GPii.56: MP62–3] and elsewhere. One of its problematic features, the extent to which it makes sense to name possible but non-actual individuals, is discussed by Sellars (pp. 26 ff.) [also (38) sect. 2]. But there are other problems, as for example that discussed by Ishiguro, whether for Leibniz a possible person who is like Caesar in all respects except, say, that he did not cross the Rubicon is, strictly, a possible *Caesar*; whether, that is, a Leibnizian possible individual can belong to more than one possible world [see (24), (44) sect. 7].

That this actual world is the best of all possible worlds is, as is well known, the reason Leibniz gives for God's creation of it rather than some other world.[4] But what he means by 'the best' is more complex than allowed for in *Candide*, Voltaire's satire on the idea. For the superiority

[4] That God exists is taken for granted in the *Discourse* and the *Correspondence*, but elsewhere various proofs are given; see (5), (6), (23), (39), and Nason, pp. 17–18. Further questions that might be raised here are, What is it for a world to be actual [see (2)]? and, Is there such a thing as *the* best possible world [(7)]?

of a world above others shows itself, *pace* Voltaire, not so much in the lack of serious earthquakes but in the 'general economy of the world and in the constitution of the laws of nature' [GP iv.446: L 487/316-17]. It connects, as in sections 1 to 6 [GP iv.427-32: L 465-70/303-6] and 19 to 22 [GP iv.444-8: L 485-9/315-18] of the *Discourse*, with the simplicity of the laws of nature and the possibility of our being able to appeal to final causes in scientific explanation; it connects so closely, indeed, that Snell's law of light refraction can be derived by appeal to it [(20), (22), (55) sect. 6, (61) sects. 4-9, 17].

But whatever the excellence of this world consists in, God could hardly fail to have created it. For this would seem to involve the absurdity either of a lack of wisdom to see what is the best, or a lack of goodness to want to create it, or a lack of power to be able to create it. But if he could not fail to create this world, in what way was God's creation free; and if it was not, are other possible worlds really possible? This is another of the questions discussed by Nason (pp. 25-6) [also (7), (35), (50), (53), (67)]. There is, moreover, a further problem for the idea of God's freely creating a contingent world, in that Leibniz sometimes says things that seem flatly inconsistent with it. He speaks at times as though the best possible world *creates itself* because 'all possible things . . . tend . . . towards existence according . . . to the degree of perfection which they contain' [GP vii.303: W 347]. This state of affairs, besides making a creative God redundant, would again mean that other possible worlds are not really possible. David Blumenfeld's article in this collection is devoted to a discussion of this Leibnizian theory of 'the striving possibles' [also (29), (71) sect. 4].

Leibniz claims, we have noted, that his understanding of truth as conceptual containment is uncontentious and that his account of substances as having complete concepts follows quickly and directly from it. Nevertheless he does concede, not merely under pressure from Arnauld, but quite openly in the *Discourse* that he derives from it 'surprising consequences' [GP ii.57: MP 64] and 'important paradoxes' [GP iv.433: L 472/308]. One of these is the principle of the identity of indiscernibles, the thesis that 'it is not true that two substances can resemble each other completely and differ only in number' [GP iv.433: L 472/308] [see (12) 25-39, (26), (40), (65), (66) 173-80]. Another is that a substance's 'succeeding state is a sequel (although free or contingent) of its preceding state, as though only God and it existed in the world; thus each individual substance . . . is like a world apart, independent of everything except God' [GP ii.57: LG 64].[5]

[5] In section 26 of the *Discourse* Leibniz says that it 'is in accord with my

It is often supposed that in thus holding that substances are self-contained, isolated from each other, dependent only on God, Leibniz must also hold that the appearance that substances are related is just that, an appearance; and that propositions expressing such relations must therefore be redundant and reducible in some way to propositions not expressing relations. Whether he really does hold this or how, if he does, the reductions are to be effected, are areas of considerable discussion. Sellars (sections III and IV) and Nason (pp. 14-17) each have something to say on the matter, which is treated at greater length by F. B. D'Agostino (pp. 97-102) in his article reprinted here, 'Leibniz on Compossibility and Relational Predicates', [also (13) sect. 6 f., (17), (31), (32) chaps. 5, 6, (42) sect. 6, (59)].

The issue of Leibniz's dealings with relations has consequences beyond itself in that there is, it seems, a reason for its being absolutely essential to him that there genuinely are relations between substances. As D'Agostino explains, Leibniz makes a distinction between individual substances that in themselves are *possible* but which amongst themselves are not *compossible*. Thus something might be 'possible in an absolute sense . . . because it does not imply a contradiction', yet might be such that for it actually to exist 'it would be necessary for the rest of the universe . . . to be . . . different from what it is' [GP iii.573: L 1075/661] [for more on this topic see (13), (28), (42) sect. 3]. But now, as D'Agostino points out in his discussion of the whole question of compossibility, if substances can ultimately be characterized in purely non-relational terms then they cannot fail to be compossible.

There is, moreover, a further difficulty with the thesis that each substance is 'like a world apart', isolated, self-contained. For Leibniz combines it with the view that they are so intimately connected and interrelated that 'every substance is . . . like a mirror . . . of the whole universe which it expresses' [GP iv. 434: L 473/308]. In their papers Nason and Russell discuss these apparently irreconcilable views, but approach the matter in different ways. Nason (pp. 28-9) uses it as the basis of a concluding objection that Leibniz is just inconsistent and self-contradictory whereas Russell uses it to set the scene for an account of the post-*Discourse* development of Leibniz's notion of substance.

Relevant to the opposition between the isolatedness and inter-connectedness of substances is the idea of pre-established harmony between them, the idea that God brings it about that 'the nature proper to each substance involves that what happens to one corresponds to what happens

principles' [GP iv.441:L 492/320] that there are ideas 'innate' in our minds. For this much discussed topic see (16) 299–312, (27), (58), and (62).

to all the others, without their acting upon one another directly' [GP ii.13: L–/311] [see also particularly (32) 111 ff., (33)].[6]

Leibniz's account of substances as having complete concepts has, so far, been seen to involve, either directly or indirectly, their being self-contained, their being each big with their own future, and their being capable of initiating and fully explaining changes in their properties and states. But this is not all it involves for, in section 9 of the *Discourse*, there follow from it further 'important paradoxes'—as that a substance 'cannot come into being except by creation, or perish except by annihilation; that a substance cannot be divided into two, or one substance made out of two' [GP iv.434: L 473/308]. Now in holding these things Leibniz begins to come into conflict with Descartes for whom matter, whose essence is extension, is substance. Substances, Leibniz argues (sections 10 ff.) cannot consist of extension for, because of its infinite divisibility, extension is incapable of providing a principle of identity for their crucially important unity and integrity [see (25), (41) sects. 3, 4, (45)]. Only the possession of a complete concept—which Leibniz begins at this point to identify with the 'substantial forms' and 'entelechies' of the Scholastics—is sufficient for this. Leibniz was pressingly questioned by Arnauld on this point of the indestructible unity of a substance and how 'forms', 'complete concepts', 'natures', and 'entelechies', can provide for it, and he was forced to explain himself in more detail. In later years too he discussed these aspects of his idea of substance with another correspondent, Burcher De Volder. The content of the important series of letters which passed between them is the topic of L. J. Russell's article in this collection.

Still in opposition to Descartes, Leibniz further believes that extension is insufficient by itself as the basis for the science of dynamics. For movement would not be properly real if it were merely a matter of relative change of place. The reality in it is whatever is the *cause* of these changes and this must be some force. By this line of thought Leibniz is again led to 'substantial forms' or 'entelechies':

> this force is something different from size, figure, and motion, and from this we can conclude that not everything which is conceived in a body consists solely in extension and its modifications . . . Thus we are compelled to restore . . . certain beings or forms . . . [and] it becomes more and more apparent that the general principles of corporeal nature and of mechanics themselves are nevertheless metaphysical rather than geometrical and pertain to certain forms or indivisible natures . . . than to corporeal mass. [GP iv.444: L 484–5/315]

[6] The idea of pre-established harmony was initially introduced in connection with the mind/body relation [(19), (63)].

The necessity of assuming some such force is another of the points on which De Volder pressed Leibniz and which, consequently, is a further theme in Russell's article.

Margaret D. Wilson's article, 'Leibniz's Dynamics and Contingency in Nature', has relevance to a number of the foregoing issues where Leibniz's metaphysics becomes his philosophy of science. Though her main theme is a claim which Leibniz made in 1699, to the effect that we can learn from dynamics the difference between necessary and contingent truth, she is involved along the way in discussion of the questions of the use of final causes, the inadequacy of Cartesian extension, the necessity of force, and its relation to 'forms' and 'entelechies' [also (41)].

A further element in Leibniz's anti-Cartesianism is, as Wilson explains, the idea—which appears in section 17 of the *Discourse*—that what is important in dynamics is what he calls '*vis viva*' (in fact twice what is now known as kinetic energy, $\frac{1}{2}mv^2$) rather than the Cartesian 'quantity of motion' (in fact the non-directional momentum, mv). '*Vis viva*' is associated by Leibniz with the force that constitutes the reality of motion, and as such is deeply rooted in his metaphysics of substance. But besides there being a philosophical dimension to these dynamical considerations there is also a more purely scientific one, and the '*vis viva* controversy' is an important feature in the history of seventeenth- and eighteenth-century science. The details of Leibniz's dynamical arguments and their significance and historical background are the topics of David Papineau's paper on the controversy [also (21), (30), (55), (60)].

The topic of the final paper in this collection does not crop up in the *Discourse*, though it connects with others which do and anyway is important in itself. The 'last controversy' of C. D. Broad's title was carried on towards the end of Leibniz's life in a correspondence between him and Samuel Clarke, a spokesman for Newton, and it concerns the nature of space and time [also (37), (49), (64) 22–30, 108–116, (68)]. As Broad explains, Leibniz's arguments for relative as opposed to absolute space are based on two ideas which are closely connected with his idea of substance. One of these, the principle of the identity of indiscernibles, has already been mentioned. The other, though not so termed in the *Discourse*, is the principle of sufficient reason. This is supposed to hold as a direct consequence of substances' having complete concepts and it states that there are '*a priori* proofs or reasons for the truths of each event and why one has happened rather than another' [GP ii.12: L –/310] [see (10) sect. 3, (50), (71) sect. 1].

I

LEIBNIZ AND THE LOGICAL ARGUMENT FOR INDIVIDUAL SUBSTANCES

JOHN W. NASON

THE most important single argument in support of Leibniz's doctrine of monads is that drawn from the logical nature of true affirmative propositions. Strangely enough Leibniz never made use of this argument, so far as I have been able to discover, in any of the writings which he published during his lifetime. The reason may have been, as Russell suggests,[1] that he considered the argument too abstract and technical to be convincing to the average reader. But even this consideration hardly explains his failure to give public utterance during his lifetime to that argument which more than any other appeared to him as self-evident in itself, far-reaching in its metaphysical consequences, and deep-rooted in his rationalism. In his unpublished writings he returned to it again and again with all the emphasis of irrefutable proof.[2]

The most familiar statement of the argument is in section 8 of the *Discourse on Metaphysics*, where it runs:

Now it is certain that every true predication has some basis in the nature of things, and when a proposition is not an identity, that is to say, when the predicate is not expressly contained in the subject, it must be included in it virtually. This is what philosophers call *in-esse*, when they say that the predicate *is in* the subject. So the subject term must always include the predicate term in such a way that anyone who understands perfectly

From *Mind*, vol. 51 (1942), pp. 201–22. By permission of the author and Basil Blackwell, Publisher.

[1] *Russell* 8–9. See Leibniz's comment to Arnauld who, as a logician, had raised objections: 'I indeed suspected that the argument taken from the general nature of propositions would make some impression on you; but I also admit that few are capable of appreciating truths so abstract and that perhaps anybody else but you would not so easily have perceived its force' [GP ii. 73–4: MP 91].

[2] It first appears in the manuscript entitled *Calculi universalis investigationes*, 1679 [C 68–9]; it is the burden of sect. 8 of the *Discourse on Metaphysics*, 1686, and the subject of much of the ensuing controversy with Arnauld; it also appears in *Generales Inquisitiones de Analysi Notionum et Veritatum* of the same year [C 388: P 77] and in the *Nouveaux Essais* [GP v.469: La 568–9]. See also C 16–17: PM 96; C 68–9; C 401–3: PM 93–5; C 518–21: L 411–15/267–9, PM 87–91; GP vii. 299–301; FC 179: L 405/263–4, PM 107; GP vii.309: PM 75.

the concept of the subject will also know that the predicate pertains to it. [GP iv. 433: L 471–2/307]

From this deceptively simple statement follow, according to Leibniz, all of his most important metaphysical conclusions.[3] It entails the principle of the identity of indiscernibles, the indivisibility and unity of substance, the existence of substances as depending purely on the goodwill of God, the mirroring by each substance of the entire universe, the system of pre-established harmony—in short, the windowless, world-containing, and (save for God) self-sufficient monads of the *Monadology*.

In terms made familiar since the time of Kant, Leibniz is asserting that every true affirmative proposition is *analytic*:

An affirmative truth is one whose predicate is in the subject; and so in every true affirmative proposition, necessary or contingent, universal or particular, the notion of the predicate is in some way contained in the notion of the subject, in such a way that if anyone were to understand perfectly each of the two notions just as God understands it, he would by that very fact perceive that the predicate is in the subject. [C 16–17: PM 96]

This is obvious in the case of identical propositions: A is A, an equilateral rectangle is a rectangle. It has some plausibility in propositions which are not expressly identical, such as: an equilateral triangle is equiangular, a circle is a closed plane figure all points on the circumference of which are equi-distant from the centre, all bodies are extended. But it is also true, according to Leibniz, of *every* true affirmative proposition, e.g. that Alexander conquered Darius and that Caesar crossed the Rubicon. And since the subjects of propositions are individual substances and the predicates are the properties of these substances, it follows that every substance contains within itself, once and for all, every property, quality, or characteristic which it ever has had or will have. That God alone can deduce *a priori* from an individual substance all its past and future attributes is, of course, a commentary on our human limitations. It does not affect the validity of the argument.

Leibniz appeals to Aristotle and the Schoolmen for support for his logical doctrine.[4] It is important to be on one's guard against the confusion which this spurious appeal may introduce. In the *Prior Analytics* Aristotle states propositions indifferently as 'A is B' or 'B belongs to A', and the Schoolmen used the verb 'inesse' widely to express the relation between predicate and subject. According to the Aristotelian doctrine

[3] See *Discourse*, sect. 9 [GP iv.433-4: L 472–3/308]; *Specimen inventorum* [GP vii.309–18: PM 75–86]; *Primae veritates* [C 518–23: PM 87–92, L 410–17/267–70].

[4] See C 366, 388: P 56, 77 where Aristotle is mentioned by name; *Disc.* sect. 8 [GP iv.433: L 471/307] and correspondence with Arnauld [GP ii.43: MP 47] where the reference is to 'the philosophers'.

of the categories the being of all 'accidents' is being in or inhering in substance. But it is hardly necessary to point out that neither Aristotle nor the Schoolmen interpreted these phrases in such a way as to deny synthetic propositions. It is one thing to hold that an accident, say 'white', cannot exist by itself but only as an attribute of snow or milk or some other substance; it is another to assert that the concept of X is such that I can by analysis deduce from it that it is white and liquid and of a volume of two quarts. In one passage [C 11] Leibniz describes *in-esse* as merely 'nexus praedicati cum subjecto', but even here he proceeds at once to specify the 'nexus' as one of containing and being contained. For the most part his language is unambiguous. The relation of subject to predicate is expressed when he is writing in French by the verbs 'comprendre' and 'enfermer', when he is writing in Latin by the verbs 'contineo' and 'involvo'. To the charge that this is a distortion of classic logic—a distortion which not unnaturally worried Arnauld—he retorts with magnificent self-assurance:

When I say that the individual concept of Adam contains [*enferme*] everything that will ever happen to him, I mean nothing other than what all philosophers mean when they say that the predicate is present in the subject of a true proposition. It is true that the consequences of a doctrine so evident are paradoxes, but the fault lies with philosophers, who do not take far enough the clearest concepts. [GP ii. 43: MP 47]

It may be objected that this is not in reality a logical argument, but a metaphysical one. What Leibniz really does, it will be said, is to parade his metaphysical view about individual substances in logical dress. But this is to miss the point. His thesis that all true affirmative propositions involve either formally or virtually the principle of identity, i.e. are analytic, is a consequence of his view of the nature of truth. 'The predicate or consequent therefore always inheres in the subject or antecedent. And as Aristotle, too, observed, the nature of truth in general or the connection between the terms of a proposition consists in this fact' [C 518–19: L 412/267]. Leibniz makes an even more emphatic statement in reply to one of Arnauld's objections:

Finally, I have given a decisive argument which in my view has the force of a demonstration; that always, in every true affirmative proposition, necessary or contingent, universal or particular, the concept of the predicate is in a sense included in that of the subject; the predicate is present in the subject; or else I do not know what truth is. [GP ii. 56: MP 63]

Thus, the doctrine that all true affirmative propositions are analytic is a result of Leibniz's view of truth, and his view of truth in turn is a reflection of his rationalism. Leibniz is in substance saying: take any affirmative proposition and you will find that in order to be true it must have the formal characteristic expressed by saying that the subject contains the predicate. Why must this be so? For the simple reason that to admit a synthetic proposition is to admit a breakdown in the ideal of complete rational explanation. It is to admit a gap which reason cannot bridge. It is to admit the bare conjunction of brute given fact, opaque to reason and destructive of complete rationalism.[5] It does not follow, of course, that this position is entailed by every system of logic, but it was for Leibniz the necessary consequence of what he considered to be the only sound logic. In that sense it is a logical argument for a metaphysical position and not a subterfuge by which a metaphysical argument is wrapped in the odour of logical sanctity.

However one may look upon the matter, the fact remains that Leibniz draws metaphysical conclusions of great significance from the argument. Is it true that all true affirmative propositions are analytic? This assertion would most certainly be rejected in many quarters today. It is open to attack on at least four grounds: (A) that it illegitimately presupposes that all true propositions are properly expressed in the subject-predicate form; (B) that analytic propositions necessarily presuppose synthetic propositions; (C) that it invalidates the distinction between necessary and contingent truths; and (D) that the very reasoning with which Leibniz supports his conclusions is inconsistent with the truth of his major assertion. I shall examine each of these four criticisms in order.

(A) The doctrine that all true affirmative propositions are analytic clearly presupposes the dogma that all such propositions are of the subject-predicate form or can be reduced to propositions of this form. Leibniz's insistence, which we shall examine shortly, that the basis of all truth is the principle of identity makes no other position possible. A proposition which asserts some relation other than that of predication between its terms cannot, if it be true at all, be true because of some identity between its subject and predicate. But we have just seen that it is the application of this principle of identity which constitutes the necessary formal character of all true affirmative propositions. Therefore a proposition to be true must be of the subject-predicate form.

Leibniz recognizes this conclusion. Indeed, he never appears to question it. It is one of the most striking instances of the dominating influence of the Aristotelian logic that the man who is now generally recognized

[5] See Couturat's comments in the Preface to his *La Logique de Leibniz*, xi: '"All truth is analytic." As a consequence, everything in the world must be intelligible and logically demonstrable in terms of pure concepts, and deduction is the only scientific method. This might well be called the postulate of universal intelligibility. Thus the philosophy of Leibniz appears as the most complete and systematic expression possible of intellectual rationalism.'

as one of the founders of modern logic, who with his mathematical turn of mind insists on extending, expanding, modifying the classic forms of reasoning, should accept as self-evident the doctrine that all true propositions must be of the subject-predicate form. It is surprising, but historically understandable how Aristotle failed to grasp the significance of relational propositions.[6] It is astounding that the discoverer of the calculus and the author of the *Universal Characteristic* failed to do so.

It is a commonplace of modern logic that there are relational propositions and that they are logically irreducible. The monopoly which Aristotle's authority gave to the subject-predicate form depends upon historical and accidental considerations which are not relevant here. It is true that any relational proposition may be expressed in what appears to be a subject-predicate form, and this has led many to hold that the subject-predicate form is logically basic. But the apparent reduction of the one to the other is based on a confusion between relations and relational qualities. McTaggart points out in section 85 of *The Nature of Existence* that every relation, or in his words every relationship, generates relational qualities in the things related. If A loves B, then A has the relational quality of being the lover of B and B the relational quality of being the beloved of A. 'Such qualities', McTaggart adds, 'though involved by the relations, can be clearly distinguished from them. For the quality, unlike the relation, is predicated, and predicated of a single substance even when, as in the case we have taken, the relation is not reflexive. The relation is between A and B, but the quality is predicated of A alone.' McTaggart is quite clear that relational qualities cannot take the place of relations, for the relations are primary and the relational qualities subsidiary. But the fact that I can express my meaning, A loves B, by the proposition that A is the lover of B has led some philosophers to conclude that relations may be dispensed with in favour of qualities and relational propositions in favour of subject-predicate propositions.

It is not difficult to show that the reduction is verbal and not real. If the proposition that A loves B is to be reduced to one of the subject-predicate form, it must be held that A possesses some quality which is the equivalent of his relation to B. What is that quality? If it is the quality of being in love or of being a lover, this quality will equally belong to other people besides A. Indeed, in the best of all possible romances it will belong to B as well as to A, although this is not implied in the original proposition that A loves B. Furthermore, A may be in love with or be the lover of other people besides A. And that being the sad fact, merely to say that A has the quality of being in love is clearly not to

[6] See Cook Wilson's interesting account in *Statement and Inference*, vol. ii, part ii, chap. 5.

assert the full import of the original proposition. What we must assert, then, is not that A has the quality of being in love, but that he has the quality of being in love with B. But the phrase 'in love with B' has clearly two terms. The quality which it specifies is a complex quality which involves both a state of the emotions and a specific object of those emotions. It contains, in other words, the relation within itself and has no meaning apart from the relation. A possesses a given relational quality because he stands in a certain determinate relation, and not vice versa. Thus, while there are propositions that assert the inherence of a quality in a substance, such as 'A is white' or 'A is sick', there are others which assert a relation between two or more terms and they cannot be reduced to propositions which are of the subject-predicate type. Such propositions are clearly not analytic, in Leibniz's sense of the term, and hence it is false that all true affirmative propositions are analytic.[7]

The dogma that all true propositions are of the subject-predicate form has been of great influence in metaphysics. It leads directly to the denial of external relations, as Leibniz clearly saw. In his fifth letter to Clarke he says:

> The ratio or proportion between two lines L and M, may be conceived three several ways; as a ratio of the greater L, to the lesser M; as a ratio of the lesser M, to the greater L; and lastly, as something abstracted from both, that is, as the ratio between L and M, without considering which is the antecedent, or which the consequent; which the subject, and which the object. And thus it is, that proportions are considered in music. In the first way of considering them, L the greater; in the second, M the lesser, is the subject of that accident, which philosophers call relation. But, which of them will be the subject, in the third way of considering them? It cannot be said that both of them, L and M together, are the subject of such an accident; for if so, we should have an accident in two subjects, with one leg in one, and the other in the other; which is contrary to the notion of accidents. Therefore we must say, that this relation, in this third way of considering it, is indeed out of the subjects; but being neither a substance, nor an accident, it must be a mere ideal thing, the consideration of which is nevertheless useful. [GP vii. 401: A 71]

As it stands this argument is singularly unconvincing, and its artificial character has been well demonstrated by both McTaggart and Broad.[8] If besides substances there are only accidents or qualities, and if these are defined as belonging to one substance, there is obviously no place left for relations which hold between two or more substances. But why should Leibniz and others have held so apparently absurd a view? Because they believed erroneously that all true assertions are subject-predicate

[7] See Russell, *Principles of Mathematics*, sect. 214.
[8] See McTaggart, *Nature of Existence*, sects. 80, 81; Broad, *An Examination of McTaggart's Philosophy*, vol. i, p. 84.

propositions, or can be more properly expressed in this form—i.e. as the inherence of one or more qualities in a substance.

(B) Do analytic propositions presuppose synthetic propositions? It has been claimed that they do,[9] and we must now examine the grounds for this claim. It is clear that if it is valid it destroys the contention that all true affirmative propositions are analytic.

We have seen that for Leibniz a true proposition is one in which the subject contains the predicate, and the relation of 'containing' is one of express or virtual identity. Its truth depends upon the principle of contradiction or, as Lovejoy calls it, 'the principle of the compossibility of concepts' [op. cit., 195]. Leibniz's illustrations are all too frequently tautologies: 'A is A', 'The equilateral rectangle is a rectangle' [GP v. 343: La 405]. Nevertheless, he is convinced that virtually identical propositions are both instructive and important. Now it is important to note that in propositions of this latter type the subject must be complex and the predicate merely one of the elements in the complex subject. Thus I can truly assert of Caesar that he is daring only because Caesar is a complex of many qualities, one of which I select in this instance for reaffirmation.

But is the complex of qualities which constitutes the subject a possible complex? Suppose that upon analysis it should turn out to contain the sort of contradiction expressed in the phrase 'a round square'. Leibniz is insistent that it is not enough to have ideas; we must be able to demonstrate that our ideas are possible, i.e. that their ultimate elements are compatible or compossible. On this depends his criticism of Descartes' clear and distinct ideas which for all their superficial clarity and distinctness may conceal contradictions if not analysed. On this depends also his distinction between nominal and real definitions. The former is arbitrary, the latter depends upon the nature of the thing defined; the former supplies distinguishing marks, the latter shows that the thing itself is possible.[10] On this depends finally the Leibnizian version of the ontological proof for the existence of God. It is not enough to have an idea of God to prove that he exists; one must show that it is a possible idea:

[F]or we cannot safely infer from definitions until we know that they are real or that they involve no contradiction. The reason for this is that from concepts which involve a contradiction, contradictory conclusions can be drawn simultaneously, and this is absurd. To explain this I usually

[9] See *Russell* sect. 11; Lovejoy, 'Kant's Antithesis of Dogmatism and Criticism', *Mind*, 15 (1906).

[10] The references are too numerous to cite. The argument is clearly stated in *Thoughts on Knowledge, Truth, and Ideas*, which was published in the Acta Eruditorum Lipsiensium in 1684. [GP iv.422–6: L 448–54/291–4].

make use of the example of the most rapid motion, which involves an absurdity. Suppose that a wheel turns at a most rapid rate. Then anyone can see that if a spoke of the wheel is extended beyond its rim, its extremity will move more rapidly than will a nail in the rim itself. The motion of the nail is therefore not the most rapid, contrary to hypothesis. Yet at first glance we may seem to have an idea of the most rapid motion, for we understand perfectly what we are saying. But we cannot have any idea of the impossible. Likewise it is not enough to think of a most perfect being in order to assert that we have an idea of it, and in the demonstration which I referred to above we must either prove or assume the possibility of a most perfect being in order to reason rightly. [GP iv. 424–5: L 451/293]

How are we to show the compatibility of the simple elements of any complex concept? Leibniz's view on this point leads him into a curious contradiction. Two elements which are absolutely simple can have no common quality. They are not only different; they are, as he expresses it [GP vii. 237: P 132], 'disparate'. Since they are disparate, they cannot be incompatible, for there can be no contradiction between them [C 69]. Thus, all simple elements are compossible, as Leibniz clearly recognizes in a paper, *Quod Ens Perfectissimum existit* [GP vii. 261-2: L 259-61/ 167–8], which he showed to Spinoza in 1676, and in an undated letter to the Duchess Sophia [GP iv. 296]. Since it is impossible in the nature of things for two or more simple positive qualities to be incompatible, the concept of God as the subject of all such simple qualities or 'perfections' is a self-consistent and therefore a possible concept. Therefore God exists. But if all simple positive qualities are compossible, whence arises incompatibility? The answer must be, from negation.[11] What an apparently clear and distinct idea may conceal within the bosom of its complexity is both the assertion and the denial of the same positive quality. It is this contradiction which makes the idea impossible.

If, however, the absence of contradiction is all that is necessary for a possible idea, then all complex ideas containing only positive qualities will be equally possible, and this is manifestly false. Leibniz recognizes its falsity when he insists upon the distinction between real and nominal definitions. In opposing the nominalism of Hobbes Leibniz insists that 'the reality of the definition does not depend upon our free choice and that *not all concepts can be combined with each other*'.[12] Even clearer is the admission: 'Nevertheless, it is so far unknown to men whence arises the incompossibility of different things, or how it happens that different essences are opposed to one another, since all purely positive terms seem to be compatible with each other' [GP vii. 195]. In short, it is a matter of brute fact that certain combinations of qualities occur in the world

[11] See Couturat, *La Logique de Leibniz*, chap. 6, sect. 21.

[12] *Thoughts on Knowledge, Truth, and Ideas* [GP iv.425: L 452/293–my italics].

and certain do not. So far as we can determine, sensations of colour depend upon light rays and sensations of sound upon vibrations in the air. Why these different sensations should be associated with their respective kinds of waves is impossible to answer. Again, for all we can tell, there is no logical contradiction in fish that suckle their young or in having all land animals lay eggs. But the fact remains that such combinations do not occur in *rerum natura*. The point is well made by Lovejoy:

Leibniz, now, on the one hand, always insists that the analysis of a definition must bring us to such simple and indefinable concepts; but on the other hand, he constantly insists that definition is not an arbitrary process but is always (when legitimately performed) limited from the outset by the requirement that the notions united shall be 'compossible', compatible with one another. But these two contentions taken together are equivalent to the assertion that there may subsist, even between ultimately simple and indefinable concepts, relations of incompatibility. For if there were no such relations of ultimate incompatibility, definitions *would* be arbitrary, and any conjunction of *positive* simple concepts into a single notion would be possible and legitimate. . . . If there are incompatibilities anywhere in definition, they must inhere in the original elements, the primary concepts, of which the definition is made up; and if there were, contrariwise, no such original incompatibilities–self-evident, not capable of being demonstrated by further definition, and not to be confused with mere non-identity–everything under heaven in the way of a definition would be permissible. In asserting, then, that definitions are not arbitrary, Leibniz plainly points to the affirmation of ultimate repugnancies to coinherence between distinct and positive concepts; and thus to the affirmation that *synthetic* relations of incompossibility, on the one hand, of necessary coexistence, on the other, are to be found in some cases between the ultimate and irreducible ideas upon which our thinking finally depends. [op. cit. 198–9]

Analytic propositions presuppose synthetic propositions in three distinct ways. (1) Since, with the exception of purely identical statements, the subject concept must be complex, any proposition which reasserts a part of this subject complex as the predicate presupposes the proposition that the elements in the subject complex are compatible. Now a proposition which asserts or denies compatibility is clearly synthetic. It is not an identical proposition; its subject may be, and usually is, simple; and it is a relational proposition about two or more terms. (2) The principle of contradiction, by means of which it is judged that a simple positive quality is incompatible with the corresponding negative quality, is itself synthetic. (3) Finally, in addition to synthetic propositions asserting the compatibility of any or all simple positive qualities, there must be synthetic propositions asserting the coinherence or the exclusiveness which we find among the terms of our actual world. Leibniz thinks that he deals satisfactorily with this last kind by his distinction between the necessary and the contingent and it is to the futility and confusion of Leibniz's position on this that I now turn;

(C) The distinction between necessary and contingent truths. 'Our reasonings are grounded upon *two great principles*', writes Leibniz in the *Monadology*:

the first the *principle of contradiction*, by virtue of which we judge that false which involves a contradiction, and that *true* which is opposed or contradictory to the false; and the second the *principle of sufficient reason*, by virtue of which we observe that there can be found no fact that is true or existent, or any true proposition, without there being a sufficient reason for its being so and not otherwise, although we cannot know these reasons in most cases. There are also two kinds of truths, truths of *reasoning* and truths of *fact*. Truths of reasoning are necessary, and their opposite is impossible. Truths of fact are contingent, and their opposite is possible.[13]

The principle of contradiction is applicable to the realm of possibility where one can see the connection or the contradiction between possibles. This is the realm of eternal truths best illustrated in Leibniz's mind by mathematics. The principle of sufficient reason applies to the realm of actuality. The contingent is the existent.[14] One must bear in mind Leibniz's metaphysical doctrine that there is in the mind of God an infinite number of possible worlds out of which God has chosen our world to make actual. Our world, to be sure, is the best of all the possible worlds, but it is not necessary in the sense that a different world would be a contradiction in terms. Our world, the actual world, is thus merely one of many possible worlds. It happens to be the one which God, for reasons best understood by himself, has elected to create. God might have selected a different world, however—one, let us assume, in which air waves of a certain frequency produce colours and light waves sound, or in which to know what is right would be for all men to do what is right. There is nothing contradictory in these assumptions; they are among the possibles. Consequently, the propositions which describe our world, which state actual fact, are contingent and not necessary. Their

[13] *Monadology*, sects. 31–3 [GP vi.612: L 1049/646]. This distinction is so basic and common in Leibniz's writings that there would be little point in citing all the references. See, however, GP vi.75: H 147–8; GP ii.62: MP 71; GP vii.355–6: A 15–16; GP vii.309: PM 75. Leibniz sometimes refers to the second principle as the principle of determining reason [GP vi.75: H 147] or the principle of rendering reason, and further defines it as the principle 'that every true proposition which is not known *per se* has an *a priori* proof, or, that a reason can be given for every truth, or as is commonly said, that nothing happens without a cause' [GP vii.309: PM 75].

[14] See *Discourse*, sect. 13, GP iv.439–40: L 475–8/310–11; GP ii.39: MP 41; GP vi.106–7: H 127–8.

truth must depend, not upon the principle of contradiction, but upon that of sufficient reason.

This is the reason why it is important to consider propositions asserting *de facto* compatibilities and incompatibilities in the actual world. It is a fact that in our world certain combinations of qualities are compatible and others are not. This cannot be because of latent contradictions in the combinations taken by themselves, for no such contradictions are to be found. It is, if you like, due to the fact that different combinations would not be compossible with our world or within our world. Still, these different combinations, since they contain no internal contradiction, must be members of some one or more of the infinite possible worlds. This is enough to show that the principle of contradiction will not apply to the contingent features of the existent world, and any propositions about the actual constitution of things will presuppose synthetic propositions about actual compatibility and incompatibility.

That Leibniz did not see this consequence is due to a confusion which pervades his philosophy. On the one hand, he distinguishes, as we have just seen, between necessary and contingent truths, between those which must be true because their opposite is logically impossible and those which are in fact true because God created the world in a particular way. On the other, he asserts that all true affirmative propositions are analytic, i.e. they are true because the subject includes the predicate. This is as true, he asserts, of contingent propositions as it is of necessary truths. But if it were true that all true affirmative propositions are analytic, then all such propositions are necessary and there is no contingency. If some propositions are genuinely contingent, they cannot be analytic and must be synthetic. If there is freedom of the will—and throughout his life Leibniz stoutly championed the cause of freedom—then there must be contingency, for free acts of will and absolute necessity in events are incompatible. If all propositions, contingent as well as necessary, are analytic, then there are not two ultimate logical principles, but one, namely the law of contradiction. It would not be correct to say that Leibniz was never aware of this dilemma, for the first half of his correspondence with Arnauld and much of the *Theodicy* are devoted to the attempt to show that it is not irresoluble. What I am contending is that Leibniz's account is both confused and confusing, and I shall now try to show this by appealing to a number of distinct, but closely related arguments.[15]

[15] It should be noted that the character of the argument in this section differs from that in the two preceding sections. While they support the position, contrary to Leibniz, that synthetic propositions are necessary, here I am content with showing that the metaphysical doctrine of contingency which Leibniz defends is inconsistent with his assertion that all true affirmative propositions are analytic.

(1) Arnauld, to whom Leibniz sent in 1686 a résumé of the *Discourse on Metaphysics*, criticized at once the argument of section 8 as entailing the denial of free will.[16] If the concept of an individual substance contains once and for all everything which has happened, is happening, and will happen to it, that individual substance cannot be different in any respect from what it in fact is without contradicting its nature. Freedom implies that the future is open, whereas Leibniz's argument implies that the future is rigorously determined by the original act of creation. Indeed, he admits in the *Theodicy* that 'It was true already a hundred years ago that I should write today, and it will be true after a hundred years that I have written' [GP vi. 123: H 143]. He describes the human soul as a kind of *spiritual automaton* because everything in it is certain and determined in advance [GP vi. 131: H 151].

But is not this to deny freedom? Leibniz thinks not. By means of a series of subtle distinctions between absolute and hypothetical necessity, metaphysical and moral necessity, the necessary and the certain, inclining reasons and necessitating reasons, he seeks to avoid the unpalatable

16 Strictly speaking Arnauld criticizes the Leibnizian argument as denying freedom to God, but this involves the denial of freedom to man, and in the correspondence which follows it is now God's freedom and now man's which is under dispute. 'If that is so, God was free to create or not create Adam; but supposing he wished to create him, everything that has happened since and will ever happen to the human race was and is obliged to happen through a more than fatal necessity. For the individual concept of Adam contained the consequence that he would have so many children, and the individual concept of each of these children everything that they would do and all the children they would have: and so on. There is therefore no more liberty in God regarding all that, supposing he wished to create Adam, than in maintaining that God was free, supposing he wished to create me, not to create a nature capable of thought' [GP ii.15: MP 9]. Leibniz is able to give a satisfactory answer to this contention. He never maintains that God is free to do *anything*, for not even God can do what is logically impossible [GP ii.49: MP 54–5]. God cannot make a round square or two plus two to equal five. The eternal verities are not, as with Descartes, dependent on God's will, but independent of it. If to deny that God can do the impossible is to deny him freedom, then Leibniz's God is not free. But the actual world is not necessary in the sense that a different world is logically impossible (at least he so argues in the present connection), and thus God is free to choose any one of the infinite possible worlds. And since God in his infinite wisdom acts with complete comprehension of all the consequences of his original free act of choice, it is legitimate to say that he willingly and freely chooses all the consequences of the original Adam, while at the same time once the original Adam is created all that follows follows necessarily. Leibniz sometimes expresses this by saying that God did not choose an indeterminate Adam, but a determinate Adam; i.e. he did not choose to create just some man or other only to find that this original creature behaved in an unsatisfactory manner and thus wish that he had done a better job of creating; on the contrary, he foresaw in creating this Adam all his children and his children's children and in fact all that would ever happen in the history of the world. Thus God chose not just Adam, but Adam plus the whole history of the world, and there is a sense in which it is meaningful to say that he chose it willingly. See GP ii.15, 18–20, 28–9, 37–8, 40–1, 48–55: MP 9, 14–16, 27–8, 39–40, 43–4, 53–6.

consequence. These distinctions, which all amount to the same thing, turn upon the difference between the possible and the actual. There are two kinds of necessity for Leibniz. One is logical necessity. It is the necessity expressed by saying that what is identical is true and what is contradictory is false. Its opposite is the impossible. It is what Leibniz sometimes calls 'absolute necessity' or 'metaphysical necessity'.[17] The other kind of necessity is that which depends upon the free decree of God. God having decreed this world decreed everything which is in it, everything which has occurred or will occur in it. Since God has foreseen everything which will occur, everything is *certain*. But God could have chosen another world. Therefore, the certainty, or the necessity, of this world depends upon God's free act of choice. It is only a hypothetical necessity, or, since God always chooses the best, a moral necessity. There are always reasons for any event which incline or which prevail (i.e. they make the event certain), but they do not necessitate in the sense that the opposite of the event is impossible. Thus Leibniz writes in the *Theodicy* in reply to those who would confound certainty with logical necessity:

> They say that what is foreseen cannot fail to exist, and they say so truly; but it follows not that what is foreseen is necessary, for *necessary truth* is that whereof the contrary is impossible or implies contradiction. Now this truth which states that I shall write tomorrow is not of that nature, it is not necessary. Yet supposing that God foresees it, it is necessary that it come to pass; that is, the consequence is necessary, namely, that it exist, since it has been foreseen; for God is infallible. This is what is termed a *hypothetical necessity*. But our concern is not this necessity: it is an *absolute necessity* that is required, to be able to say that an action is necessary, that it is not contingent, that it is not the effect of a free choice. [GP vi. 123–4: H 144]

I am not here concerned with the practical absurdities in Leibniz's position according to which I am constrained by the nature that God has given me to do what I shall do and to do it freely [see GP ii. 51: MP 57]. It is not the freedom which Kant and others have held to be a prerequisite of the moral life. The difficulty goes deeper than that. It is the contradiction involved in holding on the one hand that there is contingency in the world because God might have chosen differently and in maintaining on the other that every true affirmative proposition about an individual is analytic, i.e. is dependent upon the principle of contradiction. If the former is true, the latter is false. If the latter is true, then there is no contingency, no freedom even in Leibniz's diluted sense of the term, and

[17] See GP iv.437: L 476/310; GP ii.18, 20, 51–4: MP 13, 16, 57–60; GP vi.123, 125, 127–8, 131, 215, 283, 284, 333: H 144, 147, 148, 151, 233, 298, 299, 345.

the appeal to hypothetical necessity, to reasons which incline without necessitating is pure confusion.

(2) Closely related to the foregoing argument is Arnauld's criticism that Leibniz's doctrine denies the distinction between property and accident. It belongs to the concept of a sphere that every point on its circumference is equi-distant from the centre, but not that its diameter should be one foot or ten or one hundred. Likewise, he argues, that it is involved in the concept of himself that he is a thinking being, but not that he must make a certain journey [GP ii. 32–3: MP 32–3; see GP ii. 30–1: MP 29–30].

Now Leibniz does not deny that there is a certain difference between such cases, a difference which in the *Nouveaux Essais* he describes as the difference between the essential and the accidental:

I think that there is something essential to individuals and more than you suppose. It is essential to substances to act, to created substances to suffer, to minds to think, to bodies to have extension and motion. That is, there are some sorts of species to which an individual cannot (naturally at least) cease to belong, when it has once been of their number, whatever revolutions may happen in nature. But there are some sorts or species which are accidental (I admit) to the individuals, which may cease to belong to them. Thus you may cease to be healthy, beautiful, wise, and indeed to be visible and palpable, but you cannot cease to have life and organs and perception.[18]

In the correspondence with Arnauld Leibniz distinguishes between the incomplete and the complete concept. The concept of a sphere is incomplete; it is vague and indeterminate. That is why the property of having all points on the circumference equi-distant from the centre belongs to it, while its incompleteness prevents other than purely geometrical determinations concerning it. The concept of Arnauld, on the other hand, is the concept of a complete and particular substance, which must accordingly contain within itself the marks of all that will ever happen to it. Human limitations prevent us from being prophets as well as geometers, but this is a practical, not a theoretical limitation [GP ii. 45: MP 50]. Just as *this sphere* must have a certain length of diameter, a certain colour, a certain weight, none of which properties could be deduced from the abstract and incomplete concept of a sphere in general, so Arnauld must or must not make a given journey to a given place at a given time. Otherwise the true proposition that he does make such a journey would have no logical basis. The predicate, whether a property or an accident, whether essential or accidental, must be in the subject.[19]

But here again we fall into the original contradiction. If all true

[18] GP v.284: La 331. See also C 19: PM 98–9; C 117, 245, and especially 356–7.
[19] See GP ii.38–9, 43, 45–6, 51–4, 54–6: MP 41–2, 46–7, 49–50, 57–60, 61–3.

affirmative propositions are analytic, then every predicate is necessary. The distinction between properties and accidents or between the essential and the accidental may be of practical convenience, but it becomes logically unimportant. But if so, then there are no genuinely contingent propositions; there is no ultimate distinction between the world of existence and the realm of possibility; there are not two ultimate logical principles, but only one.

(3) This is the best of all possible worlds. It is an existent world because God decreed it into existence. It is the best world because God always acts for the best. Nevertheless, since other worlds were possible, it is not a necessary world. I have already sought to show that even if God were free in creating *this* world, man is not free once this world was created. I shall now try to show that on Leibniz's own principles God was not free in creating this world and therefore that he ought to have held that everything is absolutely necessary. If this is correct, it follows that the distinction between the contingent and the necessary rests upon confusion.

According to Leibniz God possesses, among other properties, perfect power which is relevant only to existence, perfect wisdom or understanding which refers to the true, and perfect will which is concerned with the good [GP vi. 105: H 127–8]. The realm of possibility exists in the mind or understanding of God. The realm of existence, i.e. the actual world, results from God's will which chooses the best and his power which is such that he can make actual anything which he chooses to will [GP vi. 105: H 127–8]. Leibniz holds that his distinction between the possible and the actual distinguishes his position from the amoral and atheistic position of Spinoza who denies God's will and who insists that everything which is possible is actual [GP vi. 217–18: H 235–6]. But if God chose anything but the best, it would be either because he did not have the wisdom to see the best or because he did not have a completely good will. On either alternative, however, God would not be God. Therefore, God on pain of contradicting his own nature must choose the best of all the possible worlds. He had in fact no choice, and since he had no choice, this world is an absolutely necessary one.

I said that God on pain of contradicting his own nature *must* choose the best of all possible worlds. But Leibniz claims that there is a distinction between a logical and a moral *must* and that in this connection it is the latter which applies. I think it will be evident from an examination of Leibniz's own words in the *Theodicy* that this is a desperate and untenable dodge. God, being intelligent, must always act with some reason [GP vi. 229: H 246]. His will is never vague and undetermined:

But God is incapable of being indeterminate in anything whatsoever: he cannot be ignorant, he cannot doubt, he cannot suspend his judgement;

his will is always decided [*arestée*], and it can only be decided by the best. God can never have a primitive [*primitive*] particular will that is, independent of laws or general acts of will [*voluntés*]; such a thing would be unreasonable. He cannot determine upon Adam, Peter, Judas or any individual without the existence of a reason for this determination; and this reason leads of necessity to some general enunciation. [GP vi. 315: H 328]

Again, in opposing an opinion of Bayle's that God would have been no less perfect if he had arranged for Spinoza to die at The Hague instead of at Leiden, he argues:

the matter was therefore indifferent in respect of the power of God. But one must not suppose that any event, however small it be, can be regarded as indifferent in respect of his wisdom and goodness. Jesus Christ has said divinely well that everything is numbered, even to the hairs of our head. Thus the wisdom of God did not permit that this event whereof M. Bayle speaks should happen otherwise than it happened, not as if by itself it would have been more deserving of choice, but on account of its connection with that entire sequence of the universe which deserved to be given preference. [GP vi. 218: H 235]

Finally, what other construction can be put on the following passage?:

It would be quite another matter if God decreed to draw from a given point one straight line to another given straight line, without any determination of the angle, either in the decree or in its circumstances. For in this case the determination would spring from the nature of the thing, the line would be perpendicular, and the angle would be right, since that is all that is determined and distinguishable. It is thus one must think of the creation of the best of all possible universes, all the more since God not only decrees to create a universe, but decrees also to create the best of all. [GP vi. 232–3: H 249]

In short, God must act upon some reason. Being perfectly wise and perfectly good, he must choose to create the best possible world. To say that he will not fail to create this sort of world, but that he is not *constrained* to do so [GP vi. 128: H 148] is to say what is not true. God cannot act contrary to his own nature. It would be contrary to his nature if he created any but the best world. Therefore, the best world, and that means for Leibniz this world, is necessary; and what is more it is necessary with absolute or metaphysical necessity, for in the last resort the assurance that this is the best of all possible worlds must rest and can only rest on the proposition that God is perfect in every respect combined with the principle of contradiction.

(4) Up to the end of his life Leibniz speaks of two distinct principles.[20] In his correspondence with Clarke in the last years of his life he describes the principle of contradiction as holding sway over the realm of

[20] See the sections of the *Monadology* quoted at the beginning of this section and the references given in that connection.

mathematics, while the principle of sufficient reason has as its domain physics, metaphysics, and theology [GP vi. 355-6: H 15-16]. In the *Theodicy* the ultimate reason of the world, i.e. of the realm of the contingent, is God who is himself necessary and eternal [sect. 7. GP vi. 106-7: H 127-8]. And in the *Generales Inquisitiones de Analysi Notionum et Veritatum*, written in 1686, section 131 asserts that the infinite regress of causes into which the contingent inevitably leads is resoluble only by God [C 388: P 77]. This is in line with the general distinction between the necessary and the contingent. Unfortunately for the distinction even this last stronghold is denied by Leibniz himself. Indeed, he has no choice. If all true affirmative propositions are analytic, the contingent as well as the necessary, then there can be but one ultimate principle, namely, the principle of contradiction. Couturat in *La Logique de Leibniz* puts this point beyond dispute by the overwhelming array of evidence gleaned from Leibniz's less known logical writings [chap. vi, sects. 17-20]. Leibniz's suggestion that necessary truths are subject to a finite analysis or resolution whereas contingent truths demand an infinite resolution does not suffice to keep the two kinds distinct. For even if God alone is capable of performing the analysis necessary to reduce contingent truths to their simple elements and thus to see the identity between predicate and subject, God could not see it unless the identity were there. And if the identity is present, the propositions are necessary according to the principle of contradiction. To be necessary is not to be seen by a finite mind, but to have the predicate contained within the subject.[21] Both principles have their origin in the true and the false, as Leibniz says in his *Remarques sur le Livre de l'origine du mal* [GP vi. 414: H 419], and this is merely another way of expressing the formal property which all true affirmative propositions must have, *predicatum subjecto inest*. It may still be true that it is useful to distinguish the two and to use now one and now the other, but in the end, as Leibniz is himself forced to admit, the principle of sufficient reason implies or is reducible to the principle of contradiction:

I use two principles in demonstrating, of which one is that that is false which implies contradiction, and the other is that every truth (which is not immediate or identical) can be given a reason—i.e. the notion of the predicate is always in the notion of the subject either expressly or implicitly, no less in extrinsic than in intrinsic assertions (*denominationibus*), no less in contingent than in necessary truths.[22]

[21] For some of Leibniz's many statements on this point see C 376: P 66; C 1-2; GP vii.200; GP vii.309: PM 75; and a passage from FC cited by Couturat in *La Logique*, p. 211, n.2.

[22] GP vii.199-200; see also C 513, 519: PM 7-8, 88.

(D) Leibniz believes that each monad is windowless; yet he holds that each monad mirrors the entire universe. On the one hand, he concludes as a direct result of his doctrine that all true affirmative propositions are analytic, that each substance contains once for all everything which can be truly predicated of it; on the other, he insists that the universe is a system ordered according to the principle of pre-established harmony. These two positions are inconsistent with one another. If a monad has no relation to anything outside itself, it cannot mirror other monads nor can it have been created by God. Indeed, if there is more than one monad, there must be at least the relation of numerical difference between them.[23] It might be argued that Leibniz does not mean to deny this kind of relatedness, that the phrase 'windowless' when applied to monads signifies, not absence of relation, but absence of any physical connection. What I am here concerned with is not so much the positions themselves as the arguments by which Leibniz seeks to establish them. While Leibniz holds that it is a formal characteristic of every true affirmative proposition that the subject contains the predicate, he presupposes the view that the universe is a system in making plausible the metaphysical consequences of his logical position—the consequence, namely, that every substance contains within itself marks of everything that has happened, is happening, and will happen to it. And having arrived at this conclusion, he then, in a sense, burns the bridge by which he has arrived at it, and asserts that each substance is isolated, windowless, a complete universe within itself.

The contradiction is contained in the last sentence of sect. 8 [GP iv. 433: L 472/308] of the *Discourse on Metaphysics*. After describing how it follows from his position that there are marks in the soul of Alexander from which an omniscient mind could deduce *a priori* that he would conquer Darius, Leibniz adds: 'when we well consider the connection of things, it can be said that there are at all times in the soul of Alexander traces of all that has happened to him and marks of all that will happen to him and even traces of all that happens in the universe, though it belongs only to God to know them all'. Is the 'connection of things' necessary merely in order to deduce 'even traces of all that happens in the universe' or is it necessary in order to deduce everything that has happened or will happen to Alexander himself? Leibniz makes it clear that it is the latter:

It seems clear to us that this square of marble brought from Genoa would have been exactly the same even if it had been left there, because our

[23] Note that propositions expressing these relations of difference will be synthetic.

senses permit us to make only superficial judgements, but fundamentally, because of the connections between things the whole universe with all its parts would be quite different and would have been another universe from the beginning if the least thing were to happen other than it does.[24]

Leibniz is here asserting the doctrine of internal relations. The universe is one interconnected whole of such a sort that any change in one part would entail a change in every other part. Now if this is true, it follows that every part must in a sense contain within itself marks of everything that ever has happened or ever will happen anywhere in the universe.[25] But this position is incompatible with the characteristic and irreducible pluralism for which Leibniz is famous. Leibniz needs to appeal to the interconnection of things in order to render plausible his doctrine that every substance contains analytically within itself marks of all that happens to it. Having arrived at that conclusion, he then turns around and by isolating each individual substance denies the very relatedness which gave some initial plausibility to his position. Another way of putting the argument would be that Leibniz first holds that A is related to B; second, that A has the relational quality of being related to B and B has the relational quality of being related to A; and third, that therefore there is no real relation between A and B, but each is a universe all of its own which in some sense reflects or mirrors the universe of the other.

There is only one way of avoiding this contradiction, and that is the way of Spinoza and absolute idealism. The metaphysical doctrine that every substance contains all its past, present, and future predicates can be maintained only by asserting that there is in the last analysis only one substance. In this connection it is interesting to recall Bradley's famous dictum that reality as a whole is the logical subject of all true judgements.[26] I am not suggesting that even for Bradley all true affirmative propositions are analytic, for we have seen that analytic propositions presuppose synthetic propositions. But at least it would avoid the contradiction into which Leibniz's pluralism forces him.

[24] GP ii.42: MP 46; see also GP ii.46: MP 50. Leibniz adds directly after the sentence quoted in the text: 'This does not mean that events are necessary, but the fact is that they are certain from the time God has made his choice of this possible universe, the concept of which embraces this sequence of things'. See section (C) above for a discussion of Leibniz's distinction between necessary and certain.

[25] See Ewing, *Idealism*, chap. 4.

[26] Bradley, *Logic*.

II

MEDITATIONS LEIBNIZIENNES

WILFRID SELLARS

I

MY purpose in this paper is to explore the thesis, so central to Leibniz's philosophy, that the world in which we live is but one of many possible worlds, decidedly more numerous than blackberries. The exploration I have in mind is partly historical, concerned with the questions: 'How exactly is Leibniz's thesis to be understood?' and 'How did he defend it?'. But I also have in mind the question, 'Is this thesis, or something reasonably like it, true?'. My starting point will be Leibniz's contention —so brusquely rejected by Arnauld in his first letter—that 'the individual concept of each person includes once for all everything which can ever happen to him' [GP ii. 15: MP 9].

Now the phrase 'individual concept' will be at the centre of the stage, once the argument is fully under way. For the moment it will suffice to characterize the individual concept of a substance as the sense of God's proper name for that individual; thus, the individual concept of Julius Caesar is the sense of the divine name for the individual substance we refer to as Julius Caesar. Although Leibniz insists that we have a confused grasp of this sense, which consists of our *petites perceptions* in so far as they represent Julius Caesar, this confused grasp of the individual concept is not, of course, *our* concept of Julius Caesar. For the sense of the term 'Julius Caesar', as we use it, is not, strictly speaking, an individual concept at all but—one is tempted to say—a peculiar kind of general concept which applies to many *possible* individuals, though only to one *actual* individual. And, indeed, one is tempted to say that for

From *American Philosophical Quarterly*, vol. 2 (1965), pp. 105–17. By permission of the author and Basil Blackwell, Publisher.

A shortened form of this essay was read as the opening paper in a symposium on Rationalism at the May, 1958, meeting of the American Philosophical Association. In preparing the manuscript for publication I have limited myself to stylistic changes and, where matters of substance were involved, to the omission of less fortunate passages. I have, however, added a brief discussion (section III) of Leibniz's general theory of relations to provide a background for the more specific discussion of causality.

Leibniz, the 'names' we use are not really names at all, but a peculiar kind of general term.

But more about names, divine and human, individual concepts, and possible individuals later. For our present purposes, the important thing about the individual concept of an existing substance is that though as *concept* it exists in the *divine understanding*, it exists *in re* as the *nature* of the substance. This gives us a second formulation of the contention which so startled Dr. Arnauld, to wit, *'the nature of each individual substance includes once for all everything which can ever happen to it'*.

The notion of the nature of an individual substance is a venerable one, though not without its puzzles. But this notion has obviously taken a new twist in Leibniz's hands. Leibniz was not the first to conceive of the *nature* of an individual substance as accounting for its individuality. He was, however, the first to see clearly that the individuality of a substance can only be understood in terms of *episodes* in its history, and to conclude that if the nature of a substance is to account for its individuality, it must account for episodes, and not merely the capacities, powers, dispositions—all, in principle, repeatable—which were traditionally connected with the natures of things.

If we meant by the *nature* of an individual, the criteria in terms of which we identify it as that individual, there would be no puzzle to the idea that natures individuate. But, of course, this is not how we use that expression. We may identify a certain automobile as the one owned by Smith, but in no ordinary sense of the term is *to be owned by Smith* the nature of the automobile. However difficult it may be to make the notion of the nature of a thing precise, this nature is not that in terms of which we identify it, but that in terms of which, *if we but knew it*, we could explain why it behaves as it does in the circumstances in which it is placed.

Now if we take as our model for interpreting the physical conception of the nature of the substance the kind of account we find in Broad,[1] we can by suitable oversimplification construe the nature of a substance S in terms of facts of the form 'if at any time S were to be involved in an episode of kind E_1, it would be involved in an episode of kind E_2'. Thus, suppose that on a certain occasion S is found to have been involved in an episode of kind E_2, then the nature of S would account for this fact in the sense that if we knew the nature of S and if we were to discover that S had obviously been involved in an episode of kind E_1, we would be in a position to say

S was involved in an E_2 because it was previously involved in an E_1

[1] C. D. Broad, *Examination of McTaggart's Philosophy*, vol. i (Cambridge, 1933), 264–78.

If one accepts the above as a crude model for the classical account of the nature of the thing, the first thing one is tempted to say about Leibniz's conception of the nature of a substance is that it not only provides the general hypotheticals, but the episodic premisses as well. Such a nature would, in Hegelian terms, be a set of syllogisms *in re*.

II

How are we to account for this strange twist, in Leibniz's hands, to a familiar notion? It might be thought that the explanation is to be found in his denial of interaction. If the explanation of what goes on in a substance is not to be found in what goes on in another substance, must it not be found in that substance itself, and hence in its nature? Now there is indeed a connection between his conception of the nature of the substance and his denial of the reality of relations between substances. But the latter by itself does not account for the peculiarity of his view as can be seen when we notice that Spinoza is in his own way committed to the idea that the nature of a substance provides not only the hypotheticals (laws) but *affirms the antecedents* as well. For, conceived under the attribute of extension, the nature of Spinoza's one substance specifies not merely that if the physical world were at any time to be in a certain state, it would subsequently be in a certain other state, but specifies whether or not, at a given time, it is in the former state. The nature of substance not only provides the *if* but turns it into *since*.[2] At the heart, then, of Spinoza's conception of the nature of substance is the demand that the occurrence of any *episode* has (in principle) an explanation which is not simply of the form

This episode because that episode

Such an explanation is, of course, legitimate as far as it goes. It is, however, a *relative* explanation of one episode in terms of another. Spinoza demands, in Kantian terms, that the series of other-grounded episodes must have its ground in something, obviously not an episode, which accounts for its own existence. This self-explainer is substance (*Deus sive Natura*); and, of course, in thinking of it as a self-explainer, he is thinking of an argument *in re* of which one premiss says that substance *can* exist, another premiss says that what *can* exist *must* exist if there could be nothing incompatible with its existence, and another premiss, itself a conclusion from a prior argument, says that nothing could be

[2] Hegel did well to point out that the central concept of traditional rationalism was that of syllogisms *in re*. He also saw that the argument *in re* which, according to a thoroughgoing rationalism, has as its conclusion the reality of *this* natural order rather than another—let alone the reality of *any* natural order—cannot itself be syllogistic in form.

incompatible with the existence of substance. Let us be quite clear that whatever rationalists may have said about abstractions, they were precluded from holding that the *esse* of possibilities is *concipi*. Now Leibniz makes exactly the same demand with exactly the same result. Reality provides the principle and affirms the antecedent of an argument *in re* which proves the existence of any episode which belongs to the history of the actual world. But, unlike Spinoza, he offers a complicated story which makes some sense of the idea that this might be the way things are—whereas Spinoza ultimately rests in the assurance that it *must be so* if the world is to be intelligible.

But, of course, the idea that the actual course of events in the world is the only possible course of events is prima facie so absurd that the principle of sufficient reason on which it rests would have no plausibility at all unless some meaning could be given to the idea that other courses of events are possible—even if *in the last analysis* they aren't really possible. Leibniz offers such an account.

A useful way to get the hang of this account is to conceive of a philosopher who is a blend of Leibniz and Spinoza; let us call him Leibnoza. Leibnoza, unlike Leibniz, is happy about the interaction of finite substances. He conceives of the universe as a set of interacting substances whose natures are *hypotheticals*. He also conceives of the universe as involving a temporal series of worldwide episodes in which these substances participate. The hypotheticals provide explanations of each such episode relative to another. But Leibnoza, by accepting the principle of sufficient reason, demands in addition that every truth be either analytic or a necessary consequence of analytic truths.

Leibnoza, as a good Christian, believes that the world of interacting finite substances was created by God. And this means to him that God chooses to create *this* world rather than any of the other possible worlds which he might have created instead. It also means that this choice is in a relevant sense free. This freedom, however, must be compatible with the idea that there is a logically valid argument *in re* with a *logically necessary* premiss which proves the existence of this world. An impossible combination? Not for Leibnoza. He simply asks us to conceive of a set of possible Creators, each one freely choosing *sub specie possibilitatis* to create a different possible world. He then points out that one of these possible Creators must be the most perfect and necessarily exists. To use a Leibnizian (and Spinozistic) turn of phrase, the possible has a *nisus* toward actuality in the sense that an *unimpeded* (or an insufficiently impeded) possibility is *ipso facto* actual. In short, what is logically necessary is not *the choosing* but *that the chooser of this choosing exist*. It is indeed logically necessary that the choosing exist, but no *existent* which is not defined in terms of the choosing logically implies the choosing. The existence of God necessitates the existence of the choosing but God is defined in terms of the choosing. In short, Leibnoza (like Leibniz) applies to God the latter's solution of the free will problem as it applies to Julius Caesar.[3]

Caesar's decision to cross the Rubicon was free in that (a) the objective of the decision is internally consistent in the way in which the objective of an (impossible) choosing to stand and sit simultaneously is not; (b) the choosing is not a logical consequence of any fact about Caesar which does not include the choosing; in particular, it is not a logical consequence of his prior state of mind. It is, however, a logical consequence of his nature, for his nature is simply a set of states of affairs which *includes* the state of affairs which is choosing to cross the Rubicon, and in no other sense can be said to constrain or necessitate the act.

As the existence of Caesar entails the existence of his free acts, so the existence of God entails the existence of His free acts. The difference is simply that Caesar exists by virtue of a choice made by God—whereas God exists as being the most perfect of a set of possible Creators. If we transfer Leibniz's attempted reconciliation of freedom with the principle of sufficient reason to Leibnoza, we get the following account of how the existence of this world can be logically necessary and yet be one of many possible worlds. For according to Leibnoza, this world necessarily exists because the possible God who freely chooses it *sub specie possibilitatis* necessarily exists. From this perspective we can see that the important difference between Leibniz and Spinoza is not that Spinoza thinks that Caesar's crossing of the Rubicon is a necessary consequence of possible being whereas Leibniz does not; but rather that Leibniz thinks that the relation of possible being to the crossing of the Rubicon is of the form:

> The possible God who freely chooses to create the possible substance which freely chooses to cross the Rubicon necessarily exists.

III

A brief excursus on the classical problem of relations will set the stage for the next step in the argument. Suppose one thinks that the truth of

This leaf is green

requires that there be an item inhering in this leaf which is its greenness in the metaphysical sense of a dependent particular numerically different from all other greennesses, even of exactly the same shade, which inhere

[3] *Discourse on Metaphysics*, sect.13 [GP iv.436–9: L 475–8/310–11].

in other substances. Then relational predication immediately generates a puzzle. Consider.

$$S_1 \text{ is } R \text{ to } S_2$$

If we treat this proposition as a special case of

$$S_1 \text{ is } P$$

thus,

$$S_1 \text{ is } R\text{-to-}S_2$$

and attempt to introduce a dependent particular which corresponds to this predicate as a particular greenness corresponds to 'This leaf is green,' we are faced by a dilemma

(1) Is the dependent particular an R-to-S_2? This would seem to require that S_2 inhere in S_1 as being a part of the R-to-S_2 which inheres in S_1.

(2) Is the dependent particular an R rather than R-to-S_2? If so then it inheres in either (a) S_1 alone, or (b) both S_1 and S_2 or (c) neither S_1 nor S_2. But not (a), for then the fact that S_1 is R to S_2 would be unaccounted for; furthermore, it would imply that S_1 could stand in the relation without having a relatum. And not (b), for 'an accident cannot have its feet in two subjects'. Even if S_1 and S_2 could share an R, S_2 might cease to exist (thus, be destroyed by God) and we would be back with the absurdity of the previous alternative. And not (c), for particulars other than substances are *dependent*, i.e. necessarily inhere in substance.

Leibniz found an interesting way out of this dilemma. In effect, he adopts a modified form of the first horn. He accepts the principle that if

$$S_1 \text{ is } R \text{ to } S_2$$

is true, then there must be an R-to-S_2 inherent in S_1, and he accepts the consequence that S_2 must be *in* S_1. But he reinterprets these commitments in the light of the Cartesian (ultimately Scholastic) distinction between 'representative' (or 'objective') and 'formal' being. Thus, the R-to-S_2 inherent in S_1 is interpreted as a representing of S_2 inherent in S_1, and Leibniz, therefore, interprets the sense in which S_2 is a 'part' of the R-to-S_2 inherent in S_1 as a matter of its being that which has objective or representative being in the representing which is the R-to-S_2. According to this analysis, the truth of statements of the form

$$S_1 \text{ is } R_i \text{ to } S_2$$

where R_i is prima facie a real relation, rests on facts of the form

$$S_1 \text{ represents (in specific manner } M_i) \; S_2$$

where, needless to say, the manner of representation M_i which *corresponds* to R_i and makes this relational fact a phenomenon *bene fundatum*, is not what common sense has in mind when is uses the term 'R_i'.[4] If it is objected that on the above account

$$S_1 \text{ is } R \text{ to } S_2$$

could be true even though S_2 did not exist, since non-existent substances can be represented, Leibniz would welcome this objection, but turn its edge by agreeing that the truth of the relational statement requires the actual existence of both S_1 and S_2, and hence that the mere fact that S_1 represents a substance in the appropriate manner does not make the corresponding relational statement true. The substance represented must have formal as well as objective being, in order for this to be the case. After all, his problem was to resolve the classical puzzle about relations, and this he has done, to his own satisfaction, by giving phenomenal relations between substances a metaphysical underpinning in which they have as their real counterparts acts of representing and mobilizing the distinction between the two modes of being which representables may have. Roughly, a true representation is one whose subject matter is a representable which, in addition to having 'objective' being in the representation has 'formal' being in the world.

IV

If we apply these considerations to causality, we can understand why Leibniz believes himself forced to interpret the fact that

S_2 is acted on by S_1 (e.g. S_1 by being in state ϕ *causes* S_2 to become ψ)

as involving, among other things, facts of two radically different types:

(1) S_2 representing the fact that S_1 is in state ϕ
(2) S_2 being caused by representing this fact to become ψ.

The first type of fact is a matter of the ideal relation of *truth* between a judgement and the actual state of affairs which makes it true. That in most if not all cases of the action of one substance on another the judgement is 'confused', is a complication which can be overlooked for our present purposes. What *is* important for our purposes is that the ideal relation between a judgement and the fact which makes it true and, in general, between 'ideas' and their 'ideata' was conceived to be the logical product of two relations, one between the idea and a content, the *being* of which was its *being represented*, and the other between this content and the 'external' object or state of affairs.

[4] Thus the statement, in the phenomenal framework of material things in space,
S_1 is linearly between S_2 and S_3
might have as its real counterpart something like
S_1 represents S_2 and S_3 more directly than S_2 and S_3 represent each other
where a representing of S_i is indirect if it is a representing of a representing of S_i.

Notice, in the light of the preceding brief exposition of Leibniz's general theory of relations, that although

S_1 by being in state ϕ caused S_2 to become ψ

implies that both S_1 and S_2 exist, so that it would be nonsense to say 'S_1 caused S_2 to become ψ but that there is no such thing as S_2', Leibniz can argue that the existence of S_1 and its being in state ϕ is *causally* irrelevant to S_2's being ψ and is relevant only to the *truth* of the representation which is the *vera causa* of S_2's being ψ. Thus S_2 is, as far as the *relation* grounding each of its episodes in other episodes is concerned, as self-contained as Leibnoza's world of interacting things. Both, however, are contingent and require a self-affirming premiss as their sufficient reason. It is, at least in part, the fact that truth is a perfection, which rules out the possibility that the universe might consist of S_2 and God, S_2's representation of S_1 being a representation of something that doesn't exist.

V

We can sum up our results to date by saying that one line of thought which underlies Leibniz's thesis that the nature of an individual substance entails episodic as well as hypothetical facts about it, stems from his commitment to the principle of sufficient reason. Yet the argument is incomplete, for granted that episodes have a sufficient reason and granted that this sufficient reason does not involve the actual being of other substances, it could still be argued that although hypothetical facts and episodic facts alike are grounded (not, of course, independently) in the First Cause, we are not thereby forced to count the episodic facts as elements in the nature of the substance. Why not continue, with Broad, to identify its nature with the hypotheticals, while granting that both episodes and hypotheticals are grounded in Necessary Being?

Part of the answer lies in the fact that we have been guilty of an anachronism in attributing to Leibniz the contemporary distinction between causal properties as general hypotheticals and occurrent states as the categoricals which co-operate with the former in generating further categoricals in an ontological two-step. The truth of the matter is that Leibniz, like most of his predecessors and many of his successors, interprets causal properties on the model of desires, plans, personal commitments. Thus, whereas *we* might be inclined to interpret the statement 'Jones has a strong desire to go to New York' in terms of conditional facts about Jones, Leibniz thinks of a strong desire as a continuing series of episodes which tends to develop into a going to New York and will so develop if not impeded. Thus, to be more precise, he tends to think of the fact that S_2 would become ψ if S_1 were to become ϕ as a matter of S_2 having the plan of becoming ψ if S_1 were to become ϕ. For becoming ψ is (*realiter*) doing something. And, having *the plan* of doing A if B is (though the *plan* is hypothetical in character) itself a categorical fact about S_2.

Actually, then, there is a sense in which for Leibniz all the fundamental facts about a substance are episodic facts. And consequently the notion of the nature of a substance as the law-like hypothetical which would provide an explanation of each episode relative to another episode, is ultimately replaced by the notion of the nature of a thing as that which *logically* explains each single episode. And, of course, the only way it can do this is by duplicating in some way the set of episodes which it is to account for.

Suppose we were to press Leibniz with the question: What is the mode of existence of the nature of a substance, and how is it related to the substance? I think that he would answer somewhat as follows. The nature of a substance is to be construed as its life-plan, and as such it has *esse intentionale* as the content of an abiding aspiration which is the core being of the substance. This connecting of *truths* about what a substance will do with an abiding plan of life raises in an acute form the problem of the relation of time to truth.

VI

That problems pertaining to truth play a central role in Leibniz's metaphysics is a familiar fact. Thus he supported the ideas that the nature of a thing includes once for all everything which can happen to it, and that the individual concept of a thing includes once for all everything that can happen to it—which so startled Arnauld—by considerations pertaining to truth. Like the argument from explanation, the argument from truth purports to show that there are entities, the sort of thing that would usually be called facts, themselves without dates, (though they are *about* dates), which account for the truth of true ideas about individual substances.

Thus suppose the following statements, made today (1958), are true

(1) S_1 was ϕ_1 in 1957
(2) S_1 is ϕ_2 now
(3) S_1 will be ϕ_3 in 1959.

To make these statements is to say that one and the same individual subject was ϕ_1, is ϕ_2, and will be ϕ_3. On the assumption of a correspondence theory of truth, each of these statements corresponds to a fact; thus

(1) corresponds to the fact that S_1 was ϕ_1 in 1957
(2) corresponds to the fact that S_1 is now ϕ_2
(3) corresponds to the fact that S_1 will be ϕ_3 in 1959

and indeed (always on the assumption of the truth of the original statements) it *is* a fact that S_1 *was* ϕ_1 in 1957; it *is* a fact that S_1 *is* ϕ_2 now; it *is* a fact that S_1 *will be* ϕ_3 in 1959.

We say of an episode that it took *place, is taking place, or will take place*. But if something is a fact, it *is* a fact—not *was* a fact nor *will be* a fact. This is not quite true, for there are contexts in which 'was a fact' and even 'will be a fact' do make sense. But these are derivative uses in which, roughly, we are viewing someone else in the past or in the future as thinking of something as a fact. Where it is *we* who are thinking of something as a fact, the proper expression of this thought is always by the use of the *present* tense of 'to be a fact'.

Now it is easy to move from the impropriety, in non-oblique contexts, of 'it will be a fact . . .' and 'it was a fact that . . .' to the idea that the 'is' of 'it is a fact that . . .' has to do with a timeless mode of being. (After all, one does not say '2 plus 2 will be 4' or '2 plus 2 was 4'. Are not facts like numbers?) In effect, Leibniz makes this move. To make it is to suppose that there is a timeless set of entities, i.e. facts, which are about what happens to a substance at different times, and such that it is by virtue of corresponding to these entities that our statements and judgements about the substance are true.

Before we take a closer look at this ontology of truth, let us notice that even if it were illuminating to say that every true statement is true because it corresponds to a timeless fact, this by itself would give no aid or comfort to the idea of the nature of a substance as a set of facts which make statements about its history true. For unless one has already denied the reality of relations, there would be many facts (i.e. relational facts) which have more than one substance as constituents. In the absence of Leibniz's theory of relations, therefore, the ontological version of the correspondence theory of truth would support at most the idea that the only thing which has a nature, strictly speaking, is the universe as a whole. But, of course, Leibniz does have his theory of relations, and so his theory of truth does dovetail with the argument from explanation. It is important, however, to note that even in combination with his theory of relations the argument from truth provides in and of itself no reason for calling the timeless set of facts about a substance its 'nature'.

Returning now to the idea of the nature of a substance as the abiding life plan of that substance, we note that to say that the statement

S_1 *will be* ϕ_3 in 1959

is true because S_1 *now* plans to be ϕ_3 in 1959 is to lose the prima facie advantages of the simple ontological theory and embark on an uncharted course. On the other hand, the notion of a timeless aspiration would seem to be nonsense. But even if Leibniz was not guilty of the category mistake of conflating the notions of timeless facts and life plans, the former notion undoubtedly guided his thinking. It is therefore appropriate to make the point, scarcely a surprising one, that this notion won't do at all. To see that this is so, one simply needs to see that the 'is' of

It *is* a fact that S_1 *will be* ϕ_3 in 1959

is exactly what it seems to be, namely the present tense of the verb 'to be', and that the 'will be' of the that-clause is exactly what it seems to be, namely 'will be' in relation to the present tense of the main verb.

But surely, it may be said, this 'is' can be in the present tense only if it *could be* a 'was'—which you have denied. But I have not denied it. I have pointed out that 'was' is appropriate, but only where we are indirectly expressing someone else's point of view. And this is the heart of the matter. For

It is a fact that S_1 will be ϕ_3 in 1959

is, in a very important sense a counterpart of

'S_1 will be ϕ_3 in 1959' is a true statement

(not, of course, as Strawson has pointed out,

'S_1 will be ϕ_3 in 1959' is a true sentence).

To refer to the statement 'S_1 will be ϕ_3 in 1959' is always to refer to the relevant sentence as used at a certain time. And when I say

'S_1 will be ϕ_3 in 1959' *is* a true statement

the time in question is *now*. If I say

'S_1 will be ϕ_3 in 1959' *was* a true statement

the reference is to the use of the sentence at a time before now; and if I say

'S_1 will be ϕ_3 in 1959' *will be* a true statement

the reference is to the use of this sentence at a time later than now. We can now see why, if we limit ourselves to fact statements which express our own point of view *hic et nunc*, there is no place for

It *was* a fact that S_1 *will be* ϕ_3 in 1959

The point can be made by supposing someone to ask why

It *was* a fact that S_1 will be ϕ_3 in 1959

doesn't correspond to

'S_1 will be ϕ_3 in 1959' was a true statement.

as

It is a fact that S_1 will be ϕ_3 in 1959

corresponds to

'S_1 will be ϕ_3 in 1959' is a true statement.

The answer is, of course, that to use the expression '*that* S_1 will be ϕ_3 in 1959' is to imply a reference to the *present* use of the sentence 'S_1 will be ϕ_3 in 1959', whereas,

'S_1 will be ϕ_3 in 1959' *was* a true statement

explicitly refers to a past use of this sentence. Thus, if we limit ourselves to fact statements which express our own point of view—that is, if we limit ourselves to fact statements which do not occur in oblique contexts—all fact statements will be counterparts of

X is a true statement

and will imply a reference to a *contemporary* use of the sentence represented by '*X*'.

There is an obvious comeback to this argument. It runs as follows: you have been considering the sentence '*S will be* ϕ_3 in 1959' and it must be granted that this sentence is used to make different statements at different times. And it is reasonable to argue that given a that-clause constructed from this sentence, i.e. a *tensed* that-clause, the 'is' of 'it is a fact that' must be in the *present* tense. But this reasoning no longer holds if we turn our attention to the sentences 'S_1 is ϕ_3 in 1959', 'S_1 is ϕ_2 in 1958', and 'S_1 is ϕ_1 in 1957' where these sentences have been detensed. These sentences, the objection continues, make the same statement whenever they are used, and consequently the statements

It is a fact that S_1 is ϕ_3 in 1959
It is a fact that S_1 is ϕ_2 in 1958
It is a fact that S_1 is ϕ_1 in 1957

no longer need to be construed as being in the present tense, save in that 'timeless' use of the present found in '2 plus 2 is equal to 4'. The answer to this objection consists in showing that the *contrived* sentence 'S_1 is ϕ_3 in 1959' makes sense only as introduced in terms of tensed sentence-forms and amounts to the disjunction

S_1 was ϕ_3 in 1959 or S_1 is ϕ_3 in 1959 or S_1 will be ϕ_3 in 1959.

Now for the purpose of my present argument, it will be useful to lay down an oversimplified thesis to the effect that statements of the form

It is a fact that *p*

are simply another way of saying that

'*p*' *is* a true statement in *our* language

and, to get down to fundamentals, that statements of the form

that-*p* is a proposition or state of affairs

are simply another way of saying

'*p*' is a statement in our language.

Now if these theses be granted, it follows that to say that

The statement 'S_1 will be ϕ_3 in 1959' is true
because
It is a fact that S_1 will be ϕ_3 in 1959

is like saying

we're here because we are here.

The 'because' is out of place because nothing is explained. There is indeed a proper because-statement in the neighbourhood, but it must be formulated, rather, as follows

The statement 'S_1 will be ϕ_3 in 1959' is true because S_1 *will be* ϕ_3 in 1959.

If the truth of statements about substances requires no ontology of *facts*, the argument from truth collapses. Furthermore, the implication is unavoidable that insofar as the concept of the nature of thing is a legitimate one, it can be formulated in such a way that it requires no use of 'fact' which is incompatible with the schema

It is a fact that-*p* if and only if '*p*' *is* a true statement of our language.

This, I believe, can be done. Of more immediate concern, however, is what might be called the promissory note character of the idea that things have natures. This promissory note character is a pervasive feature of the statements we are in a position to make about the world. But before I expand on this theme, there is one more strand to be disentangled from the thinking which finds expression in the thesis that the individual concept of a substance includes once for all everything which can ever happen to it. This I shall call the argument from proper names.

VII

Before exploring the cluster of reasonings which I propose to sum up by the phrase 'the argument from proper names' I shall set the stage by some informal remarks which will show how the land lies with respect to my own views on the matter. As I see it, proper names of things and persons play an indispensable role in discourse. Although essentially related on the one hand to definite descriptions and on the other to demonstratives, they are reducible to neither. The fact that any *single* name can be dropped and replaced by a descriptive phrase, at least in a specific context, should not deceive us into thinking that all names can be dropped from the language in favour of definite descriptions.

Again, the use of demonstratives presupposes that the speaker locates himself and his hearers in a common world of objects in space and time; and the framework in terms of which this locating is done is constituted by the use of names and definite descriptions of abiding things. But if the use of demonstratives presupposes the use of names and descriptions, the use of names and descriptions in their turn presupposes the use of demonstratives. The meaning of names and descriptions alike requires that I be able to recognize a named or described object as *this* object. No one of these modes of reference is, so to speak, the foundation of reference, the Atlas which supports all the rest.

That proper names presuppose definite descriptions is scarcely controversial. To use a name '*N*' is to purport to be ready to make at least one statement of the form

N is the f-thing.

Thus names presuppose the statement form 'Something is f'. But in their turn statements of the form 'Something is f' presuppose that we have some way of referring to objects other than by making general statements. The idea that the Atlas of reference is bound variables is as mistaken as the once popular idea that it is demonstratives. The statement

Something is red: $(\exists x)(x \text{ is red})$

is a functioning part of language only because there are names and demonstratives to function in determinate singular reference.

It is not, however, my purpose to *argue* that descriptions and demonstratives presuppose names (and vice versa). I shall simply assume that this is so. For my concern is with the question, 'Granted that names are an irreducible mode of reference, what are the implications of the idea that every individual thing is *nameable*?' For if anything is a central fact in Leibniz's metaphysics, it is that he clearly assumes that every substance is nameable, and I believe that the recognition of this fact throws a flood of light on his system.

Let us call the idea that every substance is nameable the 'Principle of Nameability'. The first thing to note about this principle is that it stands in a certain interesting relation to the principle of the identity of indiscernibles (or the dissimilarity of the diverse). To begin with, if names were shorthand for definite descriptions (which they are not), to stipulate that every individual is nameable would be to stipulate that

$$(x)(\exists y)(\exists f)[x = (\imath y)fy]$$

from which it follows that

$$(x)(y)[x \neq y \rightarrow (\exists f)(fx \,\&\, \sim fy)]$$

The important thing to see is that even if one doesn't *equate* names with definite descriptions, the same conclusion follows from the principle of nameability if one makes the related claim that every name has a *sense* which consists of one (or more) definite descriptions. For one can hold that *being the f-thing* is a *criterion* for being correctly called *N* without holding that '*N*' is *shorthand* for 'the *f*-thing'.

It is sometimes thought that the reason why it is incorrect to characterize names as shorthand for definite descriptions lies in the precariousness of our beliefs about the world which makes it advisable to avoid pinning a name down to only one definite description. In short, it is thought that there are *practical* reasons independent of vagueness, open-texture and the like for refusing to equate names with descriptions—for one can grant that the use of names rests on a fallible inductive footing which warrants a looseness in the connection of names with descriptions, without construing this connection on the model of logical shorthand.

In the event, I am going to stipulate for the purposes of my argument, that names have definite descriptions as their senses, in that definite descriptions serve as the criteria for the application of names. Statements about named objects, then, presuppose (in Strawson's sense) the truth of statements affirming the existence of a unique descriptum. Because, thus construed, names presuppose states of affairs, one can appreciate why those who seek an ultimate mode of reference which involves no commitment to something's being the case either deny (with Wittgenstein in the *Tractatus*) that names have a sense—or equate the sense with the referent—or, with Quine, deny that naming is an ultimate mode of reference and seek to reduce it to the use of bound variables. But this notion of a presuppositionless mode of reference is but another manifestation of the idea that empirical knowledge has a foundation, other facets of which I have explored in 'Empiricism and the Philosophy of Mind'.[5]

Now I am implying that Frege's conception of proper names—though not his theory of definite descriptions—is not only sound, but closer to the tradition than certain modern alternatives. In particular, I am implying that it is in close harmony with Leibniz's treatment of names, though the latter nowhere develops an explicit theory of names along these

[5] *Minnesota Studies in the Philosophy of Science* (Minneapolis, 1956), vol. i, ed. H. Feigl, M. Scriven.

lines. Assuming this to be so, the first point I wish to make is that Leibniz is clearly committed to the idea, indeed takes for granted, that every individual substance is *nameable*, and that this acceptance of the Principle of Nameability carries with it the principle of the Identity of Indiscernibles. For according to the above theory of names, the name of each properly (and not merely putatively) named substance will have as its sense a criterion which distinguishes its nominatum from all other substances. Let us call this *sense* the 'individual concept' which the name 'stands for'.

Now this is exactly the sort of thing Leibniz means by the phrase 'individual concept'. But whereas *we* would think that the individual concept for which a name stands need specify only a few facts about the nominatum, for we think that a few facts suffice to single it out from other things, Leibniz interprets the individual concept associated with the name as specifying everything that the nominatum does or suffers throughout its entire career.

Why should Leibniz think that the sense of a proper name must include a complete description of the nominatum? The answer to this question is surprisingly simple once one realizes that Leibniz is concerned not with *our* names for substances–indeed as we have already pointed out he thinks that the so-called names we use are not really names at all but a peculiar kind of general term–but with *God's* names for things. Thus the principle of nameability is the principle that every individual substance is nameable by God. If, now, we bear in mind the argument that the sense of a name must serve to distinguish its nominatum from all other substances, we see right away what is going on. For Leibniz simply takes it for granted that it makes sense to speak of naming possible substances! And it is by no means implausible that, though an incomplete description of an object may serve to distinguish it from all other *actual* things, only a complete description which pins the object down in all conceivable respects in accordance with the law of excluded middle can distinguish it from all other *possible* things. If it were to be granted that God has names for all possible substances, it would seem indeed that the individual concepts for which these names stand must be as Leibniz characterizes them.

Now even before we turn the cold light of analysis on the idea of names of possible substances, we can put our finger on an ambiguity in this conception. We have pointed out that the sense of a name serves to discriminate its nominatum from the other members of a set of mutually discernible substances. Now, granted that the set of all logically possible substances is a mutually discernible set, the question arises 'Is the mutually discernible set *which is relevant to the naming of a possible substance* the set of all *logically* possible substances?'. The point is an important one, for it is only if the former is the case—only, that is, if the names of possible substances are prior to any *more restrictive* principles of compossibility which build logically possible substances into possible worlds—that it would be true that their 'individual concepts' must describe them exhaustively. If the set of mutual discernibles relevant to the naming of a possible substance coincides with the more restricted notion of a possible world having extra-logical coherence, the individual concept of a possible substance could discriminate it from other substances in its world without having to describe it completely; and its distinguishability from all possible substances in other possible worlds would follow from the distinguishability of the worlds. To take this line in applying the principle of nameability is to deny that there are any possible substances apart from coherent possible worlds.

Now it seems to be quite clear that Leibniz actually thinks of the individual concept of each possible substance as specifying its place in a system of mutually adjusting substances which develops in the orderly lawful way characteristic of a possible world. In so doing, I shall argue, he has undercut his demand, insofar as it is based on the idea of a name, that the individual concept of a possible substance selects that substance in terms of a *complete* description. Instead, however, of supporting this criticism directly, I shall do so indirectly by turning my attention to the question, What sense is there to the notion of the name of a possible substance?

VIII

Are there such things as possible substances? That question is best approached by considering a familiar case for the negative. It rests on the idea that the primary use of the term 'possible' is in such contexts as

It is possible that Tom will get well.

It rests, in short, on the idea that it is states of affairs rather than things which are said, in the first instance at least, to be possible or impossible. And, it is argued, the statement that such and such a *state of affairs* is possible presupposes the actual existence of the *things* with respect to which this possibility obtains. Thus, the possibility that Tom will get well presupposes that there actually is such a person as Tom.

It might be thought that this argument is self-refuting. How can one properly argue that there are no *possible* things on the ground that possible states of affairs concern *actual* things? Surely to speak of 'actual things' is to imply that it makes sense to speak of 'non-actual' or 'merely possible' things. But of course, the argument didn't say that in order for there to be the possibility that Tom will get well, Tom must be an actual thing, but only that there must actually be such a person as Tom.

Having made plausible the idea that the primary use of 'possible' is in connection with *states of affairs*, the case for the negative now grants that a derivative use of 'possible' might be introduced in which one would speak of possible *things* in accordance with the following schema

> There is a possible man in the corner = it is possible that there is a man in the corner.

In this stipulated sense there would be possible things–for to deny it is to deny that sentences such as 'It is possible that there is a man in the corner' can ever be used to make a true statement.

Now I take it to be common ground that such sentences as 'It is possible that Tom will get well' and 'It is possible that there is a man in the corner' are often used to make true statements. I also take it to be common ground that these statements are the blood brothers of *probability* statements and as such are statements in the *present* tense which imply a reference to evidence now 'at hand' or 'available'. Just as the probability statement

> Tom will probably get well

has roughly the force of

> There is a balance of evidence at hand in favour of the statement
> Tom will get well

so the possibility statement

> It is possible that Tom will get well

has the force of

> There is no conclusive evidence at hand against the statement
> Tom will get well;

and just as when more evidence becomes available, it may become proper to say

> It is still very likely that Tom will get well

so, if the evidence is unfavourable, it may become proper to say

> It is no longer possible that Tom will get well

or

> The possibility that Tom will get well no longer exists.

IX

Now if we have reason to believe that there is a man in the corner, we can properly say 'let's call him Jack'. In this case 'Jack' has as its sense 'the man in the corner'. As long as we have reason to think that there was a man in the corner at that time, we have reason to think that 'Jack' is our name for a man. On the other hand, as soon as we have reason to think that no man was actually there, we have reason to think that in the use we gave to it, the word 'Jack' does not name anything. For a word in a certain use, say 'Jack', to be a name for something there must be such a thing as is specified by the sense we have given to the word—there must be such a thing as Jack. This is the insight contained in the slogan: A name isn't a name unless it names something. If, therefore, we discover that there was no man in the corner, we are no longer entitled to regard 'Jack' in that use as a name. To be sure, we can *now* use it as *short for* 'the man who was in the corner'. But if we do so, we are no longer using this descriptive phrase as the criterion of a *name*, and we can no longer say that this phrase gives the sense of a name. In short, we cannot say that 'Jack' as we are *now* using it is a name.

It would be obviously absurd to say

> It is possible that there is a man in the corner: Let's call him Jack.

If, however, we have made the move from

> It is possible that there is a man in the corner

to

> There is a possible man in the corner

we may not see the absurdity. For if it makes sense to say

> There is a tall man in the corner, let's call him Jack

one might ask why it shouldn't make sense to say

> There is a possible man in the corner, let's call him Jack.

The mistake is obvious, for the latter simply repeats the absurdity of

> It is possible that there is a (unique) man in the corner; let's call him Jack.

In short, it is only if one construes 'naming' as introducing an abbreviation for a definite description that one will regard it as proper to speak of naming in this connection. For one would then construe

> It is possible that there is a man in the corner; let's call him Jack

as a paradoxical way of saying

> It is possible that there is a unique man in the corner; let's use 'Jack' as short for 'the man in the corner'.

Notice, however, that even this could not be construed as naming a 'possible man' whose status as possible was independent of epistemic vicissitudes. For, if 'Jack is a possible man' has the sense of 'It is possible that there is a (unique) man in the corner', as soon as new available evidence about the status of the corner at that time requires us to say 'It is not possible that there was a man in the corner', we would have to say 'Jack is an impossible man'.

X

This last point reminds us that the case for the negative has been built on what might be called the 'epistemic' sense of the terms 'possible' and 'impossible'. This sense is not, of course, independent of the 'nomological' senses of these terms, but must not be confused with them. In the epistemic sense, statements of possibility are relative to evidence available to the speaker. They pertain to the world not as it is 'in itself' but to the world as known by someone in some circumstances at some time. And, as a first approximation, we can say that the more evidence that is available concerning a spatio-temporal region, the fewer possible objects and states of affairs it will admit.[6]

If we mobilize the Peircean idea of an inductive community, a community consisting of ourselves and those who join us, and suppose that our remote descendants in this chain have evidence and principles which enable them to decide with respect to every earthly spatio-temporal region whether or not it contained a man, we could imagine them to say

> At such and such places and times there were men; at such and such other places and times there were no men

and, by way of epistimic commentary on the latter statement,

> It is not possible that there were men at the latter places and times

or, by an extended usage,

> There were no possible men at those places and times

The truth of these future statements is no more incompatible with the truth of *my*

> It is possible that there is a man in the corner

or

> There is a possible man in the corner

(given that there is no man in the corner) than the truth of the croupier's statement

[6] If one allows that 'there is a man in the corner' entails 'it is possible that there is a man in the corner', where 'possible' is used in the epistemic sense–which does some violence to ordinary usage–then one should say '. . . the fewer *merely* possible objects and states of affairs it will admit'.

It is impossible that the dice showed seven

is incompatible with the truth of my prior statement

It is probable that the dice showed seven

(given that I know my dice to be loaded).
It is worth pausing to note that these philosophers who argue that determinism implies that the possible coincides with the actual are guilty of two confusions:

(1) they are telescoping epistemic and nomological possibility into one concept;
(2) they are fallaciously supposing that because it would be true for a demon who knows a cross-section and the laws of a LaPlacean universe to say (with respect to any time *t*) 'it is not possible that the state of object *O* at time *t* should have been other than *S*', my statement 'it is possible that *O* is not *S* at *t*' must be false.

The fact that determinism implies that an ideal knower could make no true statement of the form 'both *p* and not-*p* are possible', where the *epistemic* sense of 'possible' is involved, does not imply that it cannot be true for imperfect knowers to say 'both *p* and not-*p* are possible'. If, speaking as convinced determinists, *we* say that 'when you come right down to it only what *actually* happens is *really* possible' this simply expresses our sense of community with those ideal members of the republic of investigators, the concept of which is the regulative ideal of the life of reason.

XI

At this stage, we may imagine the opponent of possible-but-not-actual things to grant that the epistemic sense of 'possible' permits the truth of statements of the form 'it is possible that-*p*' where not-*p* is, in fact, the case; and also that correctly construed, sense can be made of such statements as 'there is a possible man in the corner'. But, he adds, it is only if indeterminism is true that these possible-but-not-actual things are anything more than expressions of human ignorance. And even if there are possible-but-not-actual things (in the epistemic sense) which are *not* relative to ignorance, they presuppose the actual existence of the known evidential context (objects and states of affairs) which fails to pin them down. Mere possibilities in the epistemic sense cannot, in the nature of the case, be prior to actual existence in the sense required by Leibniz's system.

All this, however, would be readily granted by Leibniz. For he is committed to the view that *in the sense of the previous discussion* there are no possible but-not-actual substances save in relation to human ignorance.

For, according to Leibniz, God creates one of the possible worlds (in a sense of 'possible' to be explored) and each possible world being a maximum set of *compossibles* it follows that there are no states of affairs compossible with but not included in a given possible world to be the careers of substances which are possible-but-not-actual relatively to that possible world. Consequently, whichever possible world is the actual one, it could only be in relation to incomplete evidence that a knower in that world would be entitled to say 'it is possible that there is a man in the corner' when in point of fact there is not.

Now given a set of qualities and relations and supposing all simple qualities and relations to be compatible, i.e. supposing no extra-logical limitations on compossibility, it is not possible to define more than one maximum set of compossible objects.[7] In short, it is not possible to define more than one maximum world involving these qualities and relations. (And what a queer world that would be!) This means that in order for there to be more than one maximum world of compossible substances, an additional restriction must be introduced. And this additional restriction pertains to the coherence of possible worlds. The way in which Leibniz introduces this additional restriction is instructive. He introduces a reference to the decrees of the Creator into the defining traits of a possible world. After all, since the proximate possibility of a possible world is the possibility of the act of creation by which it would come into existence, the logical consistency of the world is but the possibility of this proximate possibility. Leibniz tells us that the possibility of *choosing* to perform a certain act presupposes that the description of the act is not self-inconsistent. To illustrate: the impossibility of *choosing* to stand and sit simultaneously stems from the impossibility of standing and sitting simultaneously. On the other hand, simply because a state of affairs is self-consistent, it does not follow that it is possible that I choose it. If, therefore, we assume that extra-logical modes of coherence are perfections, there would presumably be more than one maximum system of objects which a possible creator might choose to create, only one of which, however, could be chosen by the best possible creator, who necessarily exists. For, as we have seen, the possible, the actual, and the necessary coincide *in the last analysis* for Leibniz as for Spinoza. In this sense the actual world is the only one that is *really* possible.

XII

We have seen that Leibniz's notion of possible-but-not-actual things cannot be justified in terms of the inductive or epistemic use of 'possible',

[7] Objects must be carefully distinguished from states of affairs (possible facts). Among the latter are negative states of affairs, and there would be many systems of states of affairs (state descriptions) with respect to the objects in question.

and this for two reasons: (1) there is no such thing as naming possible objects in any sense of 'possible' springing from this use; (2) a commitment to determinism involves a commitment to the idea that 'the *really* possible coincides with the actual'.

Is there any other line of thought which enables us to understand what was at the back of Leibniz's mind? The answer lies in the fact that it does make sense to speak of the *actual* world, and, by contrast, possible-but-not-actual worlds. Now it might be thought that to speak of 'the actual world' is to refer to the actual course of *the world*, as contrasted with possible-but-not-actual courses of *the world*. If this were the case, the possibility involved would be analogous to the possibility that Tom will get well, and would be either the inductive possibility expressed by

It is (on the evidence at hand) possible that Tom will get well

or would be a misnomer for the *contingency* of the state of affairs–i.e. the fact that the idea that Tom will get well is neither analytic nor self-contradictory. But as we have seen, both the possibility that Tom will get well and the contingent character of this state of affairs presuppose the existence of Tom and of the world which includes him.

But what can the contrast between the actual world and possible-but-not-actual worlds amount to if it is neither of these? The general lines of the answer emerge if we remember that to think of the *actual* world is to think of what it would be *known as* by our ideal inductive descendents, that is, by ideal members of *our* scientific community. *This* world is essentially *our* world. *This* is what I am perceiving, and can talk about with *you*. What, then, does it mean to conceive another world? It means to conceive not only of a different set of substances than those which make up this world, but a set which does not include *us*.

Now if to think of an object is to use an expression which refers to it, we can't think of these other substances by using the referring expressions of the language we actually use. They refer *ex hypothesi* to the objects of the actual world. It would seem, then, that to think of the objects of a non-actual world, we would have to use a language we don't have. Again, one cannot specify what object a referring expression refers to save by *referring* to it by means of another referring expression. And this referring expression would be one which belongs to the language we use and which talks about 'actual things'.

Fortunately there is a simple model at hand for talking coherently about non-existent things, and using names which don't really name anything. This model is fictional discourse. Thus, to 'imagine' that there was such a person as Oliver Twist is to do what we would call purporting to describe an actual person, if the description didn't occur in a rubric ('once upon a time') which brackets discourse in a way which frees it from responsibility to inductive confirmation.

Thus to imagine a possible but not actual world is to place discourse which, if *seriously* intended, would purport to describe this *world*, in a rubric which marks it as fiction. And, of course, the 'names' in this fictional discourse are only *fictional* names, and the sentences which constitute their *principia individuationis* are fictional sentences. The referring expressions in this fictional discourse do not translate into the language we seriously use. Language about a possible world is not a *different* language simply in the sense in which Italian is different from English—for '*Parigi*' does translate into 'Paris' and we can say that '*Parigi*' refers to Paris.

To say what a language about a possible world is about we have to make *fictional* use of another language into which the *fictional* object language translates.

Furthermore, *to imagine* a possible world is to imagine that 'I' belong to this world and am a member of an inductive community ferreting out its secrets. For the concept of *actuality* includes a reference to us and ultimately—if ungrammatically—to 'I'. Consequently, imagined actuality involves a reference to an imagined 'I'.

Is it not self-contradictory to speak of imagining that I am in a different world? Am I not, by definition, in *this* world? No, for to imagine that I am in a different world is simply to suppose that the states of affairs by virtue of which the general criteria associated with the term 'I' are satisfied are other than they actually are; it is to suppose that these states of affairs are among those which belong to the fictional rubric.

But this is not the place to ferret out the truth in Kant's conception of the transcendental unity of apperception as the fundamental form of experience. Our task is rather to illuminate Leibniz's conception of the actual world as one of an infinite number of possible worlds. What I am suggesting is that at the back of Leibniz's mind is the picture of God as making use, within the fictional rubric, of alternative languages, and by so doing conceiving of alternative sets of individual substances.

According to this picture, the model for *creation* is obviously the removing of the fictional rubric from one of these languages; the move, on God's part, from 'Suppose that there were such and such things' to 'There are such and such things', via 'Let there be such and such things'.

XIII

Now it is obvious that if the *esse* of possible worlds like the *esse* of Oliver Twist consists in fictional discourse about them, we have a new sense in which *actuality* is prior to possibility–roughly that in which Dickens is prior to Oliver Twist. This accords with Leibniz's contention that the Divine Understanding is the locus of possible worlds. How, then, can he extend the notion of possibility to God Himself? For God is that Being who necessarily exists if He is possible. And God *qua* possible can scarcely have a being which is dependent on God's Understanding. I shall limit myself to two points:

(1) When Leibniz tells us that the Divine Understanding is the locus of the possible he seems, on the whole, to have the contingently possible in mind, and to be telling us that the *real* or *proximate* possibility of the contingently possible lies in the possibility of its intended Creation, and hence involves a reference to God's thought of it. This is compatible with an account of possible substances which make them prior to the actuality of God.

(2) If my positive argument is correct, the actuality of God as of anything else would presuppose *our* existence as discoverers of God.

III

NECESSITY AND CONTINGENCY IN LEIBNIZ

DENNIS FRIED

I

A recurrent theme in the work of Leibniz is his attempt to reconcile his view that all truths are analytic with his view that propositions about substances (individuals) are contingent. It has been suggested, by Mates[1] and Mondadori,[2] among others, that Leibniz had available to him a clear-cut way to effect this reconciliation by relying both on his (purported) view that all propositions with a nonexemplified subject term (concept) are false, and on the contingent existence of all created substances. Thus, on this suggestion, though the proposition expressed by 'Gerald Ford is a Republican' is analytically true, it is not a necessary truth: there are possible worlds in which Ford does not exist, and the proposition expressed by 'Gerald Ford is a Republican' is false of these worlds (having there a nonexemplified subject term). However, Leibniz does not take this line in his account of contingent propositions; rather, he resorts to an extremely difficult and unsatisfactory account based on the analysis of terms, and the reduction of truths to identities. Why Leibniz forgoes the simpler solution in favour of the more obscure has been called by Mates 'perhaps the most puzzling of all the problems here' [p. 98].

In what follows I will argue that the proposal of Mates and Mondadori fails to account for the contingency of several common classes of propositions about individual substances, and that, moreover, the proposal itself is based on a serious misinterpretation of the Leibnizian semantics. By showing the inadequacy of the proposed solution to Leibniz's difficulties with contingency, I hope to remove some of the puzzlement regarding Leibniz's failure to adopt it. In so doing, I believe, it will become clear why there can be no coherent account of contingency that is consistent both with Leibniz's semantics and with his complete concept theory of individuals.

From *Philosophical Review*, vol. 87 (1978), pp. 575–84. By permission of the author and the editor.

[1] Benson Mates, 'Individuals and Modality in the Philosophy of Leibniz', *Studia Leibnitiana*, 4 (1972), 94.

[2] Fabrizio Mondadori, 'Leibniz and the Doctrine of Inter-World Identity', *Studia Leibnitiana*, 7 (1975), 24.

II

The basic building block in Leibniz's logic of propositions is the term: 'by "term" I understand, not a name, but a concept, i.e. that which is signified by a name; you could also call it a notion, an idea' [C 243: P 39]. A primitive term for Leibniz is one which is 'unanalysable or assumed to be unanalysable'. A composite term is one which can be analysed into two or more terms. The concept of *A* (that is, the term expressed by '*A*') is said to 'contain' the concept of *B* if and only if every component of the latter is a component term of the former (Leibniz envisions complex terms to be built up by conjunctions of simpler terms, which will be the components).

For Leibniz, a categorical proposition, to which Leibniz believes all other propositional forms can be reduced, expressed by '*A* is B' asserts that the concept of *A* contains the concept of *B*.[3] This view of the structure of categorical propositions leads directly to what has become known as Leibniz's 'containment conception' of truth: a true proposition is one in which the predicate concept is contained in the subject concept—in modern terms, every true proposition is analytic:

> Always in every affirmative proposition whether veritable, necessary or contingent, universal or singular, the concept of the predicate is comprised in some sort in that of the subject. Either the predicate is in the subject or else I do not know what truth is. [GP ii. 56: MP 63]

> Every truth has its proof *a priori*, drawn from the meaning of the terms. [GP ii. 62: MP 71]

Since, for Leibniz, all true propositions are analytic, this seems to leave him no choice but to allow that *all* truths are necessary, including those about created beings (individual substances). But such a result is unacceptable to Leibniz, as it is in direct conflict with his theological

[3] Leibniz's characterization of a categorical proposition as one which asserts that the predicate concept is contained in the subject concept is strictly applicable only to universal propositions (which Leibniz takes to include singular propositions), and must be qualified for particular ones. The universal proposition that all gold is metal would be symbolized by Leibniz as '*G* is (contains) *M*': that is, the concept of gold 'simply and in itself' contains the concept of metal. However, the concept of metal does not in itself contain the concept of gold, and so the particular proposition that some metal is gold cannot be symbolized as '*M* is (contains) *G*'. Leibniz's solution is to interpret the particular proposition that some metal is gold as asserting that the concept of metal 'with some addition or specification' (e.g. 'that which makes up the greater part of a Hungarian ducat') does contain the concept of gold. The result of such addition or further specification to a subject concept is what Leibniz calls a 'species' of the subject. The proposition that some metal is gold is, for Leibniz, the proposition that some species of metal is gold, where 'it is not stated expressly just what the species is'. This would be symbolized as '*MX* is *G*', where '*X*' now represents the unspecified concept which, when added to the concept of metal, forms a subject term which does contain the concept of gold [C 51–7: P 18–24].

views. If all truths were necessary, then God could not have made the world differently than he did; and if it were impossible that the world be otherwise than it is, it would be nonsensical to praise God for creating this one (which, according to Leibniz, is the best of the infinity of possible worlds). Moreover, if all human actions were necessary, this would be incompatible with the status of men as moral agents, deserving of divine punishment or reward. Thus, it is crucial for Leibniz to be able to provide for the contingency of propositions concerning created substances; the effort to accomplish this is at the heart of a great deal of Leibniz's philosophy and logic.

III

We come now to the suggestion of Mates and Mondadori as to how Leibniz could have consistently accounted for the contingency of propositions concerning individual substances. Their suggestion rests on an interpretation of a crucial passage in Leibniz's *General Investigations* [C 393: B 71, P 82]. Mates translates this passage as follows:

> This however presupposes denying every proposition in which there is a term that does not exist. In order, namely, to keep [the principle] that every proposition is true or false, [I consider] as false every proposition that lacks an existent subject or real term. In the case of existential propositions this is somewhat remote from the ordinary way of talking. But there is no reason why I should care about that, since I am looking for a suitable notation [*propria signa*], not purporting to apply existing terminology [*recepta nomina*] correctly.

Mates interprets this as 'Leibniz's decision to regard as false every atomic sentence containing a singular name *N* that is non-denoting', as 'the proposal to regard "*A* is *B*" as false if *A* does not denote anything', and as stating that 'if *A* does not denote, every sentence of the form "*A* is *B*" is false, no matter what the predicate *B* may be' [p. 93]. Moreover, Mates believes that this semantics applies, not only to the actual world, but to possible worlds as well, so that '"*A* is *B*" is true of a possible world *W* just in case the concept expressed by *B* is contained in the concept expressed by *A* and the latter concept belongs to *W*'. (I take it here that by 'belonging to *W*' Mates means 'exemplified in *W*'). Similarly, Mondadori interprets the passage as 'Leibniz's view that a sentence of the form "*a* is *P*" is true of a given world *w* just in case the complete concept exemplified by *a* is a member of *w* and "contains" the property expressed by *P*' [p. 42]. I will later call into question the validity of this interpretation of Mates and Mondadori. But first I will give them their interpretation in order to see if it is as helpful as they believe.

Consider, then, the proposition expressed by the sentence 'Ford is a Republican'—how do Mates and Mondadori account for its contingency?

The proposition is true of the actual world. However, Ford, like all created substances, is not a necessary being—there are possible worlds in which he does not exist. In these worlds the name 'Ford' fails to denote, and the complete concept of Ford is not exemplified. Thus, on the Mates-Mondadori interpretation of Leibniz's semantics, in these worlds the proposition expressed by 'Ford is a Republican' is false. So the proposition, being true of some worlds and false of others, is a contingent truth rather than a necessary one, which is the result desired by Leibniz. This same move, it appears, could be used to account for the contingent truth of all (true) propositions expressed by sentences of the form '*A* is *B*', where '*A*' denotes an individual substance.

IV

Why hasn't Leibniz adopted this account of contingency? One way to answer this question would be to find some inadequacy in the Mates-Mondadori line (other than their interpretation of the semantics), one which might explain why Leibniz avoids it. Initially, there appears to be a way to do this. The first step is to point out that Leibniz wants all propositions about created substances to be contingent (other than those which express identities), the true as well as the false. Whatever explanation, then, that Leibniz offers for the distinction between necessary and contingent propositions, it must account for, not only the contingency of truths concerning individuals, but also the contingency of falsehoods concerning individuals.

Consider now the false proposition expressed by 'Ford is a non-Republican'—can the Mates-Mondadori line account for its contingency? At first sight, the answer seems to be negative. In all possible worlds in which Ford exists (including the actual world—in truth, Leibniz holds that an individual can exist in only one possible world[4]), the proposition is false because the complete concept of Ford includes the concept of being a Republican,[5] and thus if Ford exists he will be a Republican. In all possible worlds in which Ford does not exist, 'Ford' is nondenoting, and thus, on the present interpretation of Leibniz's semantics, the

[4] Leibniz's claim that an individual can exist in only one possible world is a direct consequence of his complete concept theory of individuals. A complete concept determines an individual; such a concept specifies the individual's relations, for all time, to every other entity in the universe. Such a concept thus completely specifies that universe or, in Leibniz's words, 'involves the whole sequence of the universe'. So an individual cannot exist in more than one possible world, for its complete concept determines that one, out of the infinite number of possible worlds, which it will inhabit.

[5] Proof: On Leibniz's complete concept theory, the complete concept of Ford contains the concepts of all the properties Ford would have were he to exist. Ford exists, and has the property of being a Republican: thus, the complete concept of Ford contains the concept of being a Republican.

proposition expressed by 'Ford is a non-Republican' would again be false. Hence, the proposition, being false in all possible worlds, would apparently have to be regarded as necessarily false by Mates and Mondadori. But Leibniz wants such a proposition to be contingently false. Thus, it seems to be a serious defect in the Mates–Mondadori line that false propositions expressed by sentences of the form '*A* is non-*B*', where '*A*' denotes an individual substance, come out as necessarily false.

Mates and Mondadori might make the following reply to this objection. They might claim that, for Leibniz, although propositions expressed by sentences of the form '*A* is *B*' are false of worlds in which '*A*' fails to denote, this is not the case for propositions expressed by sentences of the form '*A* is non-*B*'. In fact, they might argue, the propositions expressed by '*A* is *B*' and '*A* is non-*B*' are contradictories for Leibniz, or what he calls 'opposites'. This might be argued as follows. For Leibniz, to say that *A* is *B* is to say that *A* contains *B*, and to say that *A* is not *B* is to say that *A* does not contain *B* [C 365: B 38]. Furthermore, '"*A* is not *B*" is the same as "*A* is non-*B*"' [C 378: B53]. Finally, there is this quotation from Leibniz:

> Of these propositions: '*A* contains *B*' [*A* is *B*] and '*A* does not contain *B*' [*A* is non-*B*], one is true, the other false: or they are opposites . . . provided the terms are possible. Therefore, they are not true or false at the same time. [C369: B42–3; brackets mine]

Thus, the reply would continue, if the proposition expressed by '*A* is *B*' is false, as will be the case for a world in which '*A*' fails to denote, the proposition expressed by '*A* is non-*B*' is true. Moreover, this seems to be quite in keeping with Leibniz's adherence to the Scholastic principle that 'What does not exist has no properties'.

> Suppose that *N* is not *A*, *N* is not *B*, *N* is not *C*, and so on. Then we can say that *N* is nothing. This is what the common saying, that what does not exist has no attributes, refers to . [S 472]

> 'Non-being' is what is purely privative, or privative of all things, or non-*Y*; i.e. non-*A*, non-*B* non-*C*, etc.; and this is what is popularly stated as: there are no properties of nothing. [C 356: B 28]

At a world in which individual *A* fails to exist, it is false that *A* is *B* and true that *A* is non-*B*, false that *A* is *C* and true that *A* is non-*C*, etc.

Consider again the false proposition expressed by 'Ford is a non-Republican'. Mates and Mondadori might now claim that this proposition will be true of the worlds in which Ford does not exist, because its 'opposite', the proposition expressed by 'Ford is a Republican', is false of these worlds. Because Ford is not a necessary being, there will be possible worlds in which he does not exist, and so, according to this reply, there are possible worlds for which the proposition expressed by 'Ford is a non-Republican' is true—the proposition is now contingently false rather than necessarily false. So it might seem that the Mates–Mondadori account *can* explain the contingency of false propositions expressed by sentences of the form '*A* is non-*B*'.

However, this reply is unsatisfactory on several counts. On the one hand, it is self-defeating: such a defence of the Mates–Mondadori line against the initial objection leaves it vulnerable to another—it cannot now account for the contingency of *truths* expressed by sentences of the form '*A* is non-*B*'. For example, consider the true proposition expressed by 'Ford is a non-Democrat'. This proposition will be true of all worlds in which Ford exists, due to the complete concept theory. But it will also be true in all worlds in which Ford does not exist, for (supposedly) its 'opposite', the proposition expressed by 'Ford is a Democrat', is false at these worlds, being expressed by a sentence of the form '*A* is *B*' and having a nonexemplified subject term. So the proposition expressed by 'Ford is a non-Democrat' would now come out as a necessary truth on the Mates–Mondadori account.

In addition, the reply is not effective against the objection that the Mates–Mondadori line cannot account for the contingency of false propositions expressed by sentences of the simple form '*A* is *B*'. For instance, the proposition expressed by 'Ford is a Democrat' is false of the actual world, and is false of all possible worlds in which Ford exists, as is guaranteed by the complete concept theory. According to the Mates–Mondadori interpretation of the Leibnizian semantics, the proposition will also be false of all worlds in which Ford does not exist. Thus, this proposition is false of all possible worlds, and hence is necessarily false.

These inadequacies alone constitute ample reason for Leibniz to avoid the Mates–Mondadori account of contingency. To recapitulate, what has been shown is that, even allowing them their interpretation of Leibniz's semantics (in particular, that found in C 393: B 71, P 82). Mates and Mondadori cannot give a satisfactory account of the contingency of propositions concerning individual substances. There is also very good reason to believe that this interpretation itself is incorrect.

V

Leibniz's 'containment conception' of truth is a cornerstone of his philosophy (for example, 'either the predicate is in the subject or else I do not know what truth is'). Any interpretation of the Leibnizian semantics which is inconsistent with this conception must be suspect. On the Mates–Mondadori interpretation, propositions expressed by sentences of the form '*A* is *B*' are false of worlds in which '*A*' fails to denote; at such worlds, in accordance with Leibniz's statement about 'opposites', propositions expressed by sentences of the form '*A* is non-*B*' will be true. This gives results which are at odds with the containment conception of truth. Consider the true proposition expressed by 'Ford is a Republican'. For Leibniz, the proposition is true just because the complete concept of Ford includes, or contains, the concept of being a Republican—but this remains the case in every world, whether Ford the individual exists there or not. So, on the containment conception of truth, the proposition expressed by 'Ford is a Republican' will be true at all worlds, not just at those in which Ford the individual exists; this is actually the root of Leibniz's problem with contingency. Similarly, the complete concept of Ford does not contain the concept of being non-Republican; consequently the proposition expressed by 'Ford is a non-Republican' can be true at no worlds, contrary to the result of the Mates–Mondadori interpretation of the semantics.

What has happened is this. Mates and Mondadori have given us an extensional interpretation of the passage at C 393 [B 71, P 82]: they are concerned with the denotation of names and the exemplification of concepts. But Leibniz makes it quite clear that he prefers an intensional treatment of propositions and their logic (though he also maintains that an extensional logic would have the same set of theorems):

> The Scholastics speak differently; for they consider, not concepts, but instances which are brought under universal concepts. . . . However, I have preferred to consider universal concepts, i.e. ideas, and their combinations, as they do not depend on the existence of individuals. [C 53: P 20]

But why would Leibniz want to deny existential import to universal propositions, and thus to singular ones? The answer can be found in a letter to Arnauld:

> All that is actual can be conceived as possible and if the actual Adam will have in time a certain posterity *we cannot deny this same predicate to this Adam conceived as possible,* inasmuch as you grant that God sees in him all these predicates when he determines to create him. They therefore pertain to him. And I do not see how what you say regarding the reality of possibles could be contrary to it. In order to call anything possible, it is enough that we are able to form a notion of it when it is only in the divine understanding, which is, so to speak, the region of possible realities. *Thus, in speaking of possibles, I am satisfied if veritable propositions can be formed concerning them.* Just as we might judge, for example, that a perfect square does not imply contradiction, although there has never been a perfect square in the world, and if one tried to reject absolutely these pure possibles he would destroy contingency and liberty. For if there was nothing possible except what God has actually created, whatever God created would be necessary and God, desiring to create anything would be able to create that alone without having any freedom of choice. [GP ii. 55–6: MP 62–3; italics mine]

So, for instance, we might judge that the complete concept of Superman (if we could know this concept) 'does not imply contradiction'; God could have created Superman if he had wished. Yet, even though Superman does not exist, we cannot deny the predicates of being caped, being the strongest man in the world, etc., to this individual conceived as possible. And, in speaking of possibles Leibniz is satisfied if true propositions can be formed concerning them. Leibniz wants to be able to form true propositions about beings, and worlds, that God *could have* created. So, Leibniz wants the propositions expressed by 'Superman is caped', 'Superman is the strongest man in the world', etc., to be true. The containment conception of truth, which is intensional rather than extensional, allows Leibniz this result.

What then is the proper interpretation of the passage at C 393? The key sentence there is 'I consider as false every proposition that lacks an existent subject or real term'. What Mates and Mondadori seem to have overlooked is that, for Leibniz, terms are concepts and that subjects and predicates are terms–and 'real term', 'true term', 'possible term', and 'existent term' are all synonymous:

A-non-*A* is a *contradiction.* [C 364: B 37]

Possible is what does not contain a contradiction or '*A*-non-*A*'. [C 364: B 37]

False in general I define as what is not true (or what contains terms in which *B* and non-*B* occur. [C 371: B 45]

A false or non-true term is one which contains '*A*-non-*A*'. [C 397: B 76]

If I say '*AB* is not' [translated as '*AB* does not exist' at P 87], it is the same as if I say '*A* contains non-*B*' or '*B* contains non-*A*' or '*A* and *B* are inconsistent'. [C 399: B 77]

Thus, the proper interpretation of C 393 [B 71, P 82] is that all propositions which have as subject a term which contains a contradiction are to be regarded as false. This sense of the passage is brought out most clearly in Parkinson's translation, which reads, in part, 'So it remains that every proposition is either true or false, but that every proposition which lacks a consistent subject, i.e. a real term, is false' [P 82].

As an example, let term *C* be coincident with term *A*-non-*B*, or *C* = *A*-non-*B*. The term *CB* will be the term *A*-non-*B*-*B*; therefore, *CB* will be a contradictory term. *All* propositions that have *CB* as subject will be false, as they lack a consistent subject. So the proposition which asserts that *CB* contains *B* will be false, as will the proposition that *CB* contains non-*B*. This in no way contradicts what Leibniz has said about propositions which are 'opposites' [C 369: B 43], for he says that this applies only to propositions whose terms are possible. Leibniz does point out [C 393: B 71] that this convention does not conform to ordinary usage. That is,

Leibniz implies that we ordinarily would say that *A*-non-*B*-*B* contains *B* and also that *A*-non-*B*-*B* contains non-*B*. But he dismisses this variance as 'not a matter which concerns me, because I am seeking fitting signs, and I do not plan to apply traditional terms to these propositions'.

This also gives us a new way to interpret Leibniz's dictum that 'what does not exist has no attributes'. When applied to terms, 'existent' is, for Leibniz, synonymous with 'possible' or 'consistent'. We have just seen that if *A* is a contradictory concept, there can be no true propositions which assert that *A* contains *C*, where *C* may be any term (including *A*). Thus, we can now understand Leibniz as saying that if a term does not exist (that is, is inconsistent or contradictory) it has no attributes (that is, there is nothing which it can truly be said to contain).

VI

I have argued here that Mates and Mondadori have failed to produce a coherent account of contingency that is consistent with Leibniz's containment conception of truth. Nor do I think that one can be produced, while remaining faithful to Leibniz's complete concept theory of individual substances. The complete concept of a particular individual substance, such as Gerald Ford, contains the same component concepts in every possible world, whether or not the complete concept is exemplified in that world. On the containment conception of truth, then, any proposition which is true of Gerald Ford at one world will be true of him at all worlds, and similarly for false propositions about him. All true propositions about Ford are necessarily true and all false propositions about Ford are necessarily false.

One might attempt to fit contingency into all this by appealing to the fact that, for Leibniz, there are an infinite number of complete concepts very similar to that of Gerald Ford, and that God could have chosen to exemplify one of these other concepts in the actual world, rather than the one he did. So, one might argue, Gerald Ford might have been a Democrat, though in fact he is not, and this is all we need in order to claim that the proposition expressed by 'Gerald Ford is a Republican' is contingent rather than necessary.

This too fails because, according to Leibniz's complete concept theory, nonidentical complete concepts determine nonidentical individuals [GP ii. 42: MP 45-6]. Consequently, to try to argue for the contingency of Ford's being a Republican by pointing out that God could have created in his place a very similar individual who was a Democrate is no more helpful than to point out that Jimmy Carter is a Democrat.

IV

CONTINGENT TRUTHS AND POSSIBLE WORLDS

HIDÉ ISHIGURO

IN recent discussions of modal concepts philosophers have followed Hume and Kant in thinking that the main source of the philosophical problem of modality is a special conceptual difficulty about necessity and necessary truth. It is thought that various structures of possible worlds will clarify the nature of various kinds of necessity and enable us to compare their strength. Any such clarification will naturally bear upon the nature of contingent truths with which necessary truths are contrasted, but what philosophers in the tradition of Hume and Kant are specially concerned with are the grounds for the universal validity and necessity of certain judgements. Whatever the epistemological problems relating to contingent truths, their status was not held to be metaphysically problematic.

Matters were quite different for Leibniz, even if we owe our ideas of possible worlds to him. Leibniz thought that in a system like Spinoza's, or in the fatalism inherent in Pierre Bayle's doctrines, one would not be able to distinguish contingent truths from necessary truths. It was not the epistemological question how one can know that a truth is a contingent or a necessary one which troubled him, but the status or metaphysical foundations of contingency. And here I think we can follow him in being puzzled. What is it for a truth to be contingent? If it is contingently the case that S is P or *aRb* we have to be able to give content to our belief that it could have been otherwise. We have to do more than just express our intuitions. In what sense, if any, is it a necessary truth that the number two is even but not a necessary truth that Caesar crossed the Rubicon?

Without having immediate recourse to the familiar distinction of *de dicto* and *de re* modalities, which contains much more difficulty than one might suspect, let us try to see what lay behind Leibniz's introduction

From *Midwest Studies in Philosophy*, vol. IV, pp. 357–67, Studies in Metaphysics, University of Minnesota Press, Minneapolis.

of the notion of possible worlds in his attempt to make sense of contingency. Contrary to the views recently aired by some distinguished philosophers of logic working on Leibniz's thought,[1] it seems clear that it was this problem of modality that was intimately connected to Leibniz's talk about possible worlds. In an early critical commentary on Spinoza's *Ethics*, for example, Leibniz severely attacks Spinoza's claim that there is nothing contingent in the nature of things. Leibniz holds that such a view is only possible because 'contingent' is used by Spinoza in an idiosyncratic sense, that is, to mean 'without reason'. Leibniz uses contingency, as he claims, to mean 'that whose essence does not involve existence' [GP i. 148: L 313/203 (1678)].

The failure to give a place to contingency comes from confusing a metaphysical quest with an epistemological one: what is necessary and what is known with certainty [GP vi. 123, 284: H 143-4, 298-9 (1710)]. From the fact that one can understand and come to know more and more truths about the universe, someone may mistakenly infer that all these truths are necessary. Leibniz claims that he too was tempted to make the confusion but was 'pulled back from this precipice' by considering those possible things that neither are nor will be nor have been. For, if some possible things never exist, then existing things cannot always be necessary. It is here that Leibniz introduces descriptions of possible worlds that do not exist. 'For it cannot be denied that many stories, especially those we call novels, may be regarded as possible even if they actually do not take place in this particular sequence of the universe which God has chosen' [FC 179: L 405/263 (ca. 1679)]. Thus the description of possible worlds that do not exist, or worlds that God could have chosen but did not, shows the contingency of this world, and of the truth about things in it.

Leibniz also expressed the difference between contingency and necessity by saying that the former depends not only on God's understanding but also on his volition or free choice, in contrast to the latter which depends only on his understanding. In less theistic language, this is equivalent to the claim that contingent truths depend on how our world actually is, and would not always obtain had some state of affairs in it been different; and that necessary truths hold in all possible worlds—since such truths do not depend on how our world is—that is, they do not depend on which posssible world is the actual one. The contingency itself depends on the fact that God can understand everything that is possible.

[1] For example, Rauli Kauppi, 'Über die Leibnizsche Logik, mit besondere Berüchsichtung der Intension und Extension', *Acta Philosophica Fennica* 16; Robert Adams, 'Leibniz's theories of contingency', *Essays on the Philosophy of Leibniz*, ed. Mark Kulstad (Houston, Texas, 1977).

Thus if the proposition 'Spinoza died in The Hague' expressed a contingent truth (as Leibniz believed it did), this is because, had the world been different, Spinoza could have died in another place than The Hague. Since 'Spinoza' is the name of the philosopher who, among other things, died in The Hague, no one who died elsewhere would be identical with Spinoza. Does this not mean that it is necessary of Spinoza that he died in The Hague, and would this make it true of Spinoza that he could not have died anywhere else? No, this would be to confuse, as Leibniz says, (metaphysical) necessity with the certitude of our knowledge. The fact that we know for sure that Spinoza died in The Hague, and that therefore no one who died in, say, Leyden or London is Spinoza, is perfectly compatible with the fact that Spinoza could have died elsewhere. The fact that a good alibi exempts a man *A* from a criminal charge does not mean that it was *necessary* for the criminal *B* to have committed his crime at the time and place he did do so. We merely use our *knowledge* of a contingent fact—that is, that *A* was in a different place at the time of the crime—to conclude the non-identity of *A* and *B*. We grasp that someone who does not have all the properties of *B* could not be identified with him. The same follows for our knowledge about past and future events. Our ability to have certain knowledge of what will happen does not by itself remove the contingency of the fact [FC 179: L 405/263 (ca. 1679)]. Our ability to alter past events does not make the truths about them any less contingent.

Are there both necessary and contingent truths about one and the same individual? If we take the view that nothing can be individuated except as an individual of a certain kind, as Leibniz did [e.g. GP v. 268: La 309], and also think, as he did, that there are necessary truths about species, such that it is necessary that every individual which falls under that species has that property [GP ii. 49: L 509/332 (1686)], then it seems that there are necessary truths about individuals. For example, both, 'Caesar is a man' and 'Caesar is an animal capable of thinking', seem to state necessary truths about Caesar. Contrast this with 'Caesar crossed the Rubicon'. It pertains to the nature of the individual whom we name 'Caesar' that he is an individual man. Whereas the fact that Caesar crossed the Rubicon cannot be deduced from Caesar's nature alone.

Although Caesar had a good reason for crossing the Rubicon, which reflected his judgement, audacity, his belief about the state of affairs at the time, etc., yet his crossing of that stream depends on what the world was like—for example, on the fact that the Rubicon marked the boundary between Gaul and Italy. It is thus that Leibniz defends himself from those who accused him of making everything which happens to individuals necessary after all.

To answer it squarely, I say that there are two kinds of connection or sequence. One is absolutely necessary, for its contrary implies a contradiction, and this deductive connection occurs in eternal truths like those of geometry. The other is necessary only *ex hypothesi*, and by accident, so to speak, and this connection is contingent in itself when its contrary implies no contradiction. A connection of this kind is not based on pure ideas and on the simple understanding of God but also on his free decrees and on the sequence of events in the universe. [GP iv. 437: L 476/310 (1686)]

'Spinoza died in The Hague' expresses a contingent truth, but not (as Bertrand Russell suggested)[2] because it is actually made up of two propositions one of which is analytic, that is, 'whoever is Spinoza died in The Hague' and another proposition 'Spinoza existed', which is contingent (as it indeed is) and which is not true in all possible worlds. Even given that he existed, Spinoza's death in The Hague does not follow from his nature alone, but from the connection of other things in the world. Thus the proposition 'whoever is Spinoza died in The Hague', though true, is not a necessary truth according to Leibniz. That he died in The Hague is included in the individual concept of Spinoza, but, *pace* Russell and Couturat, this does not make the proposition analytic or necessary. If we try to derive the contingency from the fact that there are possible worlds in which Spinoza does not exist, then every singular proposition of the type 'Spinoza is a man' also becomes contingent, which is not merely problematic for us but also goes against Leibniz's own intention.[3] We would also utterly fail to see why Leibniz has to invoke two different kinds of connection between subject and predicate in his defence of contingency.

The predicate's being included in the subject (and both terms are concepts for Leibniz) does not mean that there is a necessary connection between subject and predicate; it means merely that the predicate holds of the thing that instantiates the subject concept. And Leibniz says this is an obvious (meta-linguistic) fact about any true proposition whatever. The required link between subject and predicate, he says, is that which exists only *a parte rei*, or from the side of the thing. It is only in this sense that he claims that '*praedicatum inest subjecto*; otherwise I do not know what truth is'.[4] In other words, the truth of subject-predicate

[2] And also more recently by Benson Mates and Fabrizio Mondadori. [See Dennis Fried's 'Necessity and Contingency in Leibniz', reprinted above, pp. 55–63, for criticism of Mates and Mondadori.–Ed.]

[3] This point was made by Jonathan Adler and John Earman.

[4] Letter to Arnauld (14 July 1686) [GP ii.56: MP 63]. In 'Remarks on a Letter of Arnauld' (1686) [GP ii.43: MP 46–7] Leibniz writes about the subsistence of individuals that makes different contingent propositions be about the same subject: for example, if 'I who have been in Paris am now in Germany', then 'my attributes of the earlier time and state, as well as the attributes of the later time and state, are predicates of the same subject'. Leibniz says this is what is meant by the claim that the notion of each predicate is contained in the notion of the subject.

propositions is understood in terms of satisfaction. If every subject-predicate proposition were analytic for Leibniz, as has so often been wrongly claimed, then Leibniz would have no point in distinguishing conceptual links which exist *a parte rei* from those which presumably exist *a parte dicti*, or from the side of what is said. The connection between the property of 'dying in The Hague' and the man Spinoza, then, is quite different from the property of, say, having successive twos in its expansion and π. We do not know if the property is true of π and, as the expansion of π is infinite, we may never know. But if we come across the property, it is only because we have deduced it mathematically and we know that π necessarily has the property. In contrast to this, the place of Spinoza's death is not something that follows from his nature alone even if we were to know all about it. (Omniscient God is said to know about this property only because he knows everything about the other things in the world that are contingently there by his choice and about their connections.)

What then is the point of Leibniz's analogy between contingent truth and infinite analysis? Can we make any philosophical sense of his claim that for a long time he was puzzled by the question 'how the predicate concept could be in the subject (concept) without the proposition thereby becoming necessary' and yet 'the knowledge of infinite analysis showed me light, so that I came to understand what it is for concepts to be resolvable in infinity' [C 18: PM 97]? For even if the concept of a differential quotient of a function involves infinite analysis, it can be deduced from the nature of the given function by logical means alone. Thus the relation between the two is a *necessary* one, which is precisely what the relation between the subject and predicate in a contingent proposition is said not to be. The fact of its involving infinite analysis does not throw light on the peculiar feature of contingent truths. A contingent truth cannot by any means be reduced to a necessary truth (some form of identity) by the analysis of the nature of the subject of the proposition alone.

We must understand that what Leibniz was puzzled by was not so much the danger that a contingent proposition would have the wrong modality as the question how there could be a proof at all of the truth —a way of starting from the proposition and getting to an identity— without going through an infinite number of steps. But he saw that something similar could be done in differential calculus. The analogy throws light on the problem because we can obtain a derivative of a function without going through an infinite number of steps in an analysis—which is impossible even for God—by understanding *the rule* that gets the result of an infinite analysis, i.e. the rules of differentiation. We can know exactly the limit of an infinite series even if, however long we enumerate the terms of the series, we never get to the limit. We also have a method of deciding for any number, whether it is a member of the series or not. Similarly with individual concepts and the contingent predicates that are contained in them. God has an *a priori* method of proving that the predcate is contained in the individual concept, because it is as a result of an *a priori* calculus (about, for example, the number of essences actualized in a world) which was involved in his choice of the best world that he has instantiated the individual concept anyway. Unlike God, we do not and cannot know the contents of a complete individual concept—that is, the concept which includes all true predicates of the individual (since there is an infinity of such predicates and since knowing them involves knowing everything about the universe). But we know what it is to be a complete concept of an individual and the rule that gives the contents of it. We understand what it is to have a concept *of* a particular individual. We grasp what it is to refer to a particular individual, and then understand that the complete concept of that individual should include everything that is true of him, her, or it. We therefore see that there is a method of deciding whether the predicate is included in the complete concept. The method is an empirical one for us. We refer to the individual by empirical means and establish whether it satisfies the predicate or not. And how *do* we refer to a particular and think *of* an individual? Not normally by having a set of predicates that uniquely distinguish it. Leibniz suggests that we do it by some demonstrative action like pointing, or picking features that characterize it in the given context.[5]

Our ability to grasp contingent truths, whether they are about individual things in the world, or about kinds of things, or about abstract objects, seems to depend on our being able to think *about* things without knowing many of their properties, and even without knowing any property that uniquely identifies the thing. We cannot deduce their yet unknown contingent properties from their other known properties. For these unknown properties also depend on how the other things in the world happen to be. For example, I can think of Caesar without any thought of whether he crossed or did not cross the Rubicon. And, as we have seen, the fact that he did cross the Rubicon cannot be deduced from Caesar's nature alone. Because we understand what it is to refer to individual things that have many predicates which we do not know, we understand that every individual has a corresponding concept *of* it which

[5] 'A certain individual is *this* one, whom I designate either by pointing or by adding distinguishing features. For although they cannot be features which distinguish it perfectly from every other possible individual, they are, however, features which distinguish it from other individuals which we meet.' [C 360: P 51].

contains all predicates that are true of it, even if we do not know many of them, and have no way of proving *why* any predicate is included in it. In other words, we understand that an individual concept is a decidable set, whose members are predicates. For any predicate, there is in principle a way of deciding whether it is a member of the individual or not. It is by judging whether the particular individual of whom it is a concept satisfies or does not satisfy the predicate. If it does, it is a member of the individual concept.

The analogy then with the infinite analysis seems to be the following. We have a way of deciding whether a contingent predicate is included in an individual concept—even if the examination of the latter by enumeration would involve infinite steps and hence be impossible for God as well as for ourselves. This is because we have a method—which is not the *a priori* one only available to God—but a method that involves referring by empirical means to the individual, and of determining in principle whether the individual satisfies the predicate or not.

A complete concept or a full concept means a concept that includes all the predicates that are true of the entities that fall under the concept. This is contrasted with a partial concept. Concepts of species, or kinds of things, are only incomplete concepts. Leibniz did not think that kinds of things existed apart from the individuals that fall under them, and thus the concept of species did not include every predicate that was true of the individuals that fall under it. All things of which there are complete concepts are particulars *of* which we can have thoughts and to which we can refer.[6]

And since nothing in the world happens at random, someone who knew about all the other things in the world would know why, given the relation of the particular thing to the rest of the universe, any predicate would be true of it—that is, in Leibnizian meta-jargon, why the predicate would be included in the subject (concept). The distinction between

[6] Leibniz sometimes writes that having a complete concept is a distinguishing feature of individual substances but often writes as if having a complete concept is a feature of any particular thing—whether it is an aggregate or a complex. Individual substances do have corresponding complete concepts, but other particulars have complete concepts too. For example, in a marginal note to a letter to Arnauld (14 July 1686) [GP ii.49: L 587 n.381/348 n.2, MP 45 n.3], Leibniz explains, 'A *full* concept includes all the predicates of the thing; for example, of heat. A complete concept includes all the predicates of a subject; for example, of this heat. In individual substances they coincide.' 'Ignis calidi' is Genevieve Lewis's reading in *Lettres de Leibniz à Arnauld* (Paris, 1952), p. 35. Gerhardt reads this as '*hujus calidi*' or 'this hot thing'. Whichever reading one adopts, that is, whether one takes the subject to be fire, or some physical thing like a hot pan, it is not an individual substance in the strict metaphysical sense. Fire is probably a process or a mode of a physical thing—an aggregate—and similarly a hot object like a pan is an extended physical thing—a phenomenon, based on a plurality of individual substances. Roger Woolhouse drew my attention to Genevieve Lewis's reading.

necessary truths and contingent truths about individuals, then, is the distinction between what is true of an individual, *given* the world he is in, and what would be true even if the other things in the world had been different.

Spinoza would have been a man even if the history of the world had been different, but he might not have died in the place he did if other things were not the same. This is to say that the nature of individuals does not determine all the truths about them. Each individual embodies the laws of nature of the world. But it is only *given* the state of other things that these laws determine each of his particular states through his history.[7] If the state of other things could not have been different, then, as Leibniz says, there would not be any distinction between necessary and contingent truths. This makes us realize how the concept of law of nature or regularity is intricately linked with the concept of contingency. Individuals embodying the *same* set of natural laws, would behave differently had the initial conditions that determined the relation between each been different, or had there been more or fewer individuals (or different individuals) in the world in which they find themselves. It is only because of this that we can think that many truths about individuals could have been other than they are. Even in a world which was entirely deterministic (Leibniz was slightly ambivalent about this) there would be many contingent truths about individuals. Even if we were to agree with Leibniz that when a man acts with a reason, there are dispositions and desires in him that incline him to act in a certain way without necessitating him to act in that way, we would be able to conceive that the same man would have been inclined to behave differently had the condition of the world been very different.

Two points that have often been raised have now to be discussed. The first is this. Can the existence of contingent truths about individuals—that is, that certain properties of individuals could have been otherwise—be compatible with the notion that an actual individual is only a member of the actual world and no other possible world? Many modern logicians have indeed claimed that talk about what happens in other possible worlds cannot throw any light on contingent or necessary properties of a person in our world, unless the same person occurs in other possible worlds too. For example, they say we can understand that Caesar need not have crossed the Rubicon only because we can imagine a world in

[7] For similar reasons, Leibniz distinguished what he called 'Primitive Force' and 'Derivative Force' in his works on dynamics. Primitive Force pertains to the nature of the physical object which can be examined by a law that tells how the thing would react dynamically, depending on the status of other things. Derivative force is the momentum of the object at any instant, which is how primitive force expresses itself, *given* the condition of other things.

which the very same Caesar did not cross the Rubicon and followed the laws of Rome.

Let us examine two aspects of the question in turn, the first historical and the second conceptual. First a historical clarification. Leibniz was very concerned to defend contingency and to give a content to the concept of contingency—and, as we have seen, his talk of possible worlds was very closely linked with this concern. He thought this was compatible with his view that an individual concept includes not only the nature of the individual but also all that is contingently true of the individual given the sequence and states of other things in the world. And this view about individual concepts entails that no instantiation of an individual concept—that is, no individual—could be a member of more than one possible world. Leibniz makes this point rather vividly in the *Theodicy*, where there is a description of a palace where different rooms correspond to different possible futures of Sextus, each different from that which Sextus will actually have.

> The worlds are all here, namely in thought. I will show you where one can find, not exactly the same Sextus whom you have seen (this is not possible, he contains always within himself what he will be)—but future Sextuses who will have all that you already know of the real Sextus, but not all which, without our perceiving it, is already within him, nor consequently all that will happen to the real Sextus. [GP vi. 363: H 371 (1710)]

Now someone may say that Leibniz is obviously mistaken. We are thinking of the many possible futures of one and the same person—that is, the real Sextus—and not of someone very like him. One may say, as Kripke has done, that we do not discover that another possible world contains or does not contain an actual person—we stipulate that it does. 'There is no reason why we cannot stipulate that in talking about what would have happened to Nixon in a certain counterfactual situation, we are talking about what would have happened to him.'

Now, of course, if we think what could have become of Nixon had the Watergate burglary not been found out, we are thinking about Nixon himself. Neither would Leibniz nor recent defenders of counterpart theories deny that we make meaningful counterfactual suppositions about actual men. Leibniz writes: 'what contradiction could there be had Spinoza died in Leyden and not in The Hague? There is nothing more possible than that. Thus either event was equally within the power of God' [GP vi. 218: H 235 (1710)]. To imagine a person to have a property that he does not have is to think about *him*; in doing so, however, one describes an imaginary person, that is, a person who does not actually exist in the manner we are imagining him to exist. It thus corresponds to a description of a possible world (or possible worlds) and a possible individual (or possible individuals), that is, a world different (in any way) from how our world is, and an individual different in some way from how any actual individual is. Whether we should use the proper name of the actual individual or not is a quibble about the language with which we describe such possible worlds.

If I say 'Had it stopped raining a day earlier, the landslide would not have happened', I am talking about a counterfactual situation of *this* world. I am not talking about another world. Yet the counterfactual description gives a possible world that is slightly different from the actual world. And just because I was thinking about what might have happened in our world, we would not object to calling it a different possible world. A possible world is not another world that exists side by side with the actual world. (The claim that the concept of 'actuality' is indexical might mislead us into thinking in this way.)[8] All possible worlds apart from this actual one exist only as ideas, Leibniz claims. Possible worlds are individuated by the successive states of all the individuals they contain. This entails that any coherent description of a different sequence of states of a different set of individuals gives a different possible world. And to understand Leibniz's notion of individuals and their complete concepts, one should think of individuals precisely as modal logicians think of worlds. An actual individual has its own history and all its own properties, those that are contingently true of it as well as those necessarily true of it, both the relational and the non-relational. Any individual that has different properties is not the actual individual in question.

We now come to the second point, which concerns the relation between the Leibnizian possible world analysis of counterfactual truths and recent counterpart theories. Although Leibniz explains the contingency of Spinoza's dying in The Hague by the possibility of God's making a world in which someone (very like Spinoza) dies in Leyden instead of The Hague, Leibniz does not suggest that there is a metaphysically demarcated set of possible individuals (demarcated in terms of, for example, closest similarity) which could be called 'counterparts', consisting at most of one from each of those possible worlds that are compatible with the counterfactual situation. When Leibniz talks about the nature of an individual, he is referring to the dispositions and properties it has that determine its successive states and that make the individual what it is, given the state of the rest of the world. What is this nature? He states (in the *Theodicy* among other works) that many properties are essential to any individual belonging to the species to which it belongs. For example, a man thinks. And all individual substances by definition

[8] David Lewis, *Counterfactuals* (Oxford, 1973), p. 85.

act and perceive. But none of these is a property that essentially distinguishes one thing from other things. Of course, each individual has a unique point of view in the universe. No other thing can have the same relation to the rest of the universe and represent the universe in the same way. But this is a contingent feature of God's having situated it in the world in a certain way. In Leibniz's sense of 'individual nature', it is not the case that everything that happens to the thing can be deduced from its nature by reference to the laws of logic alone or by reference to logic and the laws of nature of the world that the individual embodies. As Leibniz repeatedly says: the nature of an individual determines what happens to it only given the sequence of states of other things in the universe. Thus '. . . if one had enough insight into the inner parts of things *and also enough memory and understanding to take in all the circumstances and calculate them*, he would be a prophet' [GU i. 49: W 571, my italics; see also GP iv. 432-3: L 471-2/307-8 (1686)].

The kind of possible entities implicitly posited by counterfactual suppositions about actual individuals are varied and depend on the context (or our counterfactual thoughts). For example, in the case of the counterfactual futures of Sextus, described above, each possible world contains a person who has, so far as can be seen, a history and environment identical with that of the actual Sextus up to a certain time. However, without its having been apparent in the past, their characters were already different or some of their dispositions were different, and at a certain point this becomes manifest by virtue of what each decides to do in the same circumstance. The various Sextuses react differently to one and the same counsel of the Gods. One obeys, goes to a city, buys a small garden; another also obeys, goes to Thrace, and marries the daughter of the king . . . whereas the real Sextus defies the Gods, goes to Rome, and violates Lucretia. Since each does what he does with a reason, each has a different character which inclines him to react differently in the same situation. But parents, place of birth, etc., etc., are all similar.

When we think what would have happened had Adam not encountered Eve, or had not taken the apple, or had not fathered Cain, Leibniz suggests that we are thinking about quite different sets of possible individuals. In each of the possible worlds that correspond to our thought, Adam is the first man, who is put in a pleasure garden which he leaves through sin. This means that in physique or character he may be different from our Adam. There is no point in talking either in terms of an absolute scale of similarities or in terms of some essence common to all counterparts. That there are infinite numbers of possible worlds, some of them with individuals very much like actual individuals, is a metaphysical truth. Each counterfactual supposition about actual individuals carries implicitly a reference to some possible world and to certain individuals in it. This criterion of selection comes from our imagination and from the contexts to which our imaginings relate. It belongs to the pragmatics and not to the metaphysics or even semantics of counterfactuals. But the very possibility of such a selection reveals the contingency of the truth about the individual which is the contrary of the counterfactual we are imagining. This is a metaphysical matter. If no such selection is possible, we have not, within a Leibnizian model, given any content to contingency.

To conclude: we would all agree that individuals *do* have all the properties they do have and no other properties. No one would think that this makes all truths about individuals and their properties necessary. Leibniz's way of talking about possible individuals was such that from the uncontroversial fact just referred to, it followed that no possible individual having properties different from an actual individual could be said to be identical with the actual individual. It is important to realize that this claim does not on its own make all truths about actual individuals and their properties necessary. The (meta-)language that one uses to talk about possible worlds and possible individuals is a technical one. Possible worlds and possible individuals are intentional objects, and their principle of individuation reflects the opacity common to all intentional objects (and all the complexities and difficulties that opacity entails).

The actual world is not *merely* one of infinitely many possible worlds, and actual individuals are not merely a subset of possible entities. They are not mere objects of thought. They are actualized within a world, but since it was possible for individuals with the *same* initial constitution and nature to have been a part of a different world and to have acted, perceived, and developed in different ways, many truths about them are contingent. Indeed, possible worlds were introduced to give metaphysical content to contingent truth.

The identity conditions of Leibniz's possible individuals are such that it is misguided to ask of any possible individuals conceived to be in other possible worlds whether they are identical with any actual individual—just as it is misguided to ask of other possible worlds whether they are identical with the actual world or not. To deduce from this position that every property of an individual is necessary for it, and to ascribe to Leibniz a 'super-essentialism' is surely perverse. I have tried to show that the way in which Leibniz talks of possible worlds need not lead to the denial of the distinction between necessary truths and contingent truths about actual individuals. But if someone believes that this is so, then the right thing to say is that Leibniz's talk about possible worlds does not do the meta-logical job he wanted it to do. It is a strange interpretation that assimilates Leibniz's view about individuals and their properties to the view of Spinoza, with which he so explicitly and repeatedly disagreed.

The interpretation I oppose seems to be based on a failure to distinguish between two separate questions. One is whether one can have a meta-language in which one can meaningfully talk about individual concepts and say of a predicate that an individual contingently satisfies that it is a constituent of the individual concept—that is, the concept of the individual. I have tried to show that the answer is yes. The second question is whether a model theory of the kind Leibniz tried to devise will preserve the distinction between necessary and contingent. This is a technical question and even a negative answer to this would not imply a negative answer to the first.[9]

[9] I profited from discussions on an earlier version of this paper at the Department of Philosophy, University of Minnesota, and at Brooklyn College, in autumn 1975.

V

LEIBNIZ'S THEORY OF THE STRIVING POSSIBLES

DAVID BLUMENFELD

ALTHOUGH Leibniz seems to have taken his *Daseinstreben* theory to be intuitively evident, it more frequently strikes readers as bizarre. The reasons for this reaction will probably be clear from the following quotations which express some of the essentials of the view:

we ought first to recognize that from the very fact that something exists rather than nothing, there is in possible things . . . a certain exigent need of existence, and, so to speak, some claim to existence; in a word, that essence tends of itself towards existence. Whence it further follows that all possible things . . . tend by equal right towards existence, according to their quantity of essence or reality, or according to the degree of perfection which they contain . . . Hence it is most clearly understood that among the infinite combinations of possibles and possible series, that one actually exists by which the most of essence or of possibility is brought into existence. [GP vii. 303: W 347, L 791/487]

Everything possible demands that it should exist, and hence will exist unless something else prevents it, which also demands that it should exist and is incompatible with the former; and hence it follows that that combination of things always exists by which the greatest possible number of things exists. . . . And hence it is obvious that things exist in the most perfect way. [GP vii. 194: *Russell* 296]

And as possibility is the principle of essence, so perfection or degree of essence (through which the greatest number is at the same time possible) is the principle of existence. [GP vii. 305: W 349]

The theory expressed above appears to consist of six closely related theses: (1) that every possible thing has an internal impetus to exist (2) that this impetus is exactly proportionate to its degree of perfection (3) that the possibles vie with one another for existence by combining forces with as many other essences as they are mutually compatible with (4) that there is a unique series of compossible essences which has the greatest overall perfection and hence the greatest total thrust (5) that the inevitable result of the struggle is that the maximally perfect series (i.e. best possible world) realizes itself (6) that unless possible things contained such an impetus and behaved as described, no actual world would exist at all.

From *Studia Leibnitiana* (Franz Steiner Verlag, Wiesbaden) vol. 5 (1973), pp. 163–77. By permission of the author.

Several aspects of this theory call for further clarification. Leibniz wants to say that the most perfect possible world will exist because its total thrust toward reality is greater than that of any other. And, he indicates (above) that the total thrust of a world is a function of two factors—the internal perfection of its constituent entities and the number of possible things contained in it.[1] This may seem to conflict with his repeated assertion that the most perfect world is the one which contains the richest variety of phenomena consistent with the greatest simplicity of its laws [e.g. GP iv. 431: L 470/306; GP vi. 241: H 257; GP vi. 603: L 1039/639]. A partial resolution of this problem can be achieved by taking 'greatest number of things' to mean 'greatest number of types of things'; and, indeed, the context often makes it clear that this is his intention [e.g. GP vii. 303: L 791/487]. As far as simplicity is concerned, Leibniz tells us that this is the necessary *means* by which the greatest perfection is realized. In a letter to Malebranche he says that God used the simplest laws, 'to find room for as many things as it is possible to place together. If God had made use of other laws, it would be as if one should construct a building of round stones, which leave more space unoccupied than that which they fill'.[2] But if richness of phenomena is Leibniz's principal criterion of perfection in a world, we must still account for the role played by the internal perfection of the constituent members of the world. On this subject, however, Leibniz's view is somewhat unclear. But a reasonable conjecture is that he thought that possible worlds might be equally rich in types of phenomena. More than one, for example, might contain an infinite variety of types of beings and, in this case, greatest overall perfection would be determined by the internal perfection of the constituents.[3] Thesis (4), then, which refers to overall

[1] Leibniz speaks of possible things, or possible individuals, and he sometimes creates the impression that he recognizes the subsistence of such individuals over and above the attributes and concepts he elsewhere discusses. On the whole, however, I agree with Mates that we should 'interpret the term "possible world" as referring for Leibniz to a set of individual concepts, and not to a set of individuals'. As Mates says, 'In that way he [Leibniz] can avoid introducing a shadowy realm of "possible individuals" in addition to the abstract entities (i.e. the attributes and concepts) already involved in his metaphysics'. See Benson Mates, 'Leibniz on Possible Worlds', *Frankfurt* 335–64. In addition to the considerations raised by Mates, it is difficult to see what it would be for possible *individuals*—as opposed to individual concepts—to subsist in the mind of God.

[2] GP vii.290–1. Quoted in A. D. Lovejoy, *The Great Chain of Being* (Cambridge, Mass., 1936), chap. 5, p. 179. Chapter 5 is reprinted in *Frankfurt*, see p. 330. Leibniz says the same in *The Monadology* para. 58 [GP vi.616: L 1053/648].

[3] This is a conjecture and no more. Other widely divergent accounts have been given. Lovejoy, for example, holds [*Frankfurt* 328–330] that Leibniz's actual working theory is that all essences have equal claim to existence and that a possible world's impetus to exist is a function only of the number of types of compossible things contained in it. He acknowledges the passages in which Leibniz says that

perfection in a *world*, probably should be understood as being qualified in the manner described here.

An objection to his theory which worried Leibniz was the contention that the possibles are not real, but mere figments. If this were so, they could hardly be the metaphysical basis of the origination of things. Leibniz replied that the possibles have a certain kind of reality, since they exist from eternity in the mind of God. They exist, *qua* possible, in so far as God conceives them. The struggle for actual existence, then, takes place in the divine mind. Since Leibniz thought this premiss was necessary for the theory to have any plausibility, it should be added to our list of theses and treated as a background condition. It could be put simply: (B) God conceives the possibles which struggle among themselves for existence. Taken together with (B), the six theses are apparently thought to provide a complete account of the origination of finite existence. It is easy to understand, I think, why the metaphysical picture of an infinity of sheer possibilities existing in God's mind and battling to become actual has seemed a bit uninviting.

But mere considerations of appeal aside, it has frequently been thought that the *Daseinstreben* theory is strictly inconsistent with another account that Leibniz gives of the origination of the world. This is the more well known view that the world exists through the free will of God. Having freely chosen to subscribe to the Principle of Perfection, God selects the most perfect world from among the infinity of candidates and confers existence upon it. Now it has been pointed out that the two accounts have a great deal in common.[4] Both express Leibniz's view that

differences in the internal perfection of the component members of a possible world affect its total thrust, but thinks that such a view is not logically open to Leibniz. In fairness to Lovejoy it should be said that Leibniz often emphasizes variety as the measure of a world's perfection, failing to mention the internal nature of the component members themselves. But at other places Leibniz makes clear that this factor is also to be taken into account. Lovejoy's argument that Leibniz is not entitled to countenance this factor seems to me to be weak. Lovejoy says that if internal perfection determined a world's impetus to exist, then 'a world containing only men and no crocodiles would be better than one containing both'. For the essence of man contains far greater perfection than that of crocodile and 'the crocodiles would certainly require matter and occupy space which might be devoted to the uses of human beings'. As the author of a theodicy, however, Leibniz, is concerned to justify crocodiles as well as all the rest of the variety of the great chain of being. This consequence would only follow, however, if internal perfection were the *sole* determinant of impetus to exist. Lovejoy's argument shows that it cannot be the sole determinant, but it does not follow from this that it cannot be *one* of the determinants. The problem–which the conjecture is aimed at solving–is to find a place for all of the factors which Leibniz mentions. I concede that more discussion might be devoted to this issue, but since nothing in the main argument of the paper turns on it, I shall not press the matter further.

[4] Margaret D. Wilson, 'Possibility, Propensity, and Chance: Some Doubts about the Hacking Thesis', *Journal of Philosophy*, 63 (1971), 612.

for everything that exists there must be a sufficient reason why it exists; both give as the reason for the existence of the world the fact that it is more perfect than any other possible world; both seem to reflect an assumption that the question why anything exists is distinct from the question why things happen to be this way rather than some other way. But if the two views have been characterized correctly, it is difficult to see how Leibniz can maintain both consistently. One explains the transition from possibility to actuality solely in terms of the tendency of the possibles to come into being; the other appeals to an external force—the will of a God who chooses to create as much perfection as possible. One view makes God the active creator of the world, the other reduces him to the passive witness of a struggle that works itself out without his intervention. One stresses the contingency of the world, while the other seems to imply its necessity. Thus Lovejoy argued, with considerable plausibility, that since the possibles have an *intrinsic* drive to exist and since this logically results in a maximally perfect world, there cannot also be room for God's free selection of this world.[5] When we add to this the fact that Leibniz elsewhere says that the existent can be *defined* as that which is compatible with the most things [C 360: P 51], the case for the inconsistency of the two views becomes very impressive indeed.

Nevertheless, many commentators have hesitated to go this far, while still others have thought it possible to square the two views. Thus the able critic Margaret D. Wilson believes that it is not clear whether Leibniz regarded the *Daseinstreben* theory the metaphysically sounder of the two accounts or whether he thought they differed mainly as forms of expression [op. cit. p. 612]. Rescher, on the other hand, adopts the bolder thesis that the views are not incompatible. According to him the *Daseinstreben* theory is a secondary thesis which is not meant to be taken literally. He says that the literalist approach,

> misconceives the issue badly, for it is only because God *has chosen* to subscribe to the standard of perfection in selecting a possible world for actualization that possible substances come to have (figurative) 'claim' to existence. The relationship between 'quantity of essence' or 'perfection' on the one hand and claim or *conatus* to existence on the other is not a logical linkage at all—a thesis which would reduce Leibniz's system into a Spinozistic necessitarianism—but a connection mediated by a free act of will on the part of God. [*Rescher* 29–30; see also *Parkinson* 105]

Now it seems to me that Rescher's suggestion that the theory should be taken figuratively is correct, although, as I shall try to show later, the situation of his opponent is even worse than the one Rescher describes. In any case, we shall have to look for a fuller argument for the position.

[5] Lovejoy, op. cit., 179 or *Frankfurt* 320.

For Rescher's contention that a literal reading of the theory would involve Leibniz in inconsistency can hardly be sufficient to defeat Lovejoy and his followers; their charge just is that a close reading of relevant passages reveals a genuine conflict between the two accounts of the origination of things. Perhaps, it might be said. Leibniz was unaware of a real conflict between his two theses. Then again, it could be that he oscillated between the two views. Or, if one were impressed by Bertrand Russell's general view, he might argue that Leibniz probably was aware of the conflict but, from motives of expediency, buried his real theory (the necessitarian one) in his so-called esoteric writings.[6] Clearly, to settle these issues we must turn to the relevant passages themselves.

When we do so, however, it may appear that the job of defending Leibniz is quite difficult. For when we look at the passages mentioned so far, it seems that it is the nature of the possibles and nothing more that guarantees that the best world will exist. We have already seen that Leibniz says that essence tends *of itself* towards existence and that as a result anything possible will exist unless something else with which it is incompatible prevents it. This suggests that no external force such as the will of God would be required to actualize the possibles. But when these passages are set in their full context, a peculiar problem arises. For on numerous occasions, if not invariably, Leibniz combines the two theories as though there were not the slightest incompatibility between them. Instead, he treats them as though they complemented one another. Frequently, he asserts the views back to back within the space of a paragraph or so and on at least two occasions combines them in a single sentence. Thus, in *The Monadology*, speaking of the sufficient reason for God's choice among possible worlds he says, 'This reason can be found only in the *fitness* or in the degrees of perfection, which these worlds contain, each possible one having a right to claim existence in the measure of perfection which it enfolds' [GP vi. 616: L 1053/648]. Elsewhere he says, 'Therefore, all beings, in so far as they are involved in the first Being, have, above and beyond bare possibility, a propensity toward existing in proportion to their goodness, and they exist by the will of God unless they are incompatible with more perfect [existence candidates]' [GP vii. 309–10: *Rescher* 38]. A similar happy juxtaposition occurs in the

[6] Bertrand Russell, *A History of Western Philosophy* (New York, 1945), 581. It should be said, though, that Rescher's book contains a sustained attack on Russell's thesis that Leibniz's system degenerates into Spinozism. It is perhaps also worth noting that in working out his view in his book Russell does not emphasize the inconsistency of the free will theory with the *Daseinstreben* theory. But he does briefly call attention to the problem in his review of Couturat, 'Recent work on the philosophy of Leibniz', *Mind*, 12 (1903), 185–6, reprinted in *Frankfurt*, see p. 378.

Principles of Nature and Grace, paragraph 10. Here he begins by saying: 'It follows from the supreme perfection of God that he has chosen the best possible plan in producing the universe', and declares a sentence later that 'For as all possible things have a claim to existence in God's understanding in proportion to their perfections, the result of all these claims must be the most perfect actual world which is possible' [GP vi. 603: L 1039/639]. Finally, in the essay *On the Ultimate Origin of Things*, where the *Daseinstreben* theory is developed in detail, Leibniz concludes his exposition of the doctrine as though he had just put forth a view that made clear that the world exists contingently and that God created it of his own free will. He says, 'Thus we now have a physical necessity derived from a metaphysical necessity. For even if the world is not necessary metaphysically . . . it is nonetheless necessary physically, or determined in such a way that its contrary would imply imperfection or moral absurdity. . . . This shows at once how there may be freedom in the Author of the world . . . because he acts on the principle of wisdom or perfection' [GP vii. 304-5: L 792-3/488]. The problem that these passages present is this: if two theories are inconsistent how could Leibniz so frequently have asserted them together? If the *Daseinstreben* theory is taken literally, then its incompatibility with the free will account is so obvious that it is almost impossible to believe that Leibniz could have been oblivious to it. If he had generally kept the theories separate, it might be plausible to maintain that he was aware of the conflict but oscillated between the two accounts. Or, if he had held the *Daseinstreben* theory at one period of his life and the free will theory at another, we could believe that he simply abandoned one view in favour of the other. But in fact, as we have seen, he often brought them together as though they were a single doctrine. It is equally implausible to suggest that Leibniz was aware of the conflict, but reserved his preferred position (the unadulterated *Daseinstreben* theory) for his unpublished works, while he displayed the illogical combination of views to the public for the sake of approval. For if approval was the motive, the natural move would have been to suppress the heterodox necessitarian theory in all the published writings and publicly enunciate only the free will doctrine. Even if the obvious contradiction escaped most of an ignorant public, it is doubtful that it could have escaped all. In any case, what profit could there have been in actually blending the views in his published works? Yet this is exactly what Leibniz did. Finally, if the secret-doctrine thesis were correct we should at least expect to find the free will theory absent from the unpublished writings. But of course this is not so either. It is true that Leibniz occasionally emphasized God's role of conceiving the possibles at the expense of his creative activity, but this is relatively insignificant.

All of this tends to suggest that Leibniz did not regard the views as incompatible and that he would have taken exception to something in the characterization of the theory given in the first pages of this essay. The obvious alternative is to suppose that the theories are complementary. When Leibniz variously attributes to the possibles an 'urge', 'inclination', 'need', 'claim', or 'right' to exist, in proportion to their perfection, these are merely figurative ways of expressing the degree of attractiveness that they have to a God who is disposed to create a world. The strongest textual support for this interpretation occurs in a passage whose importance has been emphasized by Parkinson [*Parkinson* 105]. In the *Theodicy* Leibniz tells us that the conflict of possibles is 'only ideal' and he explicitly describes it as 'a conflict of reasons in the most perfect understanding' [GP vi. 236: *Parkinson* 105]. So, it appears that a possible world has a thrust to exist commensurate with its total perfection only because God wants to create the best world he can. Since he freely chose to subscribe to the Principle of Perfection the existence of the best world is contingent. Thus, on this interpretation, theses (1) and (2) are to be understood in a figurative sense, or more precisely, tendency to exist is parasitic upon God's decision to realize as much perfection as possible. Similarly, in thesis (3), the struggle should be understood merely as a way of expressing the relative appeal which the possibles have to the creative will. Thesis (4) remains intact, though subject to the qualification mentioned earlier. Thesis (5), which declares that the upshot of the struggle is the existence of the best possible world, is to be regarded as contingent. Thesis (6), which says that the striving of the possibles is a necessary condition for the existence of any world, is understood to mean that there must be an objective reason for God's choice and that this reason must be found in the intrinsic perfection of the possible worlds themselves. Finally, the background condition, (B), is to be taken literally, although it is to be thought of as expressing something that God does in addition to creating the world, rather than something he does instead of creating it.

Opponents of this interpretation will be very likely to charge that the case I have presented so far emphasizes certain elements of Leibniz's view at the expense of others. For example, no account has yet been given of the fact that in the fragments edited by Couturat Leibniz tells us that the '"existent" can be defined as "that which is compatible with more things than anything else which is incompatible with it"'.[7] This appears to reflect the suggestion of the *Daseinstreben* theory that the logical upshot of the conflict of the possibles is the maximally perfect

[7] C 360: P 51. At this point Leibniz mentions only the number of compossible things and makes no reference to the internal perfection of the component entities.

world. But if we take this seriously as a *definition* of existence, the resulting theory of the origination of things is clearly necessitarian. As Bertrand Russell puts it, 'the relations of essences are among eternal truths, and it is a problem in pure logic to construct that world which contains the greatest number of coexisting essences. This world, it would follow, exists by definition, without the need of any Divine Decree' [*Russell* vii]. In light of this, it might be added, it is difficult not to hear Leibniz's repeated claim that the existence of the best world is an *immediate consequence* of the struggle of the possibles as 'logical consequence', his claim that everything possible '*will exist* unless something else prevents it' as 'will necessarily exist' [GP vii. 194: *Russell* 296, my italics]. Passages like this can of course be multiplied. But if this is so, it seems doubtful that we can regard the interpretation given here as completely convincing, even if the considerations adduced in its favour render the literalist interpretation equally inconclusive. Perhaps there is just no available method for deciding the issue.

But I do not think things are this grim. As E. M. Curley has pointed out the context strongly suggests that Leibniz did not suppose that he was giving a definition in the strict sense [*Frankfurt* 88-90]. In fact 'the existent' occurs in a list of primitive simple terms which are either unanalysable or thought to be so. Leibniz remarks that a cause of existence *could* be defined in the manner suggested. But, as Curley notes, Leibniz goes on to say, 'But at present we keep away from these matters, as being too profound' [C 360: P 51]. At a different place he actually says that we cannot define the existent in such a way as to give us a clearer notion of it [G 325]. Furthermore, having said that the existent is that which is compatible with the most things, Leibniz goes on to give four additional 'definitions' which appear to differ radically from the one that preceded them. They are all variations on an effort to define the existent as something which would please the divine mind.[8] Nevertheless he claims that these four definitions and the earlier one come to the same thing. This is virtually incomprehensible unless we assume that he is presupposing his view that God chooses to produce the most perfect state of affairs. If he is, then we can see why he might have tried to identify the existent in either of these sorts of ways. Assuming that the greatest number of compossibles represents the maximally perfect world,

[8] The 'existent' is (i) 'what pleases something intelligent and powerful', (ii) 'what would please some mind, and would not displease another more powerful mind, if minds of any kind were assumed to exist', (iii) 'that which would not displease the most powerful mind, if it should be assumed that a most powerful mind exists', (iv) 'that which pleases some . . . mind . . . and does not displease (absolutely) the most powerful mind' [C 375-6: P 65-6]. The fourth definition is preferred to the others.

it follows that God will choose to create it.[9] Likewise, since God wants to produce as much perfection as he can, the maximally perfect world will *please* him most and, as a result, it will be his will that it should exist. It seems more reasonable, then, with Curley, to describe Leibniz as assigning a cause for existence rather than giving a strict definition [*Frankfurt* 89]. His principle that the existent is that which is compatible with the most things should be regarded instead as a corollary of the Principle of Perfection.[10] But in this case it provides no support for the literalist interpretation of the *Daseinstreben* theory.

Once we abandon the view that Leibniz gave a true definition of existence, various words and phrases that seemed to require a necessitarian interpretation now appear more or less neutral. The fact that Leibniz says, for example, that the existence of the best world is an immediate consequence of the struggle of the possibles, gives no grounds for deciding between the rival interpretations. The real issue is whether or not the possibles compete for existence independently of God's subscribing to the Principle of Perfection. But the existence of the best world is the immediate consequence whichever view we take. Much the same can be said of Leibniz's statement that everything possible, 'will exist unless something else prevents it'. This holds on both interpretations, although, to be sure, it is a necessary truth on one and only a contingent truth on the other. We will be forced to hear 'will exist' as 'will necessarily exist' only if we treat the fragment as a true definition and we have already considered the objections to doing this.

We come now to what must be regarded as the most serious difficulty for the literalist or necessitarian interpretation. As we have seen, the *Daseinstreben* theory is characterized by theses (1)–(6) plus (B), the most crucial question being whether or not thesis (5) should be understood to mean that the most perfect universe exists of necessity. The literalist, who maintains that it should be so understood, clearly wants to say that thesis (5) follows from thesis (4). But if thesis (5) asserts that the maximally perfect world exists necessarily, it is difficult to see how this can be so. To appreciate this consider that the total force (or impetus) of a possible world is always equivalent to that world's total degree of perfection. The question is whether the best conceivable world will have enough perfection (and hence enough impetus) to realize itself necessarily. But Leibniz tells us repeatedly that no concept other than that of God guarantees the existence of its object, because no other essence (or combination of essences) represents something absolutely

[9] Strictly speaking, the argument also requires the assumption (which Leibniz makes, e.g. GP vii.304: L 792/487) that being is better than non-being.

[10] Rescher [*Rescher* 65] also suggests that it should be so regarded.

infinite, i.e. something completely perfect or containing no limitations whatsoever. Necessary existence, he says, is an attribute of God alone. The reason for this—expressed in terms of the *Daseinstreben* theory—is that no essence or system of essences that falls short of absolute perfection will have an absolute impetus to exist. And, Leibniz frequently states that no possible world is *absolutely* perfect. He admits, for example, that the existing world contains limitations, but argues that this does not show that it is not the best possible world, since *any possible world would involve some degree of imperfection* [GP vi. 613: L 1051/647]. Let us refer to this assumption as the Limitation Principle (LP). If LP is true then thesis (4) cannot entail thesis (5) (as understood by the literalist), for even the maximally perfect world would not be absolutely perfect or free of all limitations. On the contrary, thesis (4) together with LP implies that no possible world exists necessarily. For if the maximally perfect world lacks the thrust to exist necessarily, so does every other. Thus, unless LP were denied, there would be no way of deriving thesis (5); whereas, if LP were presupposed, the literalist version of the theory would be internally inconsistent. Thus, when we recall Rescher's contention—that if perfection and impetus to exist were logically linked, Leibniz's system would be reduced to a Spinozistic necessitarianism—we find that the situation for the literalist is actually much worse than this. He would happily embrace the necessitarian consequence, but the basis he cites in the *Daseinstreben* theory does not appear to allow for it.

As far as I can see the only way the literalist could escape this problem would be to suppose that Leibniz meant to deny LP. This is an extremely unpromising suggestion, for it means disregarding his explicit statements that any possible world must be limited. But this is not the worst of it. LP is so deeply entrenched in the Leibnizian metaphysics that, if it is denied, the result is a virtual landslide. For example, if the maximally perfect world is absolutely perfect, then either that world is strictly identical with God—since he too is absolutely perfect—or there are two numerically distinct but qualitatively identical beings. That is, if we deny LP, we must also either dismiss the view that God and the world are distinct or *both* (a) deny the identity of indiscernibles *and* (b) affirm that there is more than one God. Neither course is at all palatable, but the second is perhaps the more obviously hopeless. I know of nowhere where Leibniz allows that there are two beings differing solely in number[11] or

[11] Leibniz almost always treats the identity of indiscernibles as a necessary truth. In his fifth letter to Clarke, however, he seems to allow that it would be possible to conceive of indiscernible but distinct entities, though he insists that there are no such entities in nature. But the passages [GP vii.394–5: A 61–2] are somewhat ambiguous and can probably be discounted. For one discussion see

that there is more than one absolutely perfect being. Presumably, then, the literalist would prefer the first alternative, treating it perhaps as further confirmation of Leibniz's secret (or incipient) Spinozism. But he can hardly afford to make this move either. For it completely destroys the picture given by both interpretations of the role of God in the theory of the possibles. God's role is passively to *conceive* the essences, while they struggle for existence among themselves. But this picture presupposes the official Leibnizian view that God and the world are distinct. If the literalist is to swallow the pantheistic consequences of his interpretation, then he must also renounce the view of God as passive observer of the war of the (possible) worlds. For on the clarified picture, God is no mere observer; he is a participant in the struggle and in fact identical with the victor. This means dropping thesis (B) which has God conceiving the essences, but *not* engaged in the battle. It would apparently have to be replaced by one which has God *both* conceiving the essences *and* struggling along with them. It is doubtful whether this is even intelligible.

Now if there were no plausible alternative to the literalist interpretation, we should perhaps have to settle for one of these unattractive consequences. But if we return to the major source of difficulty, I think we will find that the free will interpretation can handle the problem very nicely. This problem, we will recall, was that thesis (4) was inadequate for deriving the necessitarian version of thesis (5). The rest of the difficulties arose when we examined the assumptions that would be required to make it possible to do this. But the impossibility of deriving (5) is just what we should expect on the free will interpretation. For that view differs from the literalist account in two critical ways: first, it treats thesis (5) as a contingent truth and second, it holds that theses (1)-(6) plus (B) express an *incomplete* theory, one which is only coherent when supplemented by and understood in terms of the contention that God chooses to create the best possible world. On this view, the striving of the possibles is a figurative way of expressing the degree of attractiveness that each possible world has for the divine will. Thesis (4) entails the (contingent) existence of the best possible world only when we add the premiss that God freely subscribes to the Principle of Perfection.[12]

An incidental question that still remains for the free will interpretation

Russell 55 ff. If it were possible to conceive of distinct but indiscernible entities numerous difficulties would follow for Leibniz's system. For example, it would then seem to be possible to conceive of distinct but indiscernible universes, including a duplicate of the most perfect universe. In this case God would be rendered incapable of creating any universe at all.

[12] I recognize, of course, that it is often held that this account is itself implicitly necessitarian. But the issue for now is not whether the free will theory breaks down, but only how the *Daseinstreben* theory is to be taken.

is this: why should Leibniz have wanted a second, figurative version of the theory of creation, particularly if it differed from the primary view only in expression and ultimately needed to be understood in terms of it? I suspect that the explanation is to be found in Leibniz's commitment to the objectivity of goodness. In his day he saw this doctrine threatened in equally dangerous ways by Cartesians and Spinozists. The former held that things were made good by the will of God and the latter that 'the goodness which we ascribe to the works of God are nothing but the chimeras of men who think of him in terms of themselves' [GP iv. 428: L 466/304]. He objected that,

> when we say that things are not good by any rule of excellence but solely by the will of God, we unknowingly destroy, I think, all the love of God and all his glory. For why praise him for what he has done if he would be equally praiseworthy in doing exactly the opposite? [GP iv. 292: L 466/304]

In his own account of creation he wanted to emphasize that there had to be some objective reason that determined God's choice among worlds. Given that God is good and subscribes to the Principle of Perfection, this reason can only be found in the relative degrees of objective perfection in the possible worlds. 'In my opinion', Leibniz writes to Des Bosses, 'if there were no best possible series, God would have certainly created nothing, since he cannot act without a reason, or prefer the less perfect to the more perfect' [GP ii. 424-5: W 95]. Leibniz wanted to make as clear as possible that the question which world came into being was as much a matter of its objective nature as it was a function of God's choice; the two are completely correlative and one would certainly wish to emphasize the former as well as the latter. I suggest that in the *Daseinstreben* theory Leibniz is pushing the role of the intrinsic perfection of the possibles as hard as he can. Thus, in some passages he emphasizes the nature of the world as determining God's choice. But in the end there is only one theory of creation, not two. The conflict of the possibles is 'only ideal'. If we accept this overall view, I think we can handle virtually all of the passages that express the theory of the striving possibles. Furthermore we can easily understand the otherwise rather wild basis of the theory. The suggestion that the possibles literally strive to exist and that if they did not there would be no world is exceedingly strange. On the free will interpretation this can be read as the highly intuitive suggestion that worlds differ in degrees of perfection and that if there were no best world God would have had no sufficient reason for creating anything at all.

VI

LEIBNIZ ON COMPOSSIBILITY AND RELATIONAL PREDICATES

FRED D'AGOSTINO

INTRODUCTION

I shall here examine Leibniz's views on the compossibility and incompossibility of individual substances. In particular, I shall consider the relation between these views and Leibniz's views about relational predicates.

It is commonly (though not universally) held that Leibniz believed that an individual substance could be characterized completely by monadic predicates [e.g. *Rescher* 74]. I shall argue that if this is the case, then all individual substances are compossible, and Leibniz's doctrine that there are many possible worlds thus becomes unsupportable. This can be avoided, I shall argue, only by allowing relational as well as monadic predicates to characterize individual substances. I conclude by arguing that Leibniz *did* allow this possibility, and that his belief in the multiplicity of possible worlds *is* consistent with the rest of his system.

THE PROBLEM

Leibniz draws a distinction, important both for his logic and for his metaphysics, between *possible* individual substances and *compossible* individual substances [GP vii. 289: PM 145]. For Leibniz, an individual substance is characterized by its *complete individual concept* [C 403: PM 95]. This concept 'contains' all the predicates which could ever be truly ascribed to that substance. Since the individual substance named 'Caesar' did in fact cross the Rubicon, the complete individual concept of Caesar will contain, among many others, the predicate 'crossed the Rubicon'.

An individual concept is the concept of a *possible* individual if it is not a self-contradictory concept [GP iv. 425: L 452/293]. For instance, the individual substance *A* is *impossible* if its complete individual concept contains both the predicate 'is *P* at time *t*' and the predicate 'is not-*P* at time *t*'.[1] The criterion of possibility is then a logical one: all substances

From *Philosophical Quarterly*, vol. 26 (1976), pp. 125–38. Reprinted with many small stylistic changes by the author, by permission of the author and the editor.

[1] The temporal qualification is necessary since, for Leibniz, the complete individual concept of a substance contains all the predicates that could *ever* be truly be ascribed to it. Caesar might have been hirsute at the age of 20 and bald at 30, without this making him an impossible substance.

are possible whose complete individual concepts do not involve logical self-contradiction.

But for Leibniz, not all possible individual substances are actually realized in the world [GP vii. 289: PM 145]. It is important for Leibniz to make this claim, because, without it, his system collapses into Spinozistic necessitarianism of a kind he wished to avoid. The day after his meeting with Spinoza in 1676, Leibniz wrote:

> If all possibles existed, no reason for existing would be needed, and possibility alone would suffice. Therefore there would be no God except in so far as he is possible. But such a God as the pious hold to would not be possible if the opinion of those is true who believe that all possibles exist. [C 530: L 262/169]

The solution which Leibniz offered for this problem was to claim that not all possible substances are *compossible* [GP vii. 289: PM 145-6], i.e. that not all substances could *coexist*. Those which could not coexist belonged, in Leibniz's view, to different *possible worlds*. Each possible world was further taken to be a collection of all those possible substances which could coexist. One of these possible worlds—the best one—was chosen by God to be brought into existence [GP iv. 431: L 469-70/306]. All the other possible worlds remained unrealized. By this mechanism then, Leibniz ensured the preservation in his system of God's traditional role as Creator and in this way avoided the Spinozism which he dreaded.

The merits of Leibniz's solution to this problem clearly depend upon the viability of his notion of the incompossibility of substances. But many commentators have remarked that this notion is itself suspect and perhaps even incompatible with certain of Leibniz's logical doctrines.[2] Before examining this difficulty and reviewing and criticizing some proposed solutions to the problem of incompossibility, I shall first offer a brief sketch of the metaphysical and logical doctrines which are relevant to an understanding of this problem.

SOME BACKGROUND ASSUMPTIONS

Quite early in his philosophical career, Leibniz voiced the opinion that all concepts, whether individual or general (i.e. abstract) could in theory at least, be analysed completely into irreducibly simple component concepts [GP iv. 65: P 4]. These simple concepts would constitute what he called the 'alphabet of human thoughts', out of which all complex concepts could be built up by certain combinatorial operations [GP iv. 72: P 11]. These simple concepts would furthermore be few in number

[2] e.g. *Russell* 67; B. Mates, 'Leibniz on Possible Worlds', *Frankfurt* 339–40; J. Hintikka, 'Leibniz on Plenitude, Relations, and the "Reign of Law" ', *Frankfurt* 161; and *Parkinson* 82 f.

[C 430: PM 2] and mutually compatible with one another [GP iv. 296: *Ishiguro* 45].

One reason for this compatibility requirement is that these simple concepts were all taken by Leibniz to be attributes of God [GP iv. 425: L 452/293]. And in one of his proofs of the existence of God–the so-called 'Modal Proof'–God was taken to be a (necessarily) possible being [GP iv. 424: L 452/293]. But if some of these concepts, *qua* attributes of God, were incompatible with each other, then God would not be a possible being, and this proof would fail.

Another reason for this requirement may have been Leibniz's interest in devising a purely formal procedure (an algorithm) for building up complex concepts out of this finite stock of simple concepts. This could not be done, however, if some of these concepts were incompatible with each other. If two such incompatible concepts were combined, an impossible concept would result. This could be avoided, of course, if the algorithm always verified the compatibility of simple concepts before combining them. But compatibility is not a formal, but rather a *semantic* property of concepts. A purely formal algorithm for combining simple concepts into complex possible concepts thus presupposes the compatibility of these simple concepts.[3] Hence the requirement.

When Leibniz first considered the possible ways in which simple concepts might be combined to form complex concepts, he allowed only the operation of logical conjunction. If 'rational' and 'animal' are both simple concepts, then the complex concept 'rational animal' could be derived, its extension being just those substances which could truly be characterized both as rational and as animal. Leibniz realized that, by limiting his combinatorial resources in this way, he could actually arithmetize the combinatorial process. Each simple concept would be represented by a prime number. Each complex concept would then be represented as a product of primes [C 49–50: L 361–2/235–6]. This device in turn made it possible for Leibniz to consider a mechanical, arithmetical procedure for determining the truth of propositions. The Leibnizian doctrine that the predicate 'is contained in' the subject of every true proposition [GP iv. 66: P 5] would then be reflected in the fact that, for any true proposition, the number representative of the subject concept would be exactly divisible by the number representative of the predicate concept [C 55: L 367–8/239]. As long as the idea of arithmetizing truth-tests for propositions (and later even validity-tests for inferences [C 77–84: P 25–32]) seemed viable to Leibniz, he did not expand his combinatorial repertoire beyond the operation of logical conjunction. As this programme broke down, however, he gradually

[3] I have here followed the argument of *Ishiguro* 45–6.

added other operations.[4] Major developments in this area came in 1686, during the second active period of logical research in Leibniz's multifaceted career.

INCOMPOSSIBILITY

It will perhaps already be obvious that, with a finite stock of compatible simple concepts and the single combinatorial operation of logical conjunction, *no concepts of incompossible substances can be formed*. In fact, with just these resources, *no self-contradictory concepts can be formed either*. This latter fact has escaped some commentators, perhaps because the question of incompossibility is so much more important for Leibniz's metaphysical views.

It is easy to see why, with just these resources, no concepts of incompossible substances can be formed. If, for instance, the stock of available compatible simple concepts were *a, b,* and *c*, then, since all these concepts are mutually compatible (by hypothesis), there would be no reason, for example, why the concept *a&b* should be incompatible with the concept *a&c*. These two concepts would be incompatible only if the concept *a* were incompatible with either or both of the concepts *b* and *c*, which is contrary to the hypothesis. If we interpret incompossibility of substances as logical incompatibility of their complete individual concepts,[5] then it is clear that no two substances can be incompossible, given just the resources so far specified. Leibniz himself recognized this problem, noting that:

> It is yet unknown to me what is the reason of the incompossibility of things, or how it is that different essences can be opposed to each other, seeing that all purely positive terms seem to be compatible. [GP vii. 194: *Ishiguro* 47]

(This passage, by the way, seems to offer clear evidence that Leibniz *did* identify incompossibility of substances with logical incompatibility of concepts.)

Unless Leibniz can find a solution to the problem of incompatibility, his system collapses into Spinozism. Since Leibniz nowhere to my knowledge offers a completely explicit solution to this problem, I will try to reconstruct a solution which is Leibnizian in spirit. My procedure here will be heuristic: my reconstructed solution will emerge from an examination and criticism of solutions to this problem which other commentators on Leibniz have offered.

[4] It broke down in the 'Elements of a Calculus' [C 57:L 370/240] where he notes, 'What we have said, therefore, is more restricted than it should be; so we shall begin again anew.'

[5] Hintikka, op. cit., 160 suggests the identification of incompossibility of substances with the logical incompatibility of their complete individual concepts.

SOME PROPOSED SOLUTIONS

(a) *Mates' 'Solution'.* Before examining some of the important positive attempts to solve the problem of incompossibility, I shall consider Mates' equivocal discussion of this problem.

According to Mates, Leibniz himself left this problem unsolved, deciding that it was, in Mates' words, 'one of those mysteries understandable by God but not by man' [Mates, op. cit., 340]. Elsewhere Mates says, 'How two such (complete individual) concepts can fail to be compossible is a great mystery, according to Leibniz, but he clearly holds that there are infinitely many possible worlds, each of which contains infinitely many concepts' [ibid.].

As I shall point out later, this 'solution' seems to be historically inadequate: Leibniz did in fact feel that he had solved the problem of incompossibility. But whatever its merits historiographically, it is certainly inadequate as a *reconstruction* of a possible Leibnizian position: even if Leibniz himself never explicitly resolved this problem, his system might have contained just those resources required for a solution.

Mates' discussion is, however, interesting for another reason. He seems to reject the quite plausible suggestion that incompossibility of substances be identified with incompatibility of concepts. He notes in this regard that the relationship of compossibility is intended by Leibniz to be transitive—that is, if two substances *A* and *B* are each compossible with a third, *C*, then they must also be compossible with each other. But, as he points out, this is not in general true in the case of logical compatibility of concepts. Given three concepts *a*, *b*, and *c*, then, if *c* is incomplete, 'i.e. simply fails to embody any information that commits it one way or another as regards the other two', then both *a* and *b* may be compatible with *c*, without being compatible with each other.[6]

This argument, though plausible, is mistaken. Compossibility is a relationship between substances, and substances are represented by concepts which *are* complete—i.e. by their complete individual concepts. By their very nature, such concepts cannot fail to commit themselves to anything relevant to a description of the unique individual substances which they represent. Saying this does not of course solve the incompossibility problem. It does however suggest that we cannot rule out on *a priori* grounds the equation of incompossibility of substances with logical incompatibility of concepts.

(b) *Russell's Solution.* If identifying compossibility with logical incompatibility points towards an *analytic* solution of the incompossibility

[6] Mates, op. cit., 341; the definition of conceptual incompleteness stems from *Rescher* 17.

problem, then it is also possible to imagine a *synthetic* solution as well. An analytic solution would show how it would be logically impossible for two substances to be part of the same possible world. A synthetic solution, on the other hand, would show how two substances could not belong to the same possible world without violating some synthetic law governing the arrangement of substances in that world—and could not do so despite the logical compatibility of the complete individual concepts by which they are represented. This is, in essence, Russell's solution of the incompossibility problem.

Russell notes in this regard that:

> All possible worlds have general laws, analogous to the laws of motion.... Hence two or more things which cannot be brought under one and the same set of general laws are not *compossible.* [*Russell* 66]

Russell supports this interpretation by citing a passage in which Leibniz refers to the 'laws of the general order of . . . [each] possible universe', and, explicitly rejecting an analytic solution, goes on to conclude:

> without the need for *some* general laws, any two possibles would be compossible, since they cannot contradict one another. Possibles cease to be compossible *only when there is no general law whatever to which both conform.*[7]

This solution to the incompossibility problem is logically adequate. Given (i) a set of complete individual concepts, each of which is the logical conjunction of compatible simple concepts, and (ii) a set of general laws of the usual forms, then these general laws induce a partition of the set of individual substances into different possible worlds. For instance, the general law 'everything is red' partitions the set of possible substances into many different possible worlds. In one of these worlds, every substance is red; in the remaining worlds, some, but not all substances are red. Simultaneous or successive application of all such general laws to the initial set of possible substances does, in fact, induce a partition of possible substances into an infinite number of different possible worlds.

Despite the logical adequacy of this solution, it seems to be one which is peculiarly inadequate in this context. It is Leibniz's abhorrence of Spinozism which provides the background to the incompossibility problem. But Russell's solution to this problem depends on God's 'decision' to partition a set of otherwise compossible individual substances into different possible worlds, so that he might then choose to create the best of these worlds. On this interpretation, God's role as Creator logically presupposes his role as Law-Maker. Any argument of this form against necessitarian atheism is thus surely a very weak and nearly circular one.

[7] Op. cit., 66–7. Final italics added.

This difficulty seems intrinsic moreover to any synthetic solution to the incompossibility problem, and thus suggests that we must seek an analytic solution.

(c) *Couturat's Solution.* To obtain an analytic solution to the incompossibility problem we must clearly supplement the combinatorial resources which Leibniz first provided for generating complex concepts from a stock of compatible simple concepts. Leibniz has been taken as recognizing this necessity. He cited Locke's contention that 'there are *privative ideas*, as there are negative truths' [GP v. 255: La 289], and Ishiguro, for instance, has taken this as evidence that Leibniz did see the need to supplement his combinatorial resources if he were indeed to solve the problem of incompossibility. Commenting on this passage, Ishiguro says:

A complex idea is not a mere collection of simple ideas as a heap may be a collection of sand. A complex idea is a construct obtained by logical operations on simple ideas. The logical operation may be that of denial. Thus, there are complex ideas of impossible things as well as complex ideas which are incompossible with other complex ideas. [*Ishiguro* 47–8]

On this argument then—and it is one which Couturat proposes [*Frankfurt* 27 n. 20]—the incompatibility of complex concepts arises from the fact that they are formed from compatible simple concepts by the two operations of negation and conjunction.

With the operation of negation available, it is clear that impossible complex concepts can be generated. If the set of simple concepts available is *a*, *b*, and *c*, then the complex concept *a* & *b* ¬-*a* can be generated. But this concept is self-contradictory and the substance it purports to represent is thus in fact impossible. But can concepts of incompossible substances be formed with just these resources? The answer to this question is 'no' since, for instance, there are no grounds for supposing that the two concepts *a* & *b* and *a*¬-*b* are logically incompatible.

The addition of negation alone does not then suffice to solve the incompossibility problem. It does, however, answer the question—unanswerable with just the operation of conjunction—how there can be impossible substances. If Couturat's solution to the incompossibility problem were in fact Leibniz's solution, then we would have to conclude that Leibniz failed to solve this problem and that his contention that there are many possible worlds was thus unsupported.

(d) *A 'Carnapian' Solution.* Carnap has developed a rudimentary possible world semantics which may seem to offer a solution to the incompossibility problem.[8] Carnap assumes a stock of individual constants and

[8] *Logical Foundations of Probability*, 2nd ed. (Chicago, 1962), sects. 31–8. John Watkins suggested to me the possibility of this kind of solution to the incompossibility problem.

compatible monadic predicates. Each individual is then characterized in terms of every possible distribution of these predicates or their negations over the constant which designates it. Each such distribution gives rise to a different concept of the individual so designated. Furthermore, each such concept is logically incompatible with every other, since it differs in at least one place in the distribution from every other such concept—e.g. in characterizing the individual a_i as P_j rather than as not-P_j. This incompatibility, finally, forces a partition of these different concepts (of the same individual) into different possible worlds.

And so, it may seem, the incompossibility problem is solved. Despite its plausibility and elegance, however, this solution is not a genuinely Leibnizian one. It is in fact incompatible with one of Leibniz's basic doctrines—that which asserts the unique identification of an individual substance by its complete individual concept. A Carnapian solution, on the other hand, presupposes that we can identify a substance independently of its concept—i.e. by its designating individual constant—and, in fact, that the same individual can be represented by different and incompatible complete individual concepts. Any Carnapian solution to the incompossibility problem is thus ruled out.

(e) *Hintikka's Solution.* At this point, even more than before, I am forced to offer a reconstruction of Leibniz's solution of the incompossibility problem. What I am going to do now is to ask what further resources would suffice for such a solution, and whether such resources were in fact available to Leibniz.

Hintikka has pointed out that two concepts cannot be incompatible if '*relational concepts are not employed*' [op. cit., 161]. That is, unless some of the predicates 'contained in' the complete individual concept of one substance refer to some other substance(s), no incompossibility between these two substances can arise. It is easy to see why this is so. Following Hintikka, we can represent the compatibility of two complete individual concepts A and B by the expression 'M $((\exists x)(Ax)$ & $(\exists x)(Bx))$', where 'M' stands for 'it is possible that'. If A and B are simply conjunctions of compatible monadic predicates and their negations, then '$(\exists x)(Ax)$ & $(\exists x)(Bx)$' is satisfiable if and only if '$(\exists x)(Ax)$' and '$(\exists x)(Bx)$' are both separately satisfiable [ibid.]. But this will always be logically possible whenever both expressions are logically possible, Incompossibility between two substances thus collapses into the logical impossibility of one or both of them, so long as only monadic predicates are available. On the other hand, if both relational predicates and negation are available, then the incompossibility problem can be solved. If it is part of the complete individual concept of one substance A that it stands in a certain symmetric relation R to every other substance, *and* if it is part of the complete individual concept of another substance *B* that it does not stand in the relation *R* to any other substance, then *A* and *B* are clearly incompossible substances.

The availability of relational predicates and negation seem to be necessary and sufficient conditions for solving the incompossibility problem. Without negation, all concepts are possible; and without both negation and relational predicates, all possible concepts are compatible. And, of course, without the incompatibility of concepts—and thus the incompossibility of substances—Leibniz's views on the multiplicity of possible worlds become unsupportable and his metaphysical system collapses into Spinozism. In short: the solution of the incompossibility problem presupposes the availability of relational predicates. We must now therefore ask: Were relational predicates permitted in Leibniz's system?

THE MERITS OF HINTIKKA'S SOLUTION

Hintikka himself has pointed out that Leibniz's system may be 'inconsistent in an ironic manner' if relational predicates are presupposed for any solution of the incompossibility problem [op. cit. 160]. Commentators on Leibniz have long held either that he banned relational concepts altogether (the No Relations Thesis) [e.g. *Russell* 14] or that he felt that all relational concepts could be reduced to or satisfactorily replaced by non-relational ones (the Reducibility Thesis) [e.g. *Rescher* 74]. On the latter interpretation, Leibniz is held to have believed that descriptions of a substance involving relational concepts could be replaced by descriptions involving monadic predicates only. If either the Reducibility or the No Relations Thesis is correct, the incompossibility problem cannot be solved within Leibniz's system. Any solution to this problem presupposes the availability of at least some *irreducibly* relational predicates. Herein lies the ironic inconsistency whose possibility Hintikka mooted.

In arguing for Hintikka's solution I shall thus be compelled to argue against both the No Relations and the Reducibility Theses. I proceed by first considering some of the evidence that is usually adduced in support of these theses. I will argue that this evidence does not in fact support them. I shall then present some of the evidence for accepting Hintikka's solution.

(a) *Arguments against this solution.* There are at least five important pieces of evidence that might tell against Hintikka's solution of the incompossibility problem. First, there is Leibniz's doctrine that individual substances, or monads, are 'windowless'—i.e. that they are not involved in any causal relations with one another [GP vi. 607–8: L 1044–5/643]. Second, there is Leibniz's doctrine that all propositions are of the subject-predicate form. It is widely held that by 'predicate' Leibniz here means non-relational predicates only. Third, there is Leibniz's view that

> As regards relations, paternity in David is one thing and filiation in Solomon another, but the relation common to both is a *merely mental thing*, of which the modifications of singulars are the foundations. [GP ii. 486: Mates, op. cit., 351–2. Italics added]

This passage is commonly cited [e.g. *Russell* 13, *Rescher* 75] in support of the No Relations and Reducibility Theses. Fourth, in further support of the Reducibility Thesis, one may point out, with Mates [op. cit., 351], that Leibniz devoted a great deal of energy to trying to show how relational propositions could be rewritten in non-relational form [C 287: P14]. Leibniz shows, for example, that we can rewrite the relational proposition 'Peter is similar to Paul' as the conjunction of two non-relational propositions, 'Peter is *P* now' and 'Paul is *P* now'. And fifth, Leibniz's statement that there is no 'purely extrinsic denomination' [GP v. 211: La 236] is often cited in support of the Reducibility Thesis. This is a particularly strong piece of evidence, since, as Ishiguro points out, for Leibniz and his contemporaries

> Denomination is intrinsic if the property referred to inheres in the object independently of anything outside it. A denomination is extrinsic if it leads our thought beyond the object which we are characterizing to something distinct from it. [*Ishiguro* 78]

This evidence is, I think, strong enough to warrant a certain amount of caution about Hintikka's proposed solution to the incompossibility problem. But is it strong enough actually to undermine that solution? I think not.

Let me first consider the significance of Leibniz's statement that there is no 'purely extrinsic denomination'. While this certainly can be understood in the sense of the interpretation offered above, we must, I think, qualify this interpretation to take account of the following facts. (1) Leibniz has also claimed that 'there is no term so absolute or so detached as not to include relations, and the perfect analysis of which does not lead us to other things, and even to all things' [GP v. 211: La 236]. And (2) Leibniz has elsewhere claimed that '*there are no purely extrinsic denominations*, which have no foundation in the thing denominated' [C 520: PM 89]. With these passages in mind, I think that we can understand Leibniz as distinguishing between what I shall call *merely* extrinsic denominations and *intrinsically* extrinsic denominations. It is only the former that he can be held to have banned; and then, not because they involved relational terms, but because they have 'no foundation in the thing denominated'. The latter, on the other hand, were thought by Leibniz to be both relational—in 'leading our thoughts to other things'—

and yet nevertheless well-founded. It would seem then that Leibniz did *not* ban all relational concepts, but only merely extrinsic denominations. Leibniz felt, in other words, that some concepts (the intrinsically extrinsic ones) could be both irreducibly relational and (possibly) well-founded.

The obvious question now is whether any irreducible relational concepts *can* be well-founded in this sense. If not, Hintikka's solution must be rejected.

One reason for supposing that Leibniz did not countenance the existence of irreducible but well-founded relational concepts is his belief that individual substances are not in causal interaction with one another—i.e. his belief that monads are 'windowless'. An argument to this effect might have the following form: The behaviour of each individual substance, including its changes of state, is represented in its complete individual concept. Changes of state of a substance depend entirely on an 'internal principle', which an external cause—i.e. another substance—cannot influence [GP vi. 608: L 1045/643–4]. The values of the predicates describing an individual substance must therefore depend only on the state of the substance itself. But if a substance were characterized by relational predicates, the values of these predicates would depend partially on the state of other substances. Irreducibly relational predicates therefore cannot be well-founded attributes of individual substances.

This argument is attractive but is, I think, fallacious. The fallacy lies in mistaking logical for causal dependence. The value of a relational predicate is of course logically dependent on all of its arguments. But this is not to say that the substance described by that predicate is causally dependent on other substances. If all substances exist in a pre-established harmony [GP vi. 616: L 1053/648], then predicates characteristic of one substance could be logically dependent on—in the sense of reflecting changes in—other substances, without this implying any causal interaction between these substances. It is only on this interpretation, moreover, that we can make sense of Leibniz's claim here that 'any simple substance has relations which express all the others, and . . . consequently it is a perpetual living mirror of the universe'.

That individual substances are causally independent of one another does not then seem to support the contention that Leibniz did not countenance relational predicates. Furthermore, it would be difficult to understand his belief that each individual substance 'mirrors' the entire universe unless he did in fact allow relational predicates to characterize individual substances.

A second reason for supposing that Leibniz did not permit irreducible but well-founded relational predicates is his purported belief that all propositions are of the subject/monadic-predicate form. Contrary to this very widespread view however, Leibniz seems to have allowed irreducibly non-monadic predicates to appear in propositions. Using the word 'term' to refer to the subjects and predicates of propositions, Leibniz said:

A term is either 'integral', i.e. complete, or it is 'partial', i.e. incomplete. It is integral or complete if, without any addition, it can be the subject or predicate of a proposition–e.g. 'entity', 'learned', 'the same as *A*' or 'similar to *A*'. It is partial or incomplete–e.g. 'the same' or 'similar'–when something (namely 'to *A*') must be added for an integral term to arise. [C 357: P 47]

Two comments: (1) The predicates 'the same as *A*' and 'similar to *A*' are prima facie relational. Of course, it may be objected that these predicates are not irreducibly relational. In fact, I even pointed out earlier how Leibniz thought that the proposition '*B* is the same as *A*' could be reduced to a conjunction of two non-relational propositions. It could then be argued that, if this proposition is reducible in this way, then its predicate term must also be reducible. The predicate 'is the same as *A*' could, for instance, be reduced to the syntactically monadic predicate 'is *P* at time *t* and *A* is *P* at time *t*'. But the fact that we can carry out this kind of reduction does not establish that such predicates are not irreducibly relational. The syntactically monadic reducing predicate still refers to a substance, namely *A*, other than the substance of which it is predicated. And this fact seems inescapable. Such a predicate is, in my terminology, intrinsically extrinsic, whatever its syntactic status. There is a clear sense, then, in which such a predicate *is* irreducibly relational: it is so because it unavoidably refers to other substances and thus differs from *truly* monadic predicates, which do not so refer.

Notice, furthermore, that such predicates differ from truly monadic predicates in a way that is crucial to the question of incompossibility. The fact that some substance *A* can be characterized by the truly monadic predicate *P* is irrelevant to the possibility that some other substance *B* might be characterized as not-*P*. On the other hand, that *A* shares the property *P* with some other substance *B* in the same possible world *is* relevant to the possibility that *B* is not-*P*. In other words: if all predicates are truly monadic, then the incompossibility problem cannot be solved; on the other hand, if some predicates are intrinsically extrinsic, then this problem can be solved.

If those who claim that Leibniz permitted only monadic predicates mean by this that he permitted only truly monadic predicates, then Leibniz cannot be held to have solved the incompossibility problem. On the other hand, if they believe that Leibniz permitted syntactically monadic but intrinsically extrinsic predicates, then their claim cannot be distinguished from the claim that he permitted irreducibly relational predicates—except in a quibbling technical sense.

(2) Leibniz's comments about 'partial' terms may, moreover, help us to make some sense of his remark that 'paternity in David is one thing and filiation in Solomon another, but the relation common to both is a merely mental thing'. As I have already pointed out, this remark is frequently cited as evidence for the No Relations and Reducibility Theses. How can we harmonize it with the contrary view—i.e. that Leibniz *did* permit irreducibly relational predicates? We can do this, I think, in the following way: The predicates 'is the father of Solomon' and 'is the son of David' are integral terms and can therefore stand as predicates in a proposition. But the predicates 'is the father of' and 'is the son of' are not integral, but partial, terms. They cannot therefore stand alone as predicates in any proposition. And it is exactly for *this* reason that these *partial terms* must be considered 'merely mental things'. I am arguing, in other words, that Leibniz's statement that 'the relation common to both is a merely mental thing' is *not* to be understood as a condemnation of relational predicates, but rather of partial terms. If my argument here is correct, then this piece of evidence too simply fails to support the No Relations and Reducibility Theses.

The only evidence still outstanding against Hintikka's solution is the fact that Leibniz seems to have spent a great deal of time trying to reduce relational propositions to non-relational ones. Let me now consider this problem. First, as I have already remarked, Leibniz's efforts at reduction seem uniformly to have involved the reduction of relational *propositions* rather than relational *predicates*. But all that is required for Hintikka's solution is that there should be a stock of irreducibly relational predicates. Second, Ishiguro has argued forcefully that:

> In most cases the sentences into which the original sentence is rewritten still describe relational facts, and the rewriting projects do not form any part of a general programme of reduction in which non-relational attributes are attributed to the subject. [*Ishiguro* 29]

The project in effect appears to have been not so much an attempt to eliminate relational predicates as 'an attempt to render explicit certain special logical relations which hold between relational propositions and certain non-relational propositions'.[9] Leibniz's interest in this rewriting project seems then to have been less in the elimination of relations than in a fully explicit rendering of the complex logical syntax of relational propositions.

It would seem then that most of the arguments traditionally adduced in support of the thesis that Leibniz did not countenance relational

[9] Hintikka, op. cit., 161.

attributes of individual substances simply fail to sustain that position. For (1) Leibniz did allow relational terms to be predicates in propositions; (2) his rewriting project does not seem to have been intended to eliminate relational terms; (3) his stricture that 'there are no purely extrinsic denominations' does not ban all relational concepts, but only all unfounded terms; and (4) only partial terms were called by him 'merely mental things'. Finally (5), the argument that 'windowless' monads could not properly be characterized by relational predicates founders on a confusion between logical and causal independence. All the arguments against Hintikka's solution of the incompossibility problem seem then, on closer inspection, actually to support that solution.

(b) *Arguments for this solution*. In addition to this evidence, there are at least two positive arguments for accepting Hintikka's solution. First, Leibniz in several places insists that 'the concept of an individual substance involves all its changes and all its relations, even those which are commonly called extrinsic' [GP ii. 56: MP 63]. This statement is important not only for the support which it lends Hintikka's solution—for it would be difficult to see how we could accommodate this view to either the No Relations or the Reducibility Theses—but also for the light it sheds on Leibniz's belief that monads, while windowless, nevertheless mirror the whole universe. Second, in an important paper of 1686, Leibniz expanded the stock of combinatorial resources to include operations other than negation and conjunction. He noted there that 'from these there will doubtless arise various relations' [C 359: P 50]. This fact may furthermore help to draw the sting out of my suggestion that Leibniz did permit irreducibly relational predicates to characterize individual substances. Since these new combinatorial operations were not truth-functional, it may be that Leibniz felt (a) that the stock of compatible simple concepts need include only truly monadic predicates, and (b) that truth-functionally irreducible relational predicates could nevertheless be formed out of these concepts, and could then stand as predicates in statements about individual substances.

CONCLUSION

I have here argued that on most traditional accounts of Leibniz's philosophy he cannot be held to have accounted for the incompossibility of individual substances. I have noted that unless Leibniz can account for incompossibility his thesis that there are many possible worlds is insupportable. But if this is the case, then the role of God as Creator of the actual world is abrogated and Leibniz's system collapses into necessitarianism. Since Leibniz himself seems never to have offered an explicit solution of this problem, I have adopted a policy of reconstruction. First

I have examined some of the solutions of this problem which have been traditionally proposed. Finding that all of these were logically inadequate to the task, I then asked what resources would be needed to effect a satisfactory solution of this problem. Following Hintikka, I suggested that irreducibly relational concepts were needed if this problem was to be solved. Since it is traditionally held that Leibniz did not permit such relational concepts, I examined evidence usually adduced in favour of this view. I found it wanting and introduced further evidence that Leibniz did in fact employ relational concepts. I concluded, finally, that the resources necessary for a solution of the incompossibility problem were available to Leibniz and that his system need therefore be neither 'ironically inconsistent' nor Spinozistic.[10]

[10] I would like to thank John Watkins and Colin Howson for their help.

VII

THE CORRESPONDENCE BETWEEN LEIBNIZ AND DE VOLDER

L. J. RUSSELL

I

IN thinking about Leibniz, we should start with the ordinary common-sense world, containing material things, plants, animals, men; interdependent, changing; and with the Cartesian simplification of this world according to which there are, in men, souls independent of matter, and in the rest, nothing but extension variously moved: with the addition that men are corporeal substances, i.e. unities of mind and body in some way.

Leibniz does not accept the Cartesian simplification. On the one hand, he insists that the conception of body as extension and motion is incomplete, since it provides no definite substances anywhere; on the other hand, that we must include the notion of activity in some way in our conception of what is real. And activity he thinks must be interpreted by analogy with what goes on in our minds—as some kind of perception and appetition.

The extreme form of this view is to be found in the *Discourse on Metaphysics* of 1686. The universe consists of a system of individual substances, each endowed with thought and perceptions of higher or lower grade, each entirely self-contained, evolving from its own inner nature an ordered series of ever new perceptions. We are individuals of this sort; and as our perceptions correspond among themselves, and as nothing else but them can occur to us or in us, we need not ask whether they are outside us, or whether any other beings can perceive them.

This view rests mainly on logical and metaphysical grounds. The logical ground is, that whatever can be predicated of a substance must be contained in the notion of the substance. The metaphysical ground is, that the notion of a substance must be something in the substance permanently and without any alteration. From these two grounds Leibniz concludes that any substance must be completely self-contained. From the phenomena we experience he concludes that we are not only substances, but imperfect and so dependent; hence we are creates substances, hence created substances depending on God.

From *Proceedings of the Aristotelian Society*, vol. 28 (1927/28); pp. 155–76.

[I am grateful to Susan Mendus and Roland Hall for helping to get into English three passages which Russell left untranslated.—Ed.]

If this were all, Leibniz would be logically compelled in the end to resolve the universe into his own purely self-contained created substance, a mind viewing only his own perceptions, recognizing his dependence on God, and admitting the possibility of other created minds, but knowing nothing of them.

But this would not give us what we know of Leibniz. He wants, not an isolated substance, dependent on God solely, but a system of interrelated substances knit together in the closest possible way, so that nothing happens in any which is not reflected in all the rest. And he does not want this to happen merely in virtue of the notion which was implanted by God in each substance when it was created. He wants the reason for each change in every monad to be reflected at every moment not merely in each monad considered separately, but in the aggregate of monads, viewed as an interrelated system in space and time. That all things conspire together for the glory of God was as important and as true for him as that there are individual substances.

If each monad were purely self-contained, knowing nothing of other monads, it might perceive a world of space and time, but only a world of space and time of which it was a spectator, and in which it had no part; but the world the monad actually perceives is one in which it is situated, and in which the other monads are situated too.

In this world, not only do I perceive, but events occur; in other words, not only do changes occur in my perceptions considered as mine, but changes occur in me considered as a member of this common world in space and time; and Leibniz wants to show that these changes are linked with one another in accordance with uniform laws, which, like the notion implanted in each monad, persist throughout all changes.

It can be said, then, that the problem for Leibniz was, how to develop his principles, which seemed to isolate the monads, in such a way as to keep the system of the world.

That his principles were not entirely clear, he recognized; but he was not willing to give them up on that account. In working with principles, and in getting into difficulties with them, we are enabled to develop our principles. This was a constant thought with him. Leibniz was always pioneering. He thought of himself as only beginning a new movement, which he hoped would be developed by his successors. And however tenacious of his principles he was, he was always on the look out for opportunities for further development. And it was characteristic of him to take what he glimpsed ahead as if he saw fully into it. Huygens, who loved developed work and was suspicious of mere promise, contantly protested against this feature in Leibniz; it finds pointed expression in a letter to Fatio de Duillier, where he says in his dry way, 'at last I've had from Mr. Leibniz something about his inverse tangent method. The Preface, which is magnificent, in his way, takes up two pages, and though the method takes up only one and a half, it is so obscure that I could hardly finish it' [Huygens, *Oeuvres Complètes*, x. 209]. But while I think we should recognize that Leibniz saw further ahead than his critics did, it was characteristic of him to look ahead, and what he glimpsed, to make precise by means of definite propositions, which he then proceeded to develop, with one eye on logic, and one eye on the facts.

I think, then, that we may profitably consider the *Discourse on Metaphysics* as making precise for the time being the principles in accordance with which Leibniz's problems were to be handled, but as by no means regarded as final and complete.

And I think that we can regard his main problem as being, as I have said, to develop those principles in such a way that the separation of the monads shall not destroy the system of the world.

II

Leibniz's main line of campaign in his attempt to expound a new philosophy can be summed up briefly thus:—

(i) He began by attacking the notion that the essence of body consists in extension. For the essence of matter we need something more than extension and motion, more even than impenetrability and resistance [*Journal des Savants*, June 1691, GP iv. 464: W 100]. The laws of motion could not be deduced from the notion of extension and motion merely, but involved appeal to something active in bodies.

(ii) Having thus prepared the ground, he wrote two papers, one, De Primæ Philosophiae Emendatione, published in the *Acta Eruditorum* in 1694, and one in the *Journal des Savants* in 1695, the Système Nouveau, in the same year attacking in the *Acta* the Cartesian rule of the conservation of motion.

The first of these was very brief, and after some general remarks (a preface longer than the paper) introduced his view in a single paragraph. He spoke mainly with reference to bodily substance, which he said must be active and enclose an entelechy, in the sense of having eternally a conatus to motion, which will produce motion if it is not hindered by environing bodies. Through the action of various bodies limiting and determining each other's impulses to motion, the actual motions of bodies are produced. Thus a substance does not receive from another substance the power of acting, but only a limitation and determination of its own pre-existing impulse to act [GP iv. 468 f.: L 707 f./432 f.].

This, it is clear, does not involve any very radical alteration of the imaginative picture of the world. Bodies are still material bodies, moving in space and impinging on one another; but instead of being purely inert, they possess a tendency to move, which is determined as actual motion by their relations to other bodies.

In the second paper, the Système Nouveau, he still kept to the general picture of the world of bodies moving in space, but went a little further with his own special way of looking at it. To the need for activity he added the need for true unity, if we are to have anything substantial; and arguing that neither mathematical points (which are purely abstract) nor physical points or atoms (which are always divisible and so pluralities) will suffice, he concluded that we need for true substance a formal atom or a metaphysical point, endowed with entelechy or primitive active force: something analogous to sentiment and appetite in man. Starting from these, he explained that mathematical points were the points of view from which entelechies expressed the universe; they were always situated in an organic body, which could increase or diminish in size, but could never entirely perish. Thus, by utilizing the experiences of the microscopists and their theories of organisms as imperishable, he showed how an entelechy plus its organic body could be understood to be substantial in the sense of imperishable. The organic body could shrink down to the size of a physical point, while still retaining an infinitely complex structure.

He distinguished between two types of souls: rational souls, in man alone, possessing reason; lower souls, acting only as machines, for the service of man. And he was careful to insist that these lower souls were not to be utilized for the explanation of the particular phenomena of bodies, though the notion of active force in body was important for the derivation of the true laws of motion. He thus retained the system of bodies, whose changes were to be explained mechanically. And he then proceeded to his hypothesis of a pre-established harmony between events in the material universe and the perceptions in the souls of man. The Pre-established Harmony was, that is to say, published first of all as a harmony, not between all substances, but between rational minds on the one hand and the material world on the other.

The extension of this harmony to perceptions of non-rational souls was not indicated in this paper. He mentioned in a final brief paragraph that when one body impinges on another it is its own elasticity, due to the movement that is in it, that causes it to move as it does; but he left this as a mere suggestion.

Rational souls had thus their own separate life and development, but since they were situated in bodies, and their perceptions expressed what happened in bodies, and since the system of bodies was one system in space, the unity of the world of souls was not impaired.

III

These papers involved him in much controversy; and perhaps the most interesting of the discussions into which he was led are to be found in his correspondence with John Bernoulli, and with De Volder, in the years 1698–1706.

He had already convinced John Bernoulli of the correctness of his law of the conservation of energy; Bernoulli on his side had been discussing the matter with De Volder. Leibniz entered these discussion as a third party to begin with, and when he did write direct to De Volder, his letters and De Volder's replies went through Bernoulli, and were read by Bernoulli, and to a certain extent discussed between him and Leibniz. It is a triangular affair with which we have to do. De Volder was rather harder to convince of the conservation of energy than Bernoulli had been, and in the end he was led to accept it more by the purely mathematical proof of Bernoulli, based on the parallelogram of forces, than by the semi-metaphysical proofs of Leibniz. With this part of the correspondence we shall not deal. De Volder was much more interested in Leibniz's views on substance, than in the conservation of energy; for though De Volder accepted the general doctrine of his time in regard to matter and extension, he was not satisfied with it as an ultimate account, because it seemed to make matter too inert; and Leibniz had claimed to have a proof from the very definition of substance that all substance is essentially active. Leibniz's account of the pre-established harmony of mind and body had already impressed De Volder favourably. But he was not satisfied either that substantial forms really gave unity to matter, or that they could be used to show how the motions of matter arise in the last resort.

Thus, Bernoulli tells Leibniz [16/26 August 1698, GM iii. 528] that De Volder objects that body cannot be made of infinite monads, for such monads must either be extended or not: if they are extended, they are no more true unities than the body they are meant to explain, while if they are not extended, then it is difficult to see how extension can arise from them.

To this Leibniz replies [GM iii. 537], not by meeting the argument directly, but by distinguishing between materia prima and materia secunda. The first, materia in se, he calls moles; the second he calls massa. Materia secunda or mass is the matter whose nature Leibniz is trying to explain by saying that it consists of innumerable substances. For example, the human body or the body of an animal is materia secunda; it is not a substance, but an aggregate of substances, like a flock of sheep or a pond stocked with fishes. Materia prima, on the other hand, is something incomplete, in the sense [GM iii. 541] that it is the passive element in complete substance, and so, taken by itself, just as incomplete as the active entelechy taken apart from materia prima.

We have, so far, a simple scheme: complete substance consists of materia prima and entelechy taken together; these substances form aggregates which are somehow organic bodies, or materia secunda, or bodies possessing mass.

But it is no answer to the original question De Volder asked; and Bernoulli persists in seeking for a clear account of the unity that Leibniz says substance is. If materia secunda is not substance but substances, will Leibniz please show a portion of matter divided into its ultimate substances, as a flock is composed of its sheep? Leibniz has insisted that there is no smallest portion of matter; must we not then say, that we never arrive at substance, but are always dealing with substances? And, if so, is 'substantial form' successful in solving the problem of unity? [GM iii. 540]

To this, Leibniz replies [GM iii. 541–2] that there are as many substances in materia secunda as there are animals or living things; and this means two things. In the first place, every portion of matter must be taken to be like a pond stocked with fish, but we must add that any portion of the liquid in the pond (in which that is to say there are no fishes of the ordinary size) is itself a pond stocked with fishes of smaller size, and so on indefinitely, and also any portion of liquid in the body of any fish is a pond stocked with fishes, and so on to infinity. That is to say, however far you divide any mass, you have a mass of the same sort as the mass you started with. In brief, you do not come any nearer to ultimate substance by sub-division. Any mass, however small, is an aggregate of substances.

But in the second place, this means, that you must find ultimate substance here and now, in bodies of ordinary size, as well as elsewhere. If it be asked, how far we are to go in dividing, before we come to single substance, the reply is, we have substance right at the start. Every animal is such. It has an organic body, composed of innumerable substances. But these substances are not parts of the animal itself. Yet the animal's organic body, and its substantial form, taken together, compose a single complete monad.

It is clear that this does not help us very much. The organic body is an aggregate of substances; but somehow it is made into a single substance by being taken along with the mind of which it is the organic body. But if this is so, surely the organic body apart from the mind should be regarded as incomplete in the same sense as the materia prima of which he has already spoken. Indeed, if it is materia prima which taken along with our mind forms complete substance, then materia prima must be identical with the organic body.

We are back here at the position in the letter to Arnauld of September, 1687 [GP ii. 119-20: MP 153] where he says that it is the animated body, i.e. the organized body plus the mind, which is truly one being. He is even more explicit in a passage in the original draft of this letter, not included in the actual letter to Arnauld, in which he says that the body (the organized body) is the matter, the soul is the form of our substance. In this draft he further distinguished matter taken in this sense, in which it can enter and leave our substance (for our organs can change while we remain the same) from matter taken in a more primitive sense, as something always essential to the same substance. The matter which substance never loses he compared to the primitive passive power of some of the scholastics. Matter in the sense of the organic body, he said, is both extended and divisible; the more primitive matter is neither extended nor divisible, though it is the principle of divisibility.

So far, in 1687, in the passage not actually sent to Arnauld. But in the letter to Bernoulli with which we are dealing, he said nothing further about materia prima, but merely added to what he had already said about the monad, the enigmatic sentence. 'You are afraid that I shall have to make matter out of what has no quantity. I reply, that I no more make it out of minds than I do out of points' [GM iii. 542; 20/30 September 1698].

But so far there is no account of matter, except that without entelechies there is no complete substance, that complete substance needs an organized body, and that wherever there is an organized body there must be both one complete substance, consisting of the organized body and its entelechy, and an infinity of complete substances, making up the parts of the organized body. But the original thesis, that it is only by means of entelechies that real unities can be established, seems not to be confirmed, but merely asserted. How does my mind succeed in being united with my organic body so as to make one complete substance out of what, without my mind, would be merely an aggregate of substances?

Accordingly, Bernoulli insists that Leibniz must come in the end to making materia secunda out of points endowed with forms; for if the smallest corpuscle is not a substance, but substances, it will not do to regard substance as a quantum cum forma. Substance must be a punctum cum forma if it is to be indivisible [GM iii. 546-7].

IV

Meanwhile, the discussion with De Volder, in regard to the conservation of force, was proceeding; and Leibniz was endeavouring to show that for the true laws of motion we need to consider the production of motion in bodies as the effect of the action of primitive force situated in the bodies.

Of this discussion we can say that it confuses the whole issue. The metaphysical notion which Leibniz suggests to De Volder, and which he has already used elsewhere, is the notion of power, potentia, situated in a body (the nature of this 'body' not being specified; but he was thinking of the usual abstract 'particles' of mathematical physics) which, if the body were not hindered by any external obstacles, would cause it to move in a certain direction with a definite velocity. Bernoulli thought of it as an inherent conatus to motion, existing in the body as a very slow motion, standing to actual motion somewhat in the same way as infinitesimals stood to finite quantities; and he did not see that Leibniz helped the matter at all by his talk about 'forms' which were 'analogous to minds' [GM iii. 547]. But Leibniz was not content with a very slow motion. For this was derivative; potentia was more primitive. And it involved perception and appetite as well [GM iii. 552: L 830/511-12, 16 November 1698].

During the early discussions with De Volder, Leibniz spoke of this potentia or vis as an attribute of substance, and as having to overcome the general passive power of resistance which belongs to all bodies. All matter has resistance or inertia, and antitypia or impenetrability, proportional in amount to its extension. The active power implanted in the matter swings the matter into motion somewhat (as he says in the *Theodicy*, [GP vi. 119-20: H 140-1]) as a stream moves boats along. The actual motion of the body then results as a particular modification or limitation of the primary or substantial activity by the disposition of the matter or passive element in the body [GP ii. 171: L 840/517, March/April 1699].

Here we have the old view somewhat developed. The complete body, which results from the combination of the prime active and the prime passive elements, is now called materia secunda; it is materia secunda which moves, and materia secunda which possesses motive force measured by mv^2. This force possessed by materia secunda is here called secondary or motive force.

But Leibniz goes on at once to distinguish between the mind, which is the entelechy of the organic body, and the organic body itself, and to speak of the fact that each develops independently of the other. Here we have materia secunda in the previous sense, of the body considered apart from its entelechy, and it is not easy to reconcile the two passages. The only way of doing so would be to suggest that an organic body, such as that of man, can be considered as an aggregate of material particles, each of which with its own entelechy is a particle of materia secunda in the new sense; the independence of mind and body being asserted for man and denied for other entelechies. But Leibniz clearly does not mean this.

And thus De Volder naturally asks [GP ii. 180] how Leibniz's active principle can produce changes in extension. For the doctrine of pre-established harmony shows that mind (or form in general) cannot act on body. If then the active principle is distinct from extension (which for De Volder means body) it cannot act on extension; but if it is itself extension or a mode of extension, then extension is not merely passive.

Leibniz's draft reply makes the situation worse and worse. For he admits that in resistance there is something active; and he couples antitypia (previously coupled with resistance as the passive element in matter) with extension, coupling resistance with activity [GP ii. 184: L 845/520]. In the letter actually sent he says simply that vis primitiva is something prior to extension, constitutive of the substance which is in the extended. Extension is simply an attribute of the aggregate resulting from many substances. Thus the principle of action can be neither extension nor a mode of extension, and it does not act on extension, but on the extended [GP ii. 187]. And he seems to throw himself on De Volder's mercy. 'I wish', he says, 'that it were possible now to explain everything more clearly or to prove it more firmly, but at this early stage in our philosophy it is something to be able to assert undeniable truths and to draw conclusions from a few acceptable hypotheses. Especially if I can make use of your insights it may be possible to get further.' [GP ii. 187, 23 June 1699. See letter to Bernoulli, GM iii. 592, in a similar strain.]

But, as I have said, Leibniz's answers to objections seem to show rather a multitude of cross lights. All that is clear is that extension by itself is not sufficient for an explanation of the motion of bodies, and that we need something active; but what this activity is, and how it is related to body, is involved in more obscurity the more Leibniz 'explains'.

Entelechy, materia prima, materia secunda: vis primitiva being modified by materia prima and producing complete substance or materia secunda which possesses vis derivativa and motion: while yet entelechy develops by itself independently of materia secunda and materia secunda develops independently of entelechy, and yet entelechy acts on materia secunda and is the source of the mass and the forces in it—how on earth can we get all this into one consistent picture? It is no wonder that De Volder confesses that he cannot make head or tail of it. 'About this active principle which is prior to extension, I have nothing to add', he says to Leibniz, 'I am too stupid to understand anything about it.' [GP ii. 188, August 1699]

Leibniz in his reply (*a*) stresses the unity of the monad, as that which does not contain many substances, (*b*) insists that without an entelechy, an extended body is a mere aggregate of substances, (*c*) states that extension is abstract and neither a substance nor an aggregate of substances, (*d*) explains that an organic body can be looked at in two ways, first (taken apart from its entelechy), as a multitude of separate organisms, each with their own separate entelechies, and secondly (taken with its entelechy), as a single substance, because on account of the structure of the whole its entelechy is the dominating mind in the whole, and finally (*e*) reminds De Volder that rigorously speaking, for one thing to act on another is nothing but for each to correspond to the other without mutual influence [GP ii. 193–5: L 846–51/521–3].

But of course this is a mere repetition of his earlier points and does nothing to resolve the confusion into which the whole subject has been thrown. If entelechy and body together alone make a complete substance, then it is difficult to see how entelechy and body can correspond without mutual influence; and if they can thus correspond, it is difficult to see why entelechy should be needed to give body its substantiality.

And this is the point that Bernoulli stresses in a subsequent letter to Leibniz. If mind and body do not influence one another, then, says Bernoulli, De Volder insists that entelechies do nothing to matter, nor matter to entelechy. Bernoulli does not see why Leibniz has not answered this point, for it seems to need an answer [GM iii. 619, 21 October 1699]. And De Volder himself made this point shortly afterwards [GP ii. 198–9].

Leibniz's reply consists in distinguishing between the materia prima which with the entelechy makes one complete substance, and the organic body of this substance, which is an aggregate of other substances. Entelechy acts on materia prima but not on the aggregate of substances [GP ii. 205–6, 9/20 January 1700].

We see here the difficulty with which Leibniz is fighting. The complete substance, say a man, consists of his entelechy and his materia prima; but it also consists of his entelechy and his organic body. For the organic body is only made into one complete substance by the presence of the entelechy; apart from that it is only an aggregate of substances.

It would seem then that the materia prima of any part of the organic body is a part of the materia prima of the whole individual man. And this seems indicated in Leibniz's later letter of 20 June 1703 [GP ii. 250–3: L 862–6/529–31]. There is no doubt, as there has been none throughout, that the human mind makes the organic body one complete substance, or that the organic body considered apart from the mind is an aggregate of substances [GP ii. 250: L 862/529]; nor is there any doubt on this page that the primitive entelechy with its primitive passive power makes up precisely and exactly the same mass as the mass made up by the entelechies of the parts of the body with their primitive passive power. And this is repeated two pages later [GP ii. 252: L 864/530]. If you take mass as an aggregate containing many substances, he says, you can nevertheless think of it as forming one substance of higher order, that is, as being animated by an entelechy of higher rank. In this substance of higher order, he goes on, the primitive passive force is indeed the primitive passive force belonging to the whole mass of the organic body, but the subordinate monads situated in the organs are not parts of this mass, though they are 'required immediately' for it, and concur with the monad of higher rank in producing the organized bodily substance.

I am not sure of all that this means, but at least it seems to involve that the total materia prima of the subordinate monads is identical with the materia prima of the dominant monad.

Thus when Leibniz sums up his discussion by saying: I distinguish between (1) primitive entelechy or mind, (2) materia prima or primitive passive power, (3) the monad completed by these two taken together, (4) mass or materia secunda, or the organic machine, to which innumerable subordinate monads concur, (5) the animal or bodily substance, which the monad dominating in the machine makes one—when he says this, if we think of (1), (2) and (3) for the moment as referring to the dominant monad, we must regard the materia prima in (5) as identical with the materia prima in (2), the entelechies in (5) as identical with those in (4), and finally the one bodily substance in (5) as identical with the dominant monad itself.

We must, I say, if we are to hold by his previous statements. And yet we cannot do this, and keep to what he holds in general about materia prima in the monad, and to what he says about the relation of the dominant monad to the organic body.

For the most constant account he gives of materia prima is that it always belongs essentially to the monad, whereas the organic body of the monad is continually changing. And again, he insists that materia prima is not divisible, and is not extended, though it is the source of the extended and so of extension; whereas the organic body is extended and is divisible. But this means that the materia prima of any monad is peculiar to itself, and could not form part of the materia prima of any other monad. It involves also that the monad must be a strict unity in the sense of being strictly indivisible and not extended; and that thus the animate bodily substance cannot be a strict substance. The monad can have a body only in the sense of corresponding to it: the body cannot, however viewed, be a genuine part of the monad.

To sum up, the argument points on the one hand to the organic body with its mind animating it as a true substantial unity, a true monad, and on the other hand to the monad as indivisible and inextended, possessing an organic body only by way of harmonious correspondence.

If the animate body is not a true unity, there are no unities anywhere in body; but if it is a true unity, then any talk of pre-established harmony between mind and body is absurd. Again, if it is a true unity, then the problem genuinely arises as to how the mere presence of the mind can unify the infinite aggregate of substances which can be found in the body, and how the mind can perform this unifying service on a body which is constantly changing. Substance, Leibniz has throughout insisted, is not extended; but the gap between substance and the extended body has nowhere been bridged.

V

Leibniz seems to have been acutely conscious of these difficulties; for he now lays stress on a point that is new so far as this correspondence is concerned, viz. that since the bodily machine, taken apart from its animating entelechy, is only an aggregate of innumerable substances, it follows that its unity as one bodily thing is only a unity read into it by us; and the same is true of any part that we consider as one material body. Hence when we consider it as a single body made up of parts, and investigate the laws of its motion by the principles of physics, we are abstracting from the entelechies contained in it, and thus are not dealing with genuine substances at all. We are, in short, dealing only with a phenomenon. Thus the extended body of physics is only a unity 'by aggregation', and derived forces, motions, impacts, and the laws of derived forces and motions, are only 'in phenomena'. And phenomena, as Democritus said, exist only *νόμῳ* [nomo] and not *φύσει* [physei].

But so far, the word phenomenon does not mean, that what is referred to exists only 'in the mind'. The aggregation is an act of the mind; but the things aggregated are real though incomplete aspects of genuine substances. There is need of abstractions, he says, if things are to be explained scientifically [GP ii. 252: L 864/531].

A similar, though not quite the same, account, is given of space. Space and time are indeed abstract, i.e. they are not substances. But all mutations, both of spiritual and of material things, have a place both in space and in time. For though the monads are not extended, yet they have a kind of position in extension, i.e. a certain ordered relation to other co-existences, viz. through the machine over which they are set [GP ii. 253: L 865/531]. Space and time are orders of co-existence and of succession; thus they are derived from co-existent and successive states of substance.

But they are not modes of substances, though they result from substances; for space and time are invariable orders and would remain precisely the same whatever actual changes occurred [GP ii. 227: L 855/525-6]. Space designates abstractly a possible continuous plurality of co-existing things, viz. extended bodies, which are aggregates of things containing entelechies [GP ii. 195: L 850/523]. Again, an extended body can cease to exist, but not extension, just as men die, but human nature does not [GP ii. 205].

Abstract, then, space and time may be, just as number is; but none of them is purely mental.

The direction, however, in which Leibniz is going seems indicated by a phrase in his letter to Bernoulli, in which the above letter to De Volder was enclosed. He says that there is 'almost' nothing in body but entelechy (cum in corpore pene nihil aliud sit quam Entelechia) [GM iii. 720, 20 June 1703]. In his letter to De Volder of 21 January 1704, he merely repeats the point that bodies are substances and not substance, and so are only real phenomena [GP ii. 261], but in a passage in the draft letter, cut out of the letter actually sent, he goes right over to the position of the *Discourse on Metaphysics*, viz. that he does not see that there is ultimately anything but infinite percipients whose phenomena appear in an orderly succession, in harmony with those of all other percipients through their common dependence on God [GP ii. 264]. The passage was cut out; but none of the explanations actually contained in the letter itself satisfied De Volder, who still did not see how the presence of an entelechy brought about unity in a body which, however far you divided it, was infinitely divisible, and contained infinite entelechies.

And De Volder sent to Bernoulli, along with his reply reiterating this, a strong letter of protest, expressing his dissatisfaction with the whole discussion. All he gets from Leibniz, he complains, is the word entelechy, which he does not understand in the least. Bernoulli duly reported this to Leibniz [GM iii. 753, 21 June 1704]; and in his reply [30 June 1704] Leibniz explains that the notion of primitive force is very clear, since there is in it something analogous to what is in us, viz. perception and appetite; and then he takes the final plunge and lets himself go [GP ii. 270: L 876/537]. There is, he now says, strictly speaking, nothing in things but simple substances, and in simple substances nothing but perception and appetite. Matter is no longer described as an aggregate. Both matter and motion are stated to be 'phenomena of percipients', and to be derived (not by considering abstractly an aspect of a plurality of simple substances, but) from the harmony of precipients with themselves at different times, and with other precipients. There exists, in short, nothing but the ordered series of perceptions in each monad, and God as the ultimate cause [GP ii. 211: L 877/538]. He repeats this in his letter to Bernoulli of 1 July 1704 [GM iii. 756].

Wherefore De Volder, after a long silence, complains that Leibniz has now changed his ground entirely. For De Volder has all along been asking, and Leibniz has all along been answering, the question, whence come the forces belonging to bodily substance. But now Leibniz has taken bodies away entirely, and left no forces properly speaking, but only perception and appetite [GP ii. 272, 14 November 1704]. And De Volder does not understand how extended mass can appear, as the result of these purely perceiving substances. Leibniz has spoken of the extended as arising from the diffusion, or continuous repetition, of something homogeneous, but this is obscure; and unless what is diffused is itself extended, De Volder cannot see how extension can arise at all, even as an appearance [GP ii. 273–4].

In his reply, Leibniz insists that he is not taking away bodies, but showing them for what they are. His accounts show that he is still thinking of the perceptions of various monads as all expressing, in their own way, the same phenomena of the universe [GP ii. 275, 1705] and thus having reference to the whole ordered system of monads. In other words, he still feels he can keep the spatio-temporal order of monads, with organic bodies composed of materia secunda interacting according to the laws of motion, while basing the system of organic bodies on the system of purely perceiving and striving monads. For monads are not purely active, they contain essentially a passive element. And when this passive element belonging to the various monads is considered in abstraction from the complete monads themselves, it must be regarded as everywhere homogeneous; again, it forms a continuous order, for there are no gaps in the universe; and thus this continuous homogeneous plurality formed by abstraction from the infinitely varied monads, gives rise to the notion of extension. However varied the system of actual monads may be, the act of abstraction always gives rise to the same space.

I need not say how unsatisfactory all this is. If in the monads there is nothing but perception and appetite, and if the monad is really inextended, then there is nothing of it, so far as I can see, that could be perceived by another monad; it is difficult to get it into 'a' universe of events at all. Leibniz has seen this all along; he has insisted that the monads can get relation to each other and to a common universe only by their possession of an organic body. But he has been driven from one expedient to another. When the organic body has been explained as resulting from monads, he thinks of the monads as connected into one world by the homogeneity of their passive element; when the passive element has become a private aspect of the individual monad he still retains the notion that each monad, from its own point of view, mirrors the same universe (the same universe of phenomena, he says, [GP ii. 278]).

But what universe or what phenomena remain, to be mirrored, is a difficult question. For if the monads are purely perceiving and striving beings and nothing else, there is nothing of them that can be a phenomenon for any other monad. What you perceive must be distinct from your perceiving, if what I perceive is to correspond in any way to it; and, indeed, if my perceiving and your perceiving are to mirror or represent the same thing from different points of view, there must be a same thing to be mirrored. But monads as purely perceiving and striving beings cannot be mirrored or represented, even by an act of abstraction. And hence Leibniz gives his monads the impossible function of representing a universe that cannot be represented.

But while Leibniz from time to time sank back on this bed of roses in which nothing but pure perceiving and striving monads exist, yet the thorny problem of what the monads were to express, and how they were to get into the same universe, always caused him to explore further. I do not believe he ever got satisfaction, ever thought that he saw clearly the complete solution of the problem. You can, if you like, think of him throughout the whole correspondence with Arnauld, Bernoulli, and De Volder as writing with his tongue in his cheek, knowing all the time that he really believed that bodies are only well-regulated phenomena of percipients, and not even aggregates of monads. For has he not said it himself (quite privately) in the *Discourse on Metaphysics*, and does he not come out with it at the very end of his correspondence with De Volder, after he has seen that the game is up and De Volder is hopeless as a convert in any case? You can do this if you will; for myself, I am unable to do so. Throughout the correspondence he admits that he cannot prove things as he would like; that he only sees far enough into things to be able to answer objections; that he hopes by the help of his correspondents to see a little further; and I see no reason for doubting his sincerity here.

It is true that in his writing he is afraid of being misunderstood, and of ridicule, and that he hints at things sometimes instead of saying them outright; but his pen continually outran any discretion of this sort, and I feel sure that in any correspondence taken as a whole we know fairly well where he is. And in this correspondence with De Volder, it seems to me, we see him endeavouring, without success, to escape the extreme interpretation of the doctrine of substance to which his metaphysical and logical speculations of 1686 had led. But while he did not succeed, he did not give up the attempt. In the years after 1706 we still find him working with the conceptions with which he worked, and which he had elaborated, in his correspondence with De Volder; nor did success ever reward his efforts.

VIII

LEIBNIZ'S DYNAMICS AND CONTINGENCY IN NATURE

MARGARET D. WILSON

I

IN 1699 Leibniz wrote to a correspondent:

My Dynamics requires a work to itself . . . you are right in judging that it is to a great extent the foundation of my system; for it is there that we learn the difference between truths whose necessity is brute and geometrical, and truths which have their source in fitness and final causes.[1]

And about a decade later he remarks in the *Theodicy*:

This great example of the laws of motion shows us in the clearest possible way how much difference there is among these three cases, first, *an absolute necessity*, metaphysical or geometric, which can be called *blind* and which depends only on efficient causes; in the second place, *a moral necessity*, which comes from the free choice of wisdom with respect to final causes; and finally in the third place, *something absolutely arbitrary*, depending on an indifference of equilibrium which is imagined, but which cannot exist, where there is no sufficient reason either in the efficient or in the final cause. [GP vi.321: H 334]

The claims made in these passages for the philosophical importance of Dynamics are strong and in a sense unequivocal. Yet they are also rather mysterious. Leibniz of course wants to hold that the laws of nature *are* contingent—not true in all possible worlds; this in fact is a point he often makes side by side with the claim that the existence of any individual substance is contingent, and depends on the free choice of God to create the most perfect of the possible worlds. But in these passages Leibniz

Reprinted in a slightly revised and abridged version from *Motion and Time, Space and Matter: Interrelations in the History of Philosophy and Science*, edited by Peter K. Machamer and Robert G. Turnbull. Used by permission of the author, the editors, and the publisher.

[1] GP iii.645. In general, translations throughout the paper are my own unless otherwise indicated. However, I quote directly from the R. H. M. Elwes translation of Spinoza's *Ethics*, which is accurate for the passages cited; and from the admirable Lucas and Grint translation of Leibniz's *Discourse on Metaphysics* [LG]. My versions of other passages have sometimes been influenced by the published translations cited in the notes.

seems to say more than this. He says we *learn* from Dynamics the difference between necessary and contingent truths, that the laws of motion show 'in the clearest possible way how much difference there is' between the blind or brute necessity of mathematics and contingent or 'morally necessary' truths that depend on the choice of perfect reason. What is more, he speaks in the first passage specifically of 'my' Dynamics, while the second passage follows a long criticism of Cartesian physics and a statement of some of Leibniz's own physical principles. The suggestion, then, is that the specific principles that Leibniz believed he had established, in opposition to the Cartesians, help make evident the difference between necessary and contingent truths.

To a twentieth-century philosopher, this notion is apt to seem very odd. The question whether the laws of nature are necessary or contingent–assuming this is a reasonable question at all–does not seem in any way dependent on what laws are found to be the true ones. (Similarly, one would have difficulty making sense of the suggestion that the question whether individual existence is necessary or contingent must be answered with reference to what individuals actually exist.) And in fact, the contingency of laws as well as the contingency of particular existents seems often to be presented by Leibniz himself as a tenet of his system resting on purely philosophical intuitions. Nevertheless (as it will be the purpose of this paper to show), Leibniz's remarks in the passages quoted do reflect an important and persistent aspect of his thought. Further, his claims for the philosophical significance of his Dynamics, though largely anachronistic today, are tied up with some issues of considerable interest from the point of view of the history of ideas.

Leibniz's doctrine of contingency has, of course, been the subject of much controversy in the critical literature of the past seventy years. However, this controversy has tended to focus on the status of propositions about particular individuals–e.g. 'Adam ate the apple'–and largely to neglect any problems about contingency that might be specifically related to his views about the laws of nature. Most attention has been devoted to determining how, if at all, Leibniz's claims that propositions about particular existents are contingent, and true only because God freely selected the *best* possible world for creation, can be reconciled with his further doctrine that in *every* true proposition the concept of the predicate is 'in some manner' included in the concept of the subject. For the latter claim seems to imply that *all* propositions are implicit identities. But Leibniz's standard definition of a necessary truth is a proposition the negation of which implies a contradiction–in other words, an explicit or implicit identity. Thus the theory of truth suggests that even existential propositions may ultimately have to be construed as necessary, and brings in question the sense in which alternative worlds may rightly be characterized as 'possible'. (That another world is in itself consistently conceivable need not imply that it might have existed.) Of course, the theory of truth presents difficulties for any claim of contingency in Leibniz's system—not just for propositions about individuals. But some of the most interesting aspects of this particular problem are tied up with the treatment of individual substances.[2]

Naturally, it has not gone unnoticed that Leibniz regarded the laws of nature as contingent. However, their status tends to be touched on only incidentally in the literature, in connection with proposed solutions to problems deriving from the theory of truth. Thus, Louis Couturat cited the contingency of laws in Leibniz's system as evidence against the proposal that Leibniz regarded only existential judgments as contingent—and meant to *exempt* such judgments from the 'analytic' theory of truth.[3] And as part of his effort to reestablish a version of the latter interpretation, E. M. Curley has replied that 'according to Leibniz, the laws of nature are also existential propositions, so that they do not form a distinct class of contingent truths'.[4] Curley quotes a passage in which Leibniz does represent the view that the laws of nature are contingent as resting on the premiss that the existence of the 'series of things' depends on God's choice:

> [We said] these laws are not necessary and essential but contingent and existential. . . . For since it is contingent and depends on the free decrees of God that this particular series of things exists, its laws will be themselves indeed absolutely contingent, although hypothetically necessary and as it were essential once the series is given.[5]

Curley further clarifies his point by indicating that the laws of nature are 'existential' in that they rule out certain possible states of affairs from the realm of actuality:

> 'All circles are plane figures', which is given [by Leibniz] as an example of an essential proposition, says that a circle which is not a plane figure is not a possible thing. But a law of nature, such as 'unsupported bodies fall to earth', says only that an unsupported body which does not fall to earth is not an actual thing, i.e. does not exist. [Ibid., 92]

Now one may feel some hesitation about this interpretation. In particular, it seems to deny Leibniz any distinction among universal laws,

[2] For example, its connection with the claim that every substance has a 'complete concept' from which all its properties—past, present, and future—are somehow derivable.

[3] 'Sur la métaphysique de Leibniz', *Revue de métaphysique et de morale*, 10 (1902), 12.

[4] 'The Root of Contingency', *Frankfurt* 91.

[5] C 19–20: *Frankfurt* 91. I have altered Curley's wording slightly.

local law-like generalizations, 'accidental' generalizations, and hypotheticals true by virtue of the falsity of the antecedent. (The example Curley uses is, clearly, far from being universally true—and has the special disadvantage, in this context, of *mentioning* a particular existent.) Further, it seems that a philosopher could hold that more than one 'series of existents' is possible, without holding that more than one set of basic laws is possible.[6] (I will suggest below that such a view can be found in the writings of Descartes.) On the other hand, Curley is clearly right in pointing out that since Leibniz *does* believe the laws of nature are contingent, and since statements of laws of nature do have negative existential import, their truth, for Leibniz, cannot be altogether independent of God's choices of particular existents. What we need now, however, is some account of why the laws of nature should sometimes be ascribed *special importance* in illuminating the distinction between necessary and contingent truth.

In what follows I shall try to provide such an account, by placing Leibniz's interpretation of his dynamical conclusions within its historical context. Fundamentally, Leibniz was concerned to oppose—for religious reasons especially—the 'geometrical' conception of natural science exemplified (in different degrees) by his predecessors Descartes and Spinoza. That is to say, he was concerned to oppose the assimilation of physics to geometry, and of physical necessity to geometrical necessity. Leibniz shared with most of his contemporaries the view that the axioms of Euclidean geometry are among the eternal truths: within Leibniz's system this view appears as the doctrine that the axioms of geometry are true of all possible (i.e. consistently conceivable) worlds for reasons connected with the concept of space.[7] He believed he could establish that this status is *not* shared by the laws of mechanics. Leibniz believed his Dynamics yielded this conclusion in virtue of showing (1) that matter cannot be adequately conceived in purely geometrical terms—that 'the essence of matter does not consist in extension alone'; and (2) that physical laws manifest features of 'fitness and proportion', which not only are

[6] It might be questioned whether this idea would be congenial to Leibniz. A statement in one of his letters to Arnauld could be read as suggesting that he thought no two possible worlds have a law in common: 'For as there is an infinity of possible worlds, there is also an infinity of laws, some proper to one, others to another [*les unes propres à l'un, les autres à l'autre*], and each possible individual of any world includes in his notion the laws of his world'. [GP ii.40: MP 43; this passage was brought to my attention by James Alt] However, I doubt that Leibniz really means to imply that every law is peculiar to some particular possible world. Earlier in the paragraph, for instance, he indicates that the decree to create a particular substance (Adam) was distinct from the 'few free primary decrees capable of being called laws of the universe'.

[7] See J. Moreau, 'L'espace et les verités éternelles chez Leibniz', *Archives de Philosophie*, 29 (1966), 483 ff.

inconsistent with the geometrical view, but which further can only be explained with reference to the purposes of a 'wise author' of nature. (He thus claims to have discovered the basis for a new, updated version of the Argument from Design.) That his reasoning on these issues is logically impeccable can hardly be maintained; on the other hand, the reasoning has, for the most part, a definite *ad hominem* cogency against the assumptions of his opponents.

But Leibniz's rejection of the doctrine of blind or brute geometrical necessity, on the basis of his conclusions in dynamics, has a murkier aspect as well. For he also takes his Dynamics to reveal that the underlying causes of natural phenomena must be found in immaterial or soul-like entities that are governed by final causes and may be identified with Aristotelian forms or entelechies. Such immanent purposiveness he also takes to be incompatible with the concept of determination by 'geometrical necessity' (although, amazingly, he never makes clear that this is an entirely different point from those mentioned above). This view appears to reflect a good deal of wishful thinking about the possibility of partially defending the older philosophy of nature against the atheistical and 'materialistic' implications of the modern view–and, one may be tempted to think, not much else. I will suggest, however, that even this conclusion, obscure as it may be from a strictly philosophical point of view, can be partially explicated in terms of the transition away from the early geometrical conception of physics. In this case a particular sort of conceptual difficulty implicit in the transition appears partially to account for Leibniz's otherwise bewildering move.

II

All things, I repeat, are in God, and all things which come to pass, come to pass solely through the laws of the infinite nature of God, and follow (as I will shortly show) from the necessity of his essence. [I.15]

Nothing in the universe is contingent, but all things are conditioned to exist and operate in a particular manner by the necessity of the divine nature. [I. 29]

Things could not have been brought into being by God in any manner or in any order different from that which has in fact obtained. [I. 33]

These quotations from Part I of Spinoza's *Ethics* represent the strongest form of the geometricism that Leibniz wished to oppose through his Dynamics. Spinoza's extreme position can be expressed in the claim that whatever is (in the timeless sense of 'is') cannot not be, and whatever is not, cannot be. Individual existents (modes), their relations to each other, laws of nature, the two accessible attributes of thought and extension, and the world as a whole are alike in this respect. Only God is self-caused, or has an essence that includes existence; however, the causal necessity by which modes come into existence is itself in no sense weaker than the necessity of a logical deduction from necessary premisses:

From God's supreme power, or infinite nature, an infinite number of things–that is, all things have necessarily flowed forth in an infinite number of ways, or always follow with the same necessity; in the same way as from the nature of a triangle it follows from eternity and for eternity, that its three interior angles are equal to two right angles. [note to I.17]

This passage and the whole deductive format of the *Ethics* epitomize the influence of the geometrical model on scientific thought of the seventeenth century.

The geometric model was of course also a primary influence on the thinking of Spinoza's predecessor Descartes, although in some respects Descartes did not take things quite so far. Descartes does not deny that other worlds are possible; on the other hand, there is evidence that he did regard the basic laws of nature as necessary–as holding in any worlds God 'could have created'. The laws of nature, like the axioms of the geometers, are, he claimed, innate in our minds, so that 'after having reflected sufficiently upon the matter, we cannot doubt their being accurately observed in all that exists or is done in the world'.[8] Further, he remarks that in his Physics he had

pointed out what [are] the laws of Nature, and without resting my reasons on any other principle than on the infinite perfections of God, I tried to demonstrate all those of which one could have any doubt, and to show that they are such that even if God had created several worlds, there could be none in which these laws failed to be observed. [AT vi.43: HR i.108]

As this passage may suggest, Descartes in fact 'deduces' his laws of motion, such as the principle that the same 'quantity of motion' (*mv*) is always conserved, by appeal to the 'immutability of God'–an appeal which may have echoes in Spinoza. (Notoriously, though, Descartes elsewhere espouses the views that the 'eternal truths' or standards of logical and mathematical possibility themselves depend on God's will and that God enjoys a complete 'liberty of indifference' in determining

[8] 'Discourse on the Method of Rightly Conducting One's Reason and Seeking Truth in the Sciences', part 5 [AT vi.41: HR i.106]. There is a non-trivial error in the HR translation, however.

what they should be. Thus he is a source both of necessitarian thought and of the seemingly opposite tendency (also opposed by Leibniz) that views the circumstances of nature and even ordinary mathematics as 'arbitrary'.)

Descartes' conception of the laws of nature as *a priori* and necessary (like the axioms of geometry) is accompanied by a strictly geometrical conception of matter. This conception is advanced on purely intuitive grounds in his philosophical writings. The doctrine that what is 'clearly and distinctly perceived is true' yields, in the *Meditations*, the claim that the real or objective properties of body (as distinct from mere sensory appearances) are just those properties that it possesses as 'the object of pure mathematics' [AT vii.80: HR i.191]. By 'pure mathematics' Descartes means, especially, geometry;[9] extension, figure, and mutability are apprehended by the intellect as 'all that remains' when we consider a body as it is in itself, stripped of 'external forms' [AT vii.30–1: HR i.154–5]. In the *Principles of Philosophy* Descartes further argues that extension is the one property of bodies that is presupposed by all the other physical properties, without itself presupposing them. On this basis he holds that extension is *the* defining or essential attribute of body [AT viii, pt. 1.25: HR i.240]. These purely conceptual arguments ostensibly (at least) appeal only to ordinary intuitions, rather than sophisticated scientific understanding. This concept of body or matter is assumed by Descartes in deriving his laws of motion *a priori*. (The motion in the world, on the other hand, is not represented as itself part of the nature of body, but as a quantity imposed 'externally', as it were, by the prime mover.)

Extrapolating a bit from Descartes' own statements, we might suggest the following argument as an exemplar of the moderate geometricism that views the laws of nature (if not individual existents) as obtaining in any world God could have made.

1. It is a necessary truth (true in all possible worlds) that the essence of matter consists in extension alone.
2. No world could exist that is not made by God.
3. Immutability is an essential property of God, i.e. 'God is immutable' is a necessary truth.
4. The basic laws of motion, m_1-m_n, can be derived with geometrical (i.e. logical) necessity from the assumptions that the essence of

[9] Descartes's seventeenth-century French translator renders '*in purae Matheseos objecto*' as 'dans l'object de la Geometrie speculative'. See AT ix.63.

matter is just extension and that any material world is created by an immutable Being. (I take it one need not suppose the existence of motion to be a necessary truth, in order to hold that the laws of motion are true in all possible worlds.)

This series of claims is, of course, based primarily on the passage quoted above from the *Discourse.* (Fortunately, we need not be concerned here with the plausibility of these propositions, and particularly of the fourth.) It yields the conclusion:

5. The basic laws of motion are necessary (are 'observed', as Descartes puts it) in any world God could make.

Now someone concerned to dispute the conception of physical law implicit in this line of thought might very well wish to concentrate attention on the 'laws' its propounder claims to have derived in this *a priori* manner. He might, for instance, try to show that some 'laws of nature' presented as necessary either do not follow from these assumptions, or are false of the actual world (and *a fortiori* not true of all worlds that could exist). He might argue that *correct* reasoning from the geometricist's premisses yields false results. None of these approaches, to be sure, would suffice to show that the laws of nature are *not* necessary. However, a sort of minimal argument against that conclusion would consist in showing that some particular set of laws (say that espoused by the geometricist) is both possible and false (not 'observed' by nature).

In other words, one good way to refute the geometricist's conception of physics is to refute the geometricist's physics (without claiming that his principles are *necessarily* false). If such an enterprise sounds somewhat far-fetched today, this is, I think, largely because the geometricist's conception of physics sounds far-fetched. But the quotations from Descartes and from Spinoza may perhaps serve to remind us of the grip of the geometrical model in the early seventeenth century.

Some further points about the Cartesian outlook should be mentioned before we consider Leibniz's reaction to it. First, in the minds of seventeenth-century Cartesian philosophers there seems to have been a close connection between the idea that the essence of matter consists in (the geometrical property of) extension, and the idea that the laws of nature share the *necessity* of geometrical axioms. In fact, there does *not* seem to be any direct logical route between these notions: even if we suppose that Euclidean geometry is necessarily true of the world, the doctrine that the laws of nature are necessary seems neither to entail, nor to be entailed by, the proposition that only geometrical concepts are required for the statement of them.[10] But it is understandable that these ideas should be assumed to stand or fall together as twin aspects of the notion that physics (as Descartes remarked to Mersenne) 'is nothing but geometry [AT ii.268].

In the same way both necessitarianism and the Cartesian theory of matter are tied up with the exclusion of final causes from the physical world–a position shared by Descartes and Spinoza. On the one hand, it is difficult to conceive how a bare bit of extension could be endowed with a purpose or goal. On the other hand, because of the close linkage of the concept of *purpose* with that of *choice*, it might well seem natural to suppose that only efficient causality can consort with the strict necessity supposedly characteristic of geometrical axioms.[11] Thus both the necessitarianism of the geometrical conception of physics, and the attendant conception of matter, may be viewed as having *some important connection* with the denial of immanent teleology. It is understandable, therefore, that someone interested in reinstating immanent final causes should find it *necessary* to oppose the other aspects of the geometricist's view. Leibniz, as we shall see, sometimes seems to think that rejection of geometricism in physics is *sufficient* to establish that there are purposive entities throughout nature.

Finally, however, we must concede that Descartes' use of the rather inscrutable notion of *God's immutability* makes it difficult to measure with complete assurance the distance between his and Leibniz's conception of the relation between physical and mathematical truth. Thus Descartes seems to hold that the laws of nature are true in any world God could have made–on the hypothesis that God is immutable. If this hypothesis is required only for the derivation of physical laws, and not as an underpinning for geometry proper, and if, further, it is taken to introduce some reference to volition and purpose (God's immutable will), then Descartes' actual position might turn out to be much closer to Leibniz's than at first seems to be the case. It would still remain true, however, that Leibniz differs fundamentally from Descartes in his concern to emphasize rather than minimize the distinction between physical and mathematical truth.

[10] See A. Quinton, 'Matter and Space', *Mind*, 73 (1964), 347–9, for an elaboration of this point. Quinton, surprisingly, seems to go along with the view that geometry *does* provide a body of necessary truths about 'spatial qualities in the external world'. But perhaps I have misunderstood him.

[11] Spinoza, in fact, makes clear in the Appendix to Part I of the *Ethics* that he regards the claim that 'everything in nature proceeds with a sort of necessity' as incompatible with the supposition of final causes.

III

In his early years Leibniz himself accepted the geometricist conception of physics. He even attempted to derive 'abstract principles of motion' by reasoning *a priori* from the conception of matter as mere extension.[12] One of the propositions he 'proved' in this way provides the springboard for his later attacks on the doctrine of brute geometrical necessity in nature. Briefly, Leibniz had reasoned that mere extension must be 'indifferent' to both motion and rest. By this he seems to have meant that there was nothing in the purely geometrical conception of matter to provide for a force of resistance, or reaction to every action. He then proceeded to the startling conclusion that when a body in motion, however small, collides with a body at rest, however large, both bodies will then move in the direction of the original motion, and at the original speed! According to his later accounts, he was even at the time distressed by this bizarre result, and supposed that the 'wise Author of nature' would not permit such a disproportion between cause and effect. Subsequently he affirms (with a rather puzzling air of informativeness) that indeed such phenomena do not occur [GM vi.241-2: L 720-1/440-1 (1695); GP ii.170: L 838-40/516-17 (1699)]. He affirms in these later works a principle of equality of reaction, which he derives from (or perhaps equates with) the principle that there is an equality between causes and effects. This principle he seems to regard as foreign to Descartes' 'geometrical' reasoning. (Elsewhere he stresses that Descartes' disregard of the architectonic or non-geometrical principle of continuity—according to which all change is gradual—also explains fundamental errors in his physical principles) [e.g. GP vii.279: L 787-8/484 (ca. 1696); GP iv. 375: L 658/398 (1692)].

Leibniz concludes that the Cartesian conception of matter is inadequate to account for the actual phenomena of nature, so a different conception must be substituted:

> If the essence of body consisted in extension, this essence alone should suffice to explain [*rendre raison de*] all the affections of body. But that is not the case. We observe in matter a quality which some have called natural inertia [read 'resistance' or 'reaction'], through which body resists motion in some manner. [GP iv.464: W 100 (1697)]

> In order to prove *that the nature of body does not consist in extension*, I have made use of an argument . . . of which the basis is that *the natural inertia of bodies* could not be explained by extension alone. [GP iv.466: W 102 (1693)][13]

[12] GP iv.228-32: L 217-22/139-42. Leibniz makes many allusions to this 1671 paper in his later writings.

[13] As Gerd Buchdahl has pointed out, Leibniz fails clearly to distinguish *inertia*

Now we may note in passing that this argument does not depend exclusively on dynamical notions. For instance, it seems to presuppose a rather uncartesian conception of the functions of an essence: Descartes does not think that even the fundamental property of motion *follows from* the essence of matter alone. On the other hand, Descartes does assume a certain conception of body in his deductions of the basic laws. And Leibniz does not make clear exactly what he means by an 'account' of the properties of bodies. Therefore it is not easy to pinpoint the extent of their difference on this question; fortunately it does not seem very important that we do so.[14]

In at least one later writing, however, Leibniz seems to concede that this reasoning is perhaps not sufficient to clinch the case against Cartesianism. For his conclusion about impact might be staved off if only one assumed–as Descartes had assumed–that God conserves the same quantity of motion [GP iv.465: W 101]. At this point, therefore, Leibniz brings to bear another argument. This argument, based openly on the research of Galileo, purports to prove that the true conservation principle in physics is not the conservation of motion (mv), as Descartes held, but the conservation of quantity mv^2, which Leibniz identifies as *vis viva*, active force. From this fact, too, Leibniz claims, it can be seen that there is more in nature than quantity of motion, and more to matter than is dreamed of in Descartes' Geometry [ibid., also GP iv.443: LG 28-32].

(The consideration that is supposed to prove this point is, briefly, as follows. A body of 4 pounds falling freely from a height of 1 foot will rise again to a height of 1 foot (assuming elastic rebound). A body of 1 pound falling from a height of 4 feet will rise again to a height of 4 feet. This shows, Leibniz says, that the 'forces' operating in the two cases are equal (as the Cartesians would have agreed). However, Galileo had shown empirically that velocity in free fall from a state of rest is proportional not to the distance of fall but to the square root of the distance.

(a fundamental concept of Descartes' physics, taken up by Newton and re-expressed in his First Law) from *reaction* (the concept of Newton's Third Law) [*Metaphysics and the Philosophy of Science* (Oxford, 1969), 421–2]. However, it does not seem to me that Leibniz's argument against the Cartesian conception of matter depends in any important way on this confusion. In one letter to De Volder, further, Leibniz very explicitly distinguishes a version of the law of inertia ('each thing remains in its state unless there is a reason for change')–which he says is 'a principle of metaphysical necessity'–from the law of reaction [GP ii.170: L 839/516(1699)].

[14] It is rather interesting, however, to note the contrast between Descartes' *a priori* and Leibniz's *a posteriori* approach to this problem. For an illuminating account of the history of the concept of the essence of matter, see Ivor LeClerc's essay, 'Leibniz and the Analysis of Matter and Motion,' in his *The Philosophy of Leibniz and the Modern World* (Nashville, 1973). Oddly Leibniz sometimes suggests that the independence of motion from the concept of body proves the necessity of postulating God as the cause of nature [see GP vi.602: L 1038/9/639].

Thus if force were measured in the Cartesian manner (*mv*), the 'forces' of the two bodies on impact would be not equal but in a proportion of 2:1; i.e. the 1-pound body would rise to 2 feet, not 4 feet. So to get the correct results, we must introduce the quantity mv^2 as the measure of force. This argument, too, is held to manifest the principle of equality of cause and effect.)

Although Leibniz does use other dynamical arguments against the Cartesians, these two seem to have been his favourites. Sometimes, as I have indicated, he uses them in tandem; more often he presents them independently of each other. There are, to be sure, puzzling features in both arguments, from the point of view merely of the physical interpretation. In particular, it is difficult to understand in what way the second argument may be said to establish the *conservation* of *vis viva.*[15] What we are concerned with here, however, is Leibniz's *philosophical* interpretation of the arguments, his claim that they show the falsity of the doctrine of brute geometrical necessity in nature.

It is worth noting, first, that Leibniz's conclusions would provide the materials for a simple-minded but plausible repudiation of necessitarian

[15] This point is made by Carolyn Iltis, 'Leibniz and the *Vis Viva* Controversy.' *Isis*, 63 (1970), 26ff. (Iltis provides a very helpful critical analysis of several of Leibniz's dynamical arguments against Cartesianism.) One might suppose that in speaking of 'conservation' Leibniz must mean that the force of a body *immediately after* impact is the same as the force *acquired* in free fall, and that this is expressed in the quantity mv^2–not that mv^2 is constant *throughout* the fall and rebound event. Certainly some passages lend themselves to this interpretation: GM vi.117: L 455–6/296 (1686); GP iv.370: L 649 f./394 f. But R. C. Taliaferro seems to suggest a different view in *The Concept of Matter in Descartes and Leibniz*, Notre Dame Mathematical Lectures, no. 9 (Notre Dame, Ind., 1964), 29.

The controversy on this issue between Leibniz and the Cartesians is apt to seem utterly mystifying to laymen–and apparently to many physicists as well. Some of the important things to note are these.

1. The *principle* that Leibniz is particularly concerned to reject is the false principle that *mv* is conserved as a scalar quantity, not the true principle that it (understood as the 'momentum' of post-Newtonian physics) is conserved as a vector quantity. In later writings he seems to endorse the latter principle (though his concept of mass may not be identical with that of a contemporary physicist). However, he still maintains that mv^2, not *mv*, is the 'true measure' of force in nature.

2. Whether force should be expressed as proportional to the Cartesian quantity *mv*, or the Leibnizian quantity mv^2 depends on whether one is concerned with force acting through time or through distance: a body with twice the velocity of another will (in Mach's words) overcome a given force through double the time, but through four times the distance. Thus Leibniz's talk of the 'true measure' of force is not defensible.

3. Kinetic energy (represented today as the quantity $1/2\ mv^2$) is indeed conserved in perfectly elastic collisions. Leibniz of course was aware of the problem posed by inelastic collisions, and dealt with it by postulating that all collisions involve perfect elasticity on the micro-level.

claims along lines touched on above. The collision argument pretends to derive from Cartesian assumptions, 'laws' that are in fact false of the world. The free-fall argument shows (according to Leibniz) that a principle Descartes himself derived is incompatible with the true 'conservation' principle. Further, Leibniz in one place seems to go out of his way to indicate that Cartesian assumptions (as he interprets them), though false, are not impossible. He writes to the Cartesian De Volder:

> And doubtless such a world could be imagined as possible, in which matter at rest yielded to the mover without any resistance; but this world would really be pure chaos. [GP ii. 170: L 838–40/516–17]

(It might be objected that Leibniz could here be saying not that a Cartesian world *is* possible but only that we could (wrongly) suppose it to be possible. One might be particularly tempted to make this objection in view of the fact that 'pure chaos' seems incompatible with the Principle of Sufficient Reason, which Leibniz does regard as a necessary truth—as he says in this letter. However, it appears from the context that Leibniz does *not* think such a world would violate the Principle of Sufficient Reason, though it *would* violate another, contingent principle, to the effect that the better we understand things, the more they satisfy our intellect. (I admit the passage is pretty peculiar.)

If the Cartesian laws are false but not *necessarily* false, it follows of course that the basic laws of nature cannot be attributed the necessity of geometrical axioms. And, given the influence of the geometric model on seventeenth-century conceptions of physical science, this way of arguing against necessitarian conceptions might well have more effect than appeals to alleged direct intuitions of alternative possibilities. However, it does not seem that Leibniz's own reasoning ever follows quite this route.

Clearly, Leibniz thinks the need to introduce the concept of reaction, and of mv^2 as a measure of force, to describe physical phenomena shows the inadequacy of the Cartesian conception of matter, and *thereby* demonstrates the inadequacy of the conception of physics as a science of brute geometrical necessity. His reasoning here appears to be, in a way, specious, since, as we have noted, there seems to be no direct logical route between the concept of matter as mere extension and the necessitarian position concerning the laws of nature. From a historical point of view, however, Leibniz's reasoning is understandable. The Cartesian characterization of physics as nothing but geometry suggests such a close association between a necessitarian conception of the laws of nature and the conception of matter as extension, that it might well be natural to view them as standing or falling together.

Up to this point the issue of teleology has not at all entered into our discussion of Leibniz's philosophical interpretation of his results in physics. We have merely considered two ways of construing the denial of necessitarianism—one manifestly present in the Leibnizian texts, and one somewhat artificially constructed out of elements provided by the texts. This negative aspect of Leibniz's position accords well enough with the conception of the status of physical laws prevalent in contemporary philosophy—so well, in fact, that some effort of historical imagination is required to understand the prominence he accords to the contention. However, as our initial quotations clearly show, Leibniz's interest in refuting the doctrine of 'brute geometrical necessity' lay not in the bare demonstrations of *non*-necessity but rather in showing that nature manifests 'fitness and final causes'. Two points seem to be involved in this claim. First, Leibniz believes his physics provides a basis for restating and vindicating the traditional Argument from Design against the view that nature is governed not by design but by geometry. Second, he believes that his concept of force requires us to assume that underlying the phenomena of physics are purposive, mind-like metaphysical entities that somehow provide a 'foundation' for the phenomena.

IV

Many passages concerning the rejection of Cartesian physics reflect Leibniz's preoccupation with vindication of the concept of design in nature against the geometricist's view. The following are representative:

> *If mechanical rules depended on Geometry alone without metaphysics, phenomena would be quite different*. . . . One notices the counsels of [the divine] wisdom in the laws of motion in general. For if there were nothing in bodies but extended mass, and if there were nothing in motion but change of place, and if everything had to be and could be deduced from these definitions alone by a geometric necessity, it would follow, as I have shown elsewhere, that the smaller body would give to the greater which was at rest and which it met, the same speed that it had, without losing anything of its own speed. . . . But the decrees of divine wisdom to conserve always the same force and the same direction in sum has provided for this. [GP iv.446/LG 36–7]

> I have already asserted several times that the origin of mechanism itself does not spring from a material principle alone and mathematical reasons but from a certain higher and so to speak Metaphysical source.
>
> . . . One remarkable proof of this, among others, is that the *foundation of the laws of nature* must be sought not in this, that the same quantity of motion is conserved, as was commonly believed, but rather in this,

that it is necessary that the same *quantity of active power* be conserved. . . [GP iv.505–6: L 811/499 (1698)]

Perhaps someone will . . . believe that a completely geometric demonstration can be given of [the laws of motion], but in another discourse I will show that the contrary is the case, and demonstrate that they cannot be derived from their source without assuming architectonic reasons.[16]

(Again, 'architectonic reasons' means such principles as the quality of cause and effect (or of action and reaction), the principle of continuity, and certain other principles such as the law of least action, that Leibniz regards as comparable in showing the governance of a wise Author of nature.)

Leibniz himself stresses that his discernment of intelligence and a sense of perfection behind the principles that his dynamics establishes (in contrast to the 'chaotic' implications of Cartesian mechanics) is closely related to the traditional Argument from Design. He believes that he has advanced beyond the traditional form of the argument by showing that the general laws of nature, as well as its particular phenomena, manifest the workmanship of a beneficent intelligence. In the *Discourse on Metaphysics*, for example, he first endorses the traditional form of the argument (with special reference to animals in general and eyes in particular), and makes fun of its opponents. He continues:

Thus, since the wisdom of God has always been recognized in the detail of mechanical structure of some particular bodies, it ought also to show itself in the general economy of the world and in the constitution of the laws of nature. And this is so true that one notices the counsels of this wisdom in the laws of motion in general. [GP iv.466: LG 36–7; see also GP vi.603: L 1039–40/639–40 (1714)]

In the conclusion of the passage, which has already been quoted, Leibniz cites his argument against Cartesian principles that is derived from the problem of collision. In another work he claims that the dependence of the laws of his true dynamics on the principle of fitness provides 'one of the most effective and obvious proofs of the existence of God'.[17]

Without wishing to endorse any version of the Argument from Design, I would like to suggest that this is a quite understandable and rather interesting move for a determinedly pious person to make in the historical situation in which Leibniz found himself. The Cartesians rejected final causes and the Argument from Design on the grounds that

[16] *Tentamen Anagogicum* (ca.1696), GP vii.279: L 788/484. Taliaferro comments: 'The *Tentamen Anagogicum* is written for the sole purpose of showing the necessity for architectonic principles in mechanics and the insufficiency of geometry alone' [*Concept of Matter*, 31].

[17] GP vi.603: L 1040/640. (He adds the qualification, '*pour ceux qui peuvent approfondir ces choses*'.)

events in nature were determined according to a 'blind' deductive system of necessary 'geometrical' laws. Leibniz does not deny the lawfulness of nature, and he does not deny that physics is a deductive system. However, he holds that final causes, or considerations of fitness and proportion, may be said to enter into the system on the top level, once one recognizes that the Cartesian physics is false.

This move that Leibniz makes in defence of the Argument from Design (against, we may suppose, such ferocious critics as Spinoza)[18] has some affinity with a move later made in its defence in the face of the theory of natural selection. In the words of F. R. Tennant,

> The sting of Darwinism . . . lay in the suggestion that proximate and 'mechanical' causes were sufficient to produce the adaptations from which the teleology of the eighteenth century had argued to God. Assignable proximate causes, whether mechanical or not, are sufficient to dispose of the particular kind of teleological proof supplied by Paley. But the fact of organic evolution, even when the maximum of instrumentality is accredited to what is figuratively called natural selection, is not incompatible with teleology on a grander scale . . .
>
> . . . The discovery of organic evolution has caused the teleologist to shift his ground from special design in the products to directivity in the process, and plan in the primary collocations.[19]

Although Leibniz seems to present his reasoning as supplementing, rather than replacing, the traditional argument from the evidence of 'special design in the products', he too makes use of the discovery of mechanical principles—principles at first sight inimical to teleological conceptions of nature—to argue for 'teleology on a grander scale'. Whereas the later teleologist finds progress and hence purpose in the process of evolution broadly considered, Leibniz insists on the evidence of wisdom in the order and proportion that are maintained throughout nature as a result of the *sort* of mechanical laws that obtain. His claim against the geometricists is that, first, these laws are *not* those of 'brute geometrical necessity,' and second, that they can *only* be viewed as manifesting the values and aesthetic sense of a wise Creator.[20]

[18] *Ethics*, Part I, Appendix. Spinoza's criticism, though vehement, is somewhat diffuse.

[19] In *The Existence of God*, ed. John Hick (New York, 1964), 126, 127; excerpt reprinted from *Philosophical Theology* (Cambridge, 1930), vol. ii, chap. 4, pp. 79–92.

[20] Nicholas Rescher [*Rescher* 151] is therefore quite wrong in stating that, with respect to the Argument from Design, 'the only characteristic touch Leibniz adds to the classic pattern of reasoning has to do with the pre-established harmony [among substances]'. Even if Leibniz's account of contingency is ultimately untenable, his conception of the status of the laws of nature of course constitutes a major difference between his world-view and Spinozistic necessitarianism. In Leibniz's system, unlike Spinoza's, the laws of nature differ from the principles of mathematics in depending on (and even demonstrating) God's valuation of the 'fitness and proportion' in this *best* of all possible worlds.

Leibniz's theological interpretation of the laws or principles of his Dynamics is more asserted than argued; it could hardly be expected to carry conviction to anyone not highly sympathetic to the aims of the Argument from Design. One might, obviously, accept his negative claim—that not all fundamental principles of physics are 'geometrical'—while withholding credence entirely from the teleological interpretation. For there is no need to accept as exhaustive the division of geometrical necessity on the one hand and purposiveness on the other. Leibniz's point of view is, nevertheless, readily intelligible against its historical background. Indeed, it has not been altogether absent from the science and philosophy of our century.

V

As I have indicated, however, this attempted vindication of the intrinsically teleological character of the basic principles of physics is tied up in Leibniz's own thinking with a stranger and more elusive notion. Consider the following passages, from different parts of his writings.

First, from the *Discourse on Metaphysics* (1686) following a statement of the argument for the conservation of mv^2:

> And it becomes more and more apparent, although all particular phenomena of nature can be explained mathematically or mechanically by those who understand them, that nevertheless the general principles of corporeal nature and of mechanics itself are rather metaphysical than geometrical and belong rather to some indivisible forms or natures as causes of appearances than to corporeal or extended mass. [GP iv.444: LG 32]

From *Critical Thoughts on the General Part of Descartes'* Principles (1692):

> For besides extension and its variations, there is in matter a force or power of action by which the transition is made from Metaphysics to nature, from material to immaterial things. This force has its own Laws, which are deduced from the principles, not merely of absolute, and so to speak brute necessity, but of perfect reason. [GP iv.391: L 675/409]

And from *On the Elements of Natural Science* (ca.1682–4):

> Certain things take place in a body which cannot be explained by the necessity of matter alone. Such are the laws of motion which depend on the metaphysical principle of the equality of cause and effect. Therefore we must deal here with the soul, and show that all things are animated.[21]

Many other similar passages could be cited from Leibniz's work. But these three should suffice to make clear that the denial of brute necessity

[21] L 429/278. This work was translated by Loemker from an unpublished Latin manuscript.

in nature is intimately associated in his thought with the postulation of immaterial forms, entelechies, or souls as the real metaphysical basis of phenomena. Of course, Leibniz had other reasons for maintaining that extension is purely phenomenal, and that real substances are indivisible and mind-like.[22] But he seems to regard the non-geometrical nature of his 'laws of force' as providing independent reason for this view.

Bertrand Russell has with justice harshly criticized this aspect of Leibniz's position [*Russell* 87]. As far as I know, Leibniz never fills in any of the steps that might take one from 'forces' in physics to 'souls' in metaphysics. He does not indicate what it might mean to say that the latter provide a 'general explanation' of the former. And he does not provide elucidation of the relation between the two claims made about the 'general principles of corporeal nature'; i.e. that they are 'rather metaphysical than geometrical', and that they 'belong . . . to some indivisible forms or natures as causes of appearances'–he merely treats the claims as if they were obviously equivalent.

I have suggested above that there would be some natural affinities for a seventeenth-century thinker among the denial that the laws of nature have the status of geometrical axioms, the rejection of the Cartesian conception of matter, and the reaffirmation of the traditional 'forms' or immanent purposiveness in the (non-human) world. It is also quite clear and beyond question that Leibniz took an almost obsessive pride in the notion that his system offered a 'synthesis' of traditional metaphysics and modern physics, retaining the best of both views and in particular avoiding the anti-spiritualist implications of the latter. But there is a more specific and perhaps more interesting explanation, or partial explanation, of this obscurity in his system.

Despite Leibniz's opposition to the Cartesian theory, one finds in his writings a certain tendency to assimilate the concept of the material to that of the geometrical, in just the Cartesian manner:

> If nature were brute, so to speak, that is purely material or Geometric . . . [GP vii.279: L 787/484]
>
> Certain things take place in body that cannot be explained by the necessity of matter alone. [L 429/278]

Of course, Leibniz uses the term 'matter' in different ways in different

[22] For example, the paradoxes of division; also the argument that since extension involves plurality and repetition, while substance is by definition a 'true unity', we must postulate indivisible, unextended entities whose repetition somehow accounts for the well-founded phenomena of extension. Leibniz also has another sort of dynamical argument for force, derived from the relativity of motion: see *Russell* chap. 7, esp. sect. 41. This argument seems so confused that I have ignored it in the text.

contexts: it would be quite wrong to attribute to him without qualification the assumption that 'the non-material' can be equated with 'the non-geometrical'. But we may still suppose that his transition from forces in physics to 'immaterial things' reflects some implicit assumption that any entity in nature not fully describable through the concepts of geometry, and particularly anything suggesting changes not reducible to relative change of place, is by definition excluded from the realm of the material. Similarly, where the concept of efficient cause has been associated with that of geometric determination, the reintroduction of forms, entelechies, or final causes might well seem warranted or inevitable, once the geometric picture is abandoned. In such ways we can make out a path from 'mechanical' dynamics to soul-like purposive entities as underlying 'causes'.

Here someone might object that since Leibniz postulates force as part of the 'essence of body' or even of the 'essence of matter', he can hardly be said to conflate the non-geometrical with the non-material. And further support could be adduced for this objection: for example, Leibniz in one place explicitly characterizes the failure to provide a ground for the laws of force as an insufficiency in the 'common notion of matter':

> It is not possible to deduce all truths about corporeal things from logical and geometrical axioms alone, those of great and small, whole and part, figure and situation, but others of cause and effect, action and passion must be added, by which the reasons of the order of things may be preserved. Whether we call this principle Form or entelechy or Force is not important, so long as we bear in mind that it can only be intelligibly explained through the notion of force.
>
> But I cannot agree with the view of certain prominent men today, who perceiving that the common notion of matter does not suffice. . . . [GM vi.241–2: L 721/441]

What this really shows, however, is only that Leibniz's conception of matter was ambiguous. Thus, the very next paragraph after the passage quoted begins:

> Although I admit an active principle throughout bodies which is superior to material notions and so to speak vital. . . .

Similarly, while the first quotation may suggest for a minute that Leibniz's transition from 'forces' to 'entelechies' or 'souls' is after all a merely terminological issue, the second reminds us of the edifying talk of 'higher' sources and spiritual cures for those 'mired in materialist notions' that characterizes nearly all his presentations of his conclusions in physics.

'Entelechy' and 'soul' invariably connote for Leibniz the unequivocally mental qualities of sense and appetition.[23] The obscure inference to these from the concepts of Dynamics is an internally important aspect of his thinking; unfortunately it is also, as Russell remarks, 'one of the weakest points in his system'.

[23] See especially 'New System of the Nature and Communication of Substances' (1695), sect. 3 [GP iv.478: L 741/454].

IX

THE *VIS VIVA* CONTROVERSY

DAVID PAPINEAU

I INTRODUCTION

IN 1686 Leibniz published an article entitled *Brevis Demonstratio erroris memorabilis Cartesii et aliorum circa legem naturalem. . . .*[1] According to Leibniz, the memorable error in question was the identification of the 'motive force' (*vis motrix*) of a body with its 'quantity of motion', that is, with the product of its speed by its mass.[2] The argument Leibniz presents purports to show that the 'force' of a body in motion must instead be measured by the product of its mass with the *square* of its speed.

The publication of Leibniz's article marks the beginning of the '*vis viva* controversy', a dispute which occupied the attention of most European natural philosophers for about fifty years. By and large, affiliations in the dispute went by nationalities, with English Newtonians and French Cartesians following the 'old opinion' (that 'force' is proportional to mass times velocity), while Dutch, German and Italian scientists favoured the 'new opinion' put forward by Leibniz.

The *vis viva* controversy has always been something of a puzzle to historians of science. In his short textbook, *A History of Physics*, Florian Cajori calls it 'a curious dispute'.[3] He accounts for the episode by endorsing the view expressed by d'Alembert in 1743, that 'this is a dispute of words, too undignified to occupy the philosophers any longer'.[4]

Most traditional historians of science have agreed with Cajori's judgement.[5] That is, they have maintained that the expression 'force of a body

From *Studies in History and Philosophy of Science*, vol. 8 (1977), pp. 111–42.

[1] *Acta Eruditorum*, (1686), 161–3 [GM vi.117–19: L 455–63/296–301].

[2] In common with many of the other thinkers discussed in this paper, Leibniz did not have a clear concept of mass. For ease of exposition I shall ignore this where it is of no relevance to the issues being discussed.

[3] F. Cajori, *A History of Physics* (New York, 1929), 58.

[4] J. d'Alembert, *Traité de Dynamique*, 1st ed. (Paris, 1743), xxi.

[5] For a list of those holding this view see L. Laudan 'The *Vis Viva* Controversy, a Post-Mortem', *Isis*, 59 (1968).

in motion' was ambiguous, in that it was used by the participants in the *vis viva* controversy to stand for two completely different quantities, one of which was proportional to mass times velocity, while the other was proportional to mass times velocity squared. And thus they have concluded that the dispute was simply due to insufficient care in specifying the meaning of the term 'force'.

There have been a number of variations on this theme of an undetected ambiguity. Cajori follows Ernst Mach[6] in claiming that the 'force of a body's motion' simply meant the body's ability to produce effects, and consequently meant different things when different effects were considered. In particular he points out that if one has in mind as the effect in question the *time* for which a body will continue to move if uniformly retarded, one will reckon its initial 'force' to be proportional to its initial *velocity*, whereas if one is considering the *distance* through which it will continue if uniformly retarded one will think of its 'force' as proportional to the square of its velocity. The dispute, according to Cajori, was the unfortunate result of not distinguishing these two ways of considering a moving body's ability to act.

Max Jammer sees things somewhat differently in his *Concepts of Force*.[7] He reads 'force of a body's motion' as that *applied force necessary to produce (or destroy) that motion in the body*. (Where by 'applied force' is intended the familiar notion of modern physics, that is, something continuously exerted on a body from without, which at any instant produces an acceleration proportional to its magnitude.) Jammer points out that the question of what applied force is required to produce or destroy a given motion in a body is indeterminate—for in order to produce or destroy a given velocity in a body an applied force must act for some finite interval, not just for an instant. But the interval can either be considered in terms of *time*, or in terms of *space*. Given an interval of *time*, the applied force required is proportional to the given velocity; but given an interval of *space*, it is proportional to the square of the velocity. So Jammer concludes that the problem was a lack of clarity in formulating the question 'What applied force is required to produce a given velocity?'.

Others, again, have not distinguished between the Mach–Cajori line and Jammer's analysis, and have felt it sufficient simply to refer to the asymmetrical way in which time and distance are related to velocity in the equations of uniformly accelerated motion.[8]

[6] E. Mach, *The Science of Mechanics*, trans. T. McCormack, 6th ed. (LaSalle, Illinois, 1960), 365.

[7] M. Jammer, *Concepts of Force* (Cambridge, Mass., 1957), 165.

[8] See, for example, the explanation given by H. G. Alexander in the introduction to his edition of *The Leibniz–Clarke Correspondence* [A xxxi].

There is one obvious difficulty with all these versions of the traditional approach. Namely that it is not easy to see why the best minds of the seventeenth and eighteenth centuries should have been incapable of detecting an ambiguity which the modern historian apparently has no difficulty in uncovering. The natural philosophers of the time certainly knew the relationship between 'applied force' (usually called 'pressure') and acceleration,[9] and the one thing there had been no disagreement about since Galileo was the behaviour of bodies in uniformly accelerated or retarded motion.

Contemporary work on the episode has to some extent improved on the brisk analyses mentioned so far and drawn attention to some of the substantial issues involved.[10] But even the more recent commentators have in the end tended to return to the traditional but unsatisfying diagnosis that the participants in the debate were 'confused' by equivocal terminology.

My intention in this paper will be to show that the *vis viva* controversy was a perfectly serious debate between genuinely rival frameworks of physical thought. However I shall not try to do this by establishing that the two sides associated the same 'ideas' (or external physical entities) with their words. My aim will simply be to demonstrate the close structural similarity between the two theoretical systems involved. In particular, I shall show how the two sides to the dispute represented alternative ways of modifying a common system of mechanical thought handed down from the early seventeenth century.

The explanation of the longevity of the controversy will not be that the participants were talking about different things, nor that they ignored objective grounds for choosing between their views, but simply that it required time to find which of the alternative frameworks could best be developed to cope with the totality of relevant empirical data.

My exposition will proceed as follows. I shall first briefly describe the seventeenth-century framework of mechanical thought, in particular as embodied in Descartes' theory of impact, and I shall mention various critiques of this theory. Then I shall show how Leibniz's publication of *Brevis Demonstratio* can be seen as a response to the problems raised by these critiques; and I shall describe the initial reaction to Leibniz's views.

[9] See T. Hankins, 'Eighteenth-Century Attempts to Resolve the *Vis Viva* Controversy', *Isis*, 56 (1965), 286.

[10] In particular should be mentioned T. Hankins, op. cit. and C. Iltis, 'D'Alembert and the *Vis Viva* Controversy', *Studies in History and Philosophy of Science*, 1 (1970); 'Leibniz and the *Vis Viva* Controversy', *Isis*, 62 (1971); 'The Decline of Cartesianism in Mechanics', *Isis*, 64 (1973); 'The Leibnizian–Newtonian Debates: Natural Philosophy and Social Psychology', *British Journal for the History of Science* 6 (1973).

After this the respective views of the Leibnizians and their opponents on the central problem of impact are described, and it is shown that the two sides to the dispute can be seen as alternative strategies for revising the flawed Cartesian theory of impact. And finally the understanding of the dispute thus gained is used to make some sense of some of the apparently fatuous facets of the controversy.

II THE SEVENTEENTH-CENTURY BACKGROUND

The dominant philosophy of nature in the middle of the seventeenth century was mechanism. The differences between different versions of mechanism need not concern us here. What is relevant is that something like the 'principle of inertia' was generally assumed, in that it was accepted that a body would continue in any motion, with the same speed in the same direction, until subject to some external action. It was also assumed that the only way in which such action could be exercised was by *impact*; by matter with some motion coming into contact with matter with a different motion. 'Action at a distance' was considered to be absolutely impossible.

As a result, the laws governing the changes of motion which result from impacts were considered to be of fundamental importance in the seventeenth century. It was in the problem of deriving these laws that the notion of 'force of motion' had its most important application.

Descartes was the first to attempt a systematic treatment of impact. The main components of the concept of 'force of motion' can be seen in his approach to the problem. He took it that any body had a 'force', proportional to its 'quantity of motion' (its 'mass' times its speed). And he assumed that in any impact between hard bodies, any 'force' lost by one would be gained by the other. Since impact was the only possible means of changing motion, it followed that the total 'quantity of motion' in the universe was at all times conserved.

The rules that Descartes derives strike the modern eye as extremely strange.[11] This is largely because he considered 'force of motion' as a scalar quantity, and not as a vector like the modern concept of momentum. For him, an impact did not necessarily produce oppositely directed, equal-sized changes in directional motion. Instead, he saw what would happen to a body in impact as determined by the relative sizes of its 'force of motion' and the *resistance* to this force offered by the other body.[12] If the resistance of the struck body exceeds the force of the striking body then no transfer of motion takes place and the latter

[11] See R. Descartes, *Principia Philosophiae* (Holland, 1644) [AT viii.68–70].

[12] This aspect of Descartes' views is emphasised in A. Gabbey, 'Force and Inertia in Seventeenth-Century Dynamics', *Studies in History and Philosophy of Science*, 2 (1971).

rebounds with its original speed in the opposite direction. If the force exceeds the resistance then the two bodies move together in the original direction of the impacting body at such a speed as to conserve the total quantity of motion. A moving body resists the impression of the force of another proportionately to its own force of motion. Somewhat anomalously, a body at rest does not have zero resistance but resists proportionately to its mass and the speed *with which* it is struck.

Only a few of the solutions these premisses imply are now considered empirically correct (some for elastic bodies, some for inelastic). But the important things to note once again are that for Descartes all impact phenomena, and hence all changes of motion, were to be explained in terms of the 'forces of motion' of the bodies involved. All impacts involved the transference of 'force' from one body to another, in such a way that the total 'force' was conserved. The precise amount depended, as above, on the contest between 'force' and 'resistance'.

As the first systematic treatment of the problem, Descartes' rules of impact had considerable authority for his successors. However, the deficiencies of his analysis soon became apparent, once it was subject to criticism.

Huygens realized that Descartes' rules were inconsistent with something else both Descartes and he himself presupposed—the relativity of motion. Huygens considered what would happen if a series of impacts took place on a barge moving down a Dutch canal. He pointed out that an impact which seemed to a man on the barge to occur according to Descartes' rules, would not necessarily seem to do so to a man on the bank.

Huygens assumed that any rules of impact should remain true under such uniform transformations of motion. This form of argument (which came to be known simply as 'the method of the boat') is of course extremely powerful. In Huygens' case, it enabled him to dispense almost entirely with dynamic assumptions in deriving the results which we now consider to describe cases of elastic impact.

Huygens' article in the *Journal des Scavans* of 1669, which presented his results on impact, was reprinted in the *Philosophical Transactions of the Royal Society* of the same year. This was as a response to the Royal Society's invitation for accounts of the 'laws of motion'. There were two other important replies to this invitation, both published in the same year. One was by Christopher Wren, the other by John Wallis. Wren got the same results as Huygens, whereas Wallis derived the results we now accept for inelastic impacts.

Wren applied the model of the level to impact. I shall discuss this form of argument in the next section.

Wallis derived his conclusions as follows. He first imagined one of the two bodies to be at rest, and supposed it to be struck by the second, moving with its actual motion. They would then move together, with the second transferring some of its 'force' to the first, so that their common velocity is given by dividing the second body's original 'force' by their joint mass. Wallis then reversed the situation, and imagined the second body to be at rest, and the first to strike it with *its* actual motion, with a similar putative result. He then added the two resulting motions vectorially, to derive what would actually happen in the impact. What is significant about this analysis is that it implies a conception of 'force of motion' as a vectorial quantity—'force' in one direction is supposed to be 'cancelled out' by an equal amount of 'force' in the contrary direction.

The importance of the analyses given by Huygens, Wren and Wallis was soon recognized. But there was one factor which weighed heavily against their findings. This was the point on which their various analyses were in surprising agreement: they all agreed that the total 'force of motion' in the universe, measured by mass times speed, is *not* conserved. For, as mentioned above, Huygens and Wren both put forward the formulae now considered to describe cases of elastic impact; and in such cases the quantity given by mass times speed can either increase or decrease in impact (depending on what frame of reference is taken). And Wallis, in putting forward the formulae for inelastic impacts, implied that this quantity decreases whenever an impact is considered in a frame of reference in which one of the bodies changed direction.

Given the basic framework for the analysis of impact displayed in Descartes' work, these conclusions constituted a striking anomaly. For central to that framework was the principle that all impacts involved the transference of 'force' from one body to another, with the total 'force' being conserved. Insofar as the common run of natural philosophers based their understanding of impact on this principle they did not find it easy to stomach the theories put forward by Huygens, Wren, and Wallis. A. R. Hall has described[13] the initial rejection of these theories by the members of the Royal Society, on the grounds that they implied that 'motion' (mass times speed) is not conserved.

[13] A. R. Hall, 'Mechanics and the Royal Society, 1668–70', *British Journal for the History of Science*, 3 (1966).

III 'BREVIS DEMONSTRATIO' AND THE EARLY PERIOD OF THE CONTROVERSY

Leibniz was one of those who was perturbed by the possibility that the quantity of motion is not conserved in collisions between bodies. In 1680 he wrote

> M. Descartes' physics has a great defect; it is that his rules of motion are for the most part false. This is demonstrated. And his great principle, that the same quantity of motion is conserved in the world, is an error. What I say here is acknowledged by the ablest people in France and England.[14]

But, while admitting in this way the non-conservation of the *quantity* of motion, Leibniz was profoundly resistant to the idea that the total '*force* of motion' in the universe is not conserved. As he put it in *Brevis Demonstratio*:

> It conforms to reason to say that the same sum of motive force is conserved in nature; this sum does not diminish, since we never observe any body lose any force that is not transferred to another; nor does this sum increase since perpetual motion is unreal to such a degree that no machine and in consequence not even the entire world can conserve its force without new impulsion from without. [GM vi.117: L 456/296]

The natural conclusion for Leibniz to draw was that 'motive force' could not be the same thing as 'quantity of motion'. The argument of *Brevis Demonstratio* was designed to provide an independent proof of this conclusion. Leibniz first stated two premisses which he maintained are admitted by 'Cartesians as well as other philosophers and mathematicians of our times' [GM vi.118: L 456/296]. These were:

(i) that a body, in falling from a certain height, acquires just that 'force' necessary to raise itself to that height again, and

(ii) that the same 'force' is required to raise a body of 4 lb. 1 yard as is required to raise a body of 1 lb. 4 yards.

From these two premisses, together with the Galilean analysis of free fall, Leibniz deduced that 'force of motion' cannot equal quantity of motion (mass times speed).

Leibniz concluded:

> It seems from this that *force* is rather to be estimated from the quantity of effect which it can produce; for example, from the height to which it can elevate a heavy body of given magnitude and kind, but not from the velocity which it can impress upon the body. [GM vi.118: L 457/297]

(In *Brevis Demonstratio* Leibniz did not explicitly say that 'motive force' should be taken as proportional to velocity squared: but of course this would follow directly from the estimate of 'force' in terms of height).

Thus the strategy adopted by Leibniz in *Brevis Demonstratio* was to

[14] Letter to Filippi, January, 1680 [GP iv.286]. Quoted in R. Dugas, *Mechanics in the Seventeenth Century*, trans. F. Jacquot (Neuchatel, Switzerland, 1958).

turn from the analysis of impact, and to argue instead from principles accepted in other areas of natural philosophy. This should not be taken, however, to imply that the problem of impact was not of central concern for Leibniz. He was as much a mechanist as any of his contemporaries in that he thought the possibility of action at a distance absurd: as such he could not but consider the analysis of impact as central to physics. The reason for his strategy in *Brevis Demonstratio* was simply that, with the acknowledged anomaly of quantity of motion not being conserved in impact, the basic principles by which the phenomenon of impact was to be analysed had become problematic. So, if Leibniz was to discredit Descartes' measure of 'force' and suggest a measure of his own, it was essential that he draw his assumptions from other areas.

The initial responses to *Brevis Demonstratio* followed Leibniz's strategy in focussing on the premisses of his argument rather than the implications of his conclusion for the analysis of impact. It was the second premiss that was seen as most vulnerable: that is, the assumption that the same 'force' is needed to raise 4 lb. 1 yard as 1 lb. 4 yards.

In *Brevis Demonstratio* Leibniz does not state the basis for this assumption. But from the ensuing discussion it seems that he was counting on the law of the lever to get it accepted. The issue was thus what the law of moments shows about 'forces'. On Leibniz's side was the argument that the same 'force' on a lever is required to raise 4 lb. 1 yard as to raise 1 lb. (four times as far from the fulcrum) 4 yards. His critics[15] in response insisted that the *time* of the action has to be taken into account—clearly a force on a lever which lifts 4 lb. through 1 yard can lift the 1 lb. four times further from the fulcrum through any distance desired, provided it can act for a greater or lesser time. They concluded that the correct measure of a 'force' was the product of the weight it can lift and the *velocity* with which it can lift it.

Involved here is an understanding of the lever according to which a lever operates when the 'force' of a body on one arm overcomes the contrary 'force' or 'resistance' of the body on the other. This thinking was extremely common in the seventeenth century, and persisted well into the eighteenth. (It was this model of the lever that Wren used for his analysis of impact; and intimations of this model can be seen even in Descartes' theory.)

In fact it was Leibniz himself who first clearly perceived the inappropriateness of analysing the simple machines in terms of 'forces of *motion*'. He gives some idea of this in *Brevis Demonstratio*, where in considering the law of the lever, he says that one

[15] See, for example, Abbé Catalan, 'Courte Remarque de M. l'Abbé D.C.', *Nouvelles de la Rèpublique de Lettres,* 8 (1686), 1000–5.

need not wonder that in common machines . . . there is equilibrium . . . when the same quantity of motion is produced on either side. For in this special case the *quantity of effect*, or the height risen or fallen, will be the same on both sides, no matter to which side of the balance the motion is applied. It is therefore merely accidental here that the force can be estimated from the quantity of motion. [GM vi.119: L 457–8/297–8]

Leibniz elaborated this insight in response to the criticisms of his argument in *Brevis Demonstratio*. In his *Essay on Dynamics* (written in 1691) he expressed the view that

What has contributed the most to confound force with quantity of motion is the abuse of the static doctrine. [GM vi.218: La 659]

In this work he explained in some detail how this confusion should be avoided. This he did by first introducing the notion of '*dead* force' which he distinguished from '*living* force', ('force *vive*'). It was the latter which he identified with 'motive force', and urged should be measured by mass times velocity squared. 'Dead force', on the other hand, is not conditional on an actual motion, but is

the infinitely small motion which I am accustomed to call *solicitation*, which takes place when a heavy body tries to commence movement, and has not yet conceived any impetuosity. [GM vi.218: La 659–60]

In fact because of his general principle of continuity in nature Leibniz considered that 'dead force' is involved in all alterations of velocity. Moreover, he used the concept so as to imply that acceleration is proportional to dead force. Thus his concept of 'dead force' is by no means dissimilar to the 'applied force', equal to mass times acceleration, of classical physics. But it only played a subsidiary role in Leibniz's thought, as the means by which 'living force' is transferred from one body to another.

It did however enable him to give a clear account of what is involved in the analysis of the lever. There are no 'living forces' to be considered in connection with the law of moments, for 'when bodies are in equilibrium, and, trying to descend, are mutually hindered', no actual motion arises, and we have a case concerning only 'dead forces'. Thus the conditions of equilibrium specify an equation between 'dead' rather than 'living forces', and have no immediate relevance to the question of how to measure 'motive force'.

Having disposed of the argument from the simple machines as the basis for his claim that the *height* to which it can raise a body against gravity is the measure of a 'force of motion', Leibniz turned to another generally accepted principle, namely, that 'the effect is always equal to the cause'. In his *Specimen Dynamicum* of 1695, he maintained that 'motive force' is to be estimated by the effect which it produces in consuming itself. . . . Thus those things which by themselves could not easily be compared, by their effects at least might be compared accurately. I assumed, moreover, that the effect must be equal to its cause if it is produced by the expenditure or consumption of the entire force. [GM vi.243–4: L 724–5/442–3]

The principle stated here by Leibniz, that the effect must be equal to the cause which is consumed in producing it, is something which played a central role in the *vis viva* controversy. In nearly every contribution to the dispute, prior to d'Alembert's *Traité* in 1743, the author makes a point of affirming his commitment to the equality of cause and effect. Jean Bernoulli goes so far as to say:

To try and demonstrate this law would be to obscure it. Indeed, everyone regards this as an incontestable axiom, that an efficient cause cannot perish, either as a whole or in part, without producing an effect equal to its loss.[16]

However, in spite of its universal acceptance, this principle by no means sufficed to win acceptance for Leibniz's measure of force. For he had no conclusive argument to show that the *distance* to which a force could raise a body against gravity should be considered as the *effect* produced by its consumption. What he says in *Specimen Dynamicum* is less than convincing:

I chose that effect of the violent effects which is especially capable of homogeneity or division into similar and equal parts, such as exists in the ascent of a body possessed of weight: for the elevation of a heavy body two or three feet is precisely double or triple the elevation of the same heavy body one foot. [GM vi.243: L 724/442]

As will be shown in section V, the partisans of the 'old opinion' argued that the distance traversed in retarded motion is *not* the relevant measure of the effect produced by the 'force' which has been consumed in that retarded motion. Their view was that it was the *time* for which a body continues to move that measures its 'force', and that consequently 'force' is proportional to mv, not mv^2.

IV THE 'OLD' AND THE 'NEW' OPINIONS

If there had been nothing more to the '*vis viva* controversy' than a dispute as to what should count as the 'effect' produced in the 'consumption of a force' in retarded motion, then clearly there could have been no real substance to the controversy. The general insistence that 'effects equal causes' would have been no more than the mouthing of an empty slogan, which could only have served to obscure the pointlessness of the

[16] J. Bernoulli, 'Discours sur les loix de la Communication du Mouvement' *Recueil des Pièces qui a Remporté les Prix de l'Académie Royale des Sciences* (Paris, 1752), vol. i, chap. 10, sect. 1.

debate. And if that had indeed been the case the two sides in the controversy, by considering two different 'effects', would simply have been using 'force' in two quite different ways, and disputing about nothing but words.

However, retarded motion was not considered around 1700 to be the only, or even the most important, case in which effects are produced by the consumption of 'force'. More central in the minds of the mechanistic natural philosophers of the time was, of course, what happened in impacts between particles in motion. And it is in connection with this problem that the agreement on the dictum 'effects equal causes' can be seen in its true significance. For in an impact the effect produced by the annihilation of a 'force' in one body was simply assumed to be the production of the same quantity of 'force' in another. So what the general adherence to the universal 'equality of cause and effect' really indicates is that all the participants in the *vis viva* controversy continued to approach the problem of impact through the framework originally proposed by Descartes. That is, they all took for granted that all impacts are to be accounted for by the transference of 'force' from one body to the other, with the total force being conserved. Where they disagreed from Descartes, and from each other, was, of course, on the questions of how exactly 'force' should be measured, and what determined exactly how much 'force' would be transferred in a given impact.

It is precisely by attending to this common framework of presuppositions inherited from Descartes that we will be able to gain a proper understanding of the disagreement between the two sides in the *vis viva* controversy. For if we do attend to it we can see that it was *because* there was this common framework for approaching the problem of impact that the controversy amounted to a serious dispute between competing views. Far from being a mere 'dispute of words', their debate was at basis a perfectly sensible one between two alternative suggestions as to how the Cartesian theory of impact could best be modified and elaborated.

In this section I shall attempt to substantiate this view of the *vis viva* controversy by examining in some detail the views of the two sides on impact. After that I shall return to the question of retarded motion and show that even this aspect of the debate can be seen to have had some substance.

Let us first look at Leibniz's views on impact. As argued earlier, it was probably the theories of impact of Wallis, Wren, and Huygens which originally caused Leibniz to be dissatisfied with the Cartesian measure of 'motive force'. For in none of these theories is the 'quantity of motion' generally conserved. That is, it was not held to be true that the annihilation of motion in one body in an impact was always accompanied by the production of an equivalent quantity of motion in the other body.

In the *Essay on Dynamics* Leibniz notes the general recognition of this failure of conservation of quantity of motion, and observes

that we have been thrown too far into the other extreme, and do not recognize the conservation of anything absolute which might hold in the place of the quantity of motion. [GM vi.216: La 657]

What Leibniz thought should be recognized as conserved in impact was of course his 'living force', or '*vis viva*', measured by mass times velocity squared. In the *Essay on Dynamics* Leibniz specifies three equations which he believes describe all impacts between two bodies. The first is the conservation of the relative velocities; the second conservation of momentum, considered as a *vector* quantity; and the third the conservation of mass times velocity squared. Leibniz notes that any two of these equations would suffice to derive the third.

Leibniz refers the reader to Huygens and his 'method of the boat' for the derivation of these equations. However, there is the important difference that, while Huygens, as noted earlier, thought himself to be deriving theorems about perfectly hard, inflexible bodies, Leibniz intended his theory to describe the behaviour of flexible bodies, whose perfect elasticity consisted in their ability to return to their original shape after being deformed in collisions. From this assumption of the elasticity of matter Leibniz derived an analysis of the detailed mechanics of impact. This involved the 'dead forces', equal and oppositely directed, which arise *during* an impact, and act to alter the velocity of a body proportionately to the body's mass and the time for which they act.

These notions of Leibniz's were later elaborated with great sophistication by Jean Bernoulli in his important essay *Discourse on the Laws of the Communication of Motion.* After deriving the laws of elastic impact from the relativity of motion and the elasticity of matter, he uses his considerable facility with the differential relations between 'pressure' (or 'dead force'), velocity, distance and time to produce what he considered to be additional support for Leibniz's measure of 'living force'. What he does is deduce from the 'familiar law of acceleration' (pressure = mass × acceleration) the conclusion that the mass times velocity squared produced, or destroyed, by the action of a spring (elastic surface) is proportional to the length through which it expands, or contracts.

Later in the essay Bernoulli produces another argument, based on the directional resolution of velocities, to show that the number of similar springs which a body in motion can 'close' successively before being brought to rest is proportional to its mass times its velocity squared. In Bernoulli's view, these conclusions about the ability of springs to accelerate and retard bodies in motion provide an additional proof for Leibniz's measure of force. For he maintained that the 'cause' of the 'force' imparted to a body impelled by a spring must be the length through which the spring expands; and that, conversely, the effect of a 'force' consumed in closing a compound spring, or a series of springs, must be the length through which the spring or springs are closed. And so, from the necessary equality of 'causes' and 'effects', it had to follow that the 'force of a body in motion' is given by its mass times its velocity squared.

Thus we see how Leibniz, and following him, Bernoulli, articulated their theory of 'motive force' and the communication of motion, by reference to the 'pressures of elasticity', or 'dead forces', which occur in impacts between perfectly elastic bodies. It is worth emphasizing, however, that for both of them it was 'living force' which was the more important quantity; 'dead force' was simply the means by which 'living force' acted, and, indeed, 'dead force' manifested itself only in situations where 'living force' was transferring itself from one body to another. The real cause of any change in the motion of a body was its receiving the 'living force' of some other body, and, since effects had to be equal to causes, the change of motion had to be such that the 'living force' received was equal to that lost by the other body. As Bernoulli was at pains to emphasize:

> It is then clear that when the living force of a body diminishes or increases in its meeting with some other body, the living force of this other body must in exchange increase or diminish in the same quantity; the increase of one being the immediate effect of the diminution of the other, from which follows necessarily the conservation of the total quantity of living force: thus this quantity is itself absolutely unalterable in the impact of bodies.

There was, of course, one problem which this commitment to the conservation of *vis viva* raised for the Leibnizians. This was the undeniable phenomenal fact that certain bodies were such that *vis viva* was lost in their impact. For it is clearly absurd to suppose that all medium-sized physical objects are perfectly elastic. But Leibniz had no doubt as to how this should be explained:

> in the impact of such bodies a part of the force is absorbed by the small parts which compose the mass, without this force being given to the whole; and this must always happen when the pressed mass does not recover perfectly. [*Essay on Dynamics*, GM vi.230: La 669]

Leibniz repeats this view in his fifth paper of *The Leibniz-Clarke Correspondence*, where he says:

> The author objects, that two soft or un-elastic bodies meeting together, lose some of their force. I answer, no. 'Tis true, their wholes lose it with respect to their total motion; but their parts receive it, being shaken (internally) by the force of the concourse. And therefore that loss of force, is only in appearance. [GP vii.414: A 87–8]

In general, the proponents of *vis viva* as a measure of 'motive force' adopted this account of inelastic impacts, where '*vis viva*' appeared to be lost at the phenomenal level.

One might think that those who measured 'force' by mass times velocity would have had the same problem with hard bodies as did the Leibnizians. For not only is the sum of mass times velocity squared not conserved in hard body impacts, but the sum of mass times the magnitude of the velocity is not always conserved either. (Some is lost whenever either body changes direction.)

But hard bodies were not a problem for the proponents of the 'old opinion'. This was not because they denied the equality of cause and effect. They affirmed this as energetically as the Leibnizians, and it would have been equally inconceivable to them that 'force' could be created or destroyed in an impact. Instead they adopted the approach used by Wallis, and accommodated the phenomenon of inelastic impacts by conceiving of 'force' as a *vector* quantity, at least insofar as it was transmitted in impact. The effect of the annihilation of a certain 'motive force' in an impact was for them the production of an equal amount of 'force' *in the same direction.* Thus, the fact that two bodies do not rebound in an impact was argued not to imply an inequality of cause and effect. For, considered as a vector quantity, mass times velocity *is* conserved in inelastic impacts (and, for that matter, in elastic impacts as well). And so they maintained that the quantity of motion which one body loses in an impact is always transferred to the other, and that that motion, continuing to act in the same direction, combines vectorially with the 'motive force' that the latter body originally had.

V TIME OR DISTANCE

I have argued that the *vis viva* controversy should be understood as focussed on the problem of impact. The set of common assumptions about how this problem should be dealt with, and the importance with which the participants viewed it, yield an explanation of what it was that made the continued debate possible. Now that the centrality of impact in the minds of those involved in the *vis viva* controversy has been established, we are also in a better position to understand that aspect of the controversy concerned with the behaviour of bodies in retarded and accelerated motion.

To a large extent the apparently futile question of whether it is the time or the distance for which a body is accelerated (or decelerated) which measures the 'force of motion' acquired (or lost), can be seen as focussing on the possible physical *mechanisms* by which such accelerations are produced. It was generally assumed that the uncovering of the details of such mechanisms would come to show whether uniformly accelerating bodies undergo equivalent physical actions during succeeding units of time, or over succeeding units of space. The former discovery would show 'force' to be proportional to mv, the latter that it was proportional to mv^2. Thus, given the general assumption that all action involved physical contact, the apparently empty question of whether time or distance measured force was transformed into a potentially substantial dispute about the properties of the physical mechanisms producing accelerations.

Consider first the arguments about gravity. The Leibnizians said that the height to which a body can elevate itself (which is proportional to its velocity squared) is the effect which measures its 'force'. Their opponents' response was that since gravity is uniform it takes away equal forces in equal times, and so it is the *time* of ascent (proportional to initial velocity) which measures 'force'. But to this the Leibnizians replied by simply denying that gravity acts uniformly in destroying 'force' (though of course they admitted it produced a uniform deceleration). Clarke himself, in the *Correspondence*, refers to Jacob Hermann, who

> in his *Phoronomia* (arguing for Mr. Leibniz against those who hold that the forces acquired by falling bodies are proportional to the times of falling) represents that this is founded on a false supposition, that bodies thrown upwards receive from the gravity which resists them, an equal number of impulses in equal times. Which is as much as to say, that gravity is not uniform; . . . I suppose, he means that the swifter the motion of bodies is upwards, the more numerous are the impulses; because the bodies meet the (imaginary) gravitating particles. [A 124]

This argument, attributed to Hermann by Clarke, was extremely common. A body ascending against gravity would meet more particles when it was moving faster, at the beginning of its ascent. So, since it is progressively being subject to fewer impacts per unit time, it must lose decreasing amounts of 'force' per unit time in its ascent–which, by the laws of free fall, supported the measure of mv^2, rather than mv.

A closely analogous debate took place in connection with the decelerations of heavy bodies dropped into some such substance as clay.[17] William 'sGravesande showed experimentally that the volume of the cavity made by a heavy body of given shape dropped into clay is proportional to its mv^2. This was held to support the Leibnizian measure of force (cause must equal effect). But it was objected, in particular by the Swiss mathematician, Calandrin, that in general the resistance of the clay would be uniform, and that therefore it would consume equal 'forces' in equal times: from which it followed that

> the times during which two forces act on tenacious material until these forces are destroyed will always be proportional to these forces.

'sGravesande was equal to this. He granted the uniformity of the resistance (or 'pressure'). But since the 'effort of a pressure' depends on both 'the pressure *and* the speed of the points or surfaces being struck', more 'force' is taken away at first than later, and the total 'force' consumed is proportional to the distance. ('sGravesande argued that: 'force consumed' in time dt = pressure × velocity × dt. And so, by integrating, he concluded that: 'total force consumed' = pressure × distance.) 'sGravesande's argument here can be seen to be essentially the same as that used by other Leibnizians in connection with gravity.

The Leibnizian view received further support from experiments involving dropping weights onto layers of tissue paper. The number of tissues broken was proportional to mv^2. Again the Leibnizians argued that since each tissue must remove an equal amount of 'force', it must be mv^2 which measures force. But even to this the Leibnizians' opponents could find an answer. Thus, J. J. de Mairan, arguing for the 'old opinion', in 1728, admits that a uniformly retarded body 'meets more obstacles' or 'received more impressions' per unit time at the beginning of its retardation, when it is moving faster, than at the end. But, nevertheless, he argues, the 'force' lost per unit time is constant:

> the reason is, that the contrary impulsions, the resistances, or if one wishes, the contrary forces, act against those which surmount them, and which they consume, so much the more or so much the less . . . according as they are applied to them for a longer or shorter time.

That is, Mairan suggests that although a faster moving body 'meets more obstacles' than a slower, this is compensated for by the fact the obstacles have less time to act on a faster moving body.[18] This response to the Leibnizian analysis became general amongst proponents of the 'old opinion', including the English Newtonians.

[17] This debate is described in some detail in T. Hankins, 'Eighteenth-Century Attempts to Resolve the *Vis Viva* Controversy', 288–91.

[18] J. J. de Mairan. 'Dissertation sur l'Estimation et le Mesure des Forces Motrices des Corps', *Histoire de l'Academie des Sciences* (1728), sect. 32.

In the end, of course, the hope of establishing satisfactory detailed mechanistic models for the production of uniform accelerations was frustrated. In particular gravity was a problem. For, unlike clay, gravity does not only decelerate bodies moving against it, but also accelerates bodies moving 'with' it. Impact models of gravity were impotent to explain this. Bernoulli to some extent circumvented this difficulty in his *Discours*, by likening gravity to an 'elastic matter which extends vertically to infinity' (and arguing for mv^2 *via* his lemma that springs produce forces proportionally to the distance through which they act). But even this more promising reduction of gravitation to action by physical contact had nothing to say about why gravity accelerates large masses as much as small ones. (Bernoulli ignored this problem.)

In the absence of any agreed conclusions about the mechanisms behind uniform accelerations the 'time or distance' argument inevitably tended to end up going round in circles. But we have seen that this aspect of the *vis viva* controversy was at least something more than just a muddle about the equations of uniformly accelerated motion. As long as there remained the metaphysical conviction that all changes of motion must be explicable in mechanistic terms, it was perfectly coherent to discuss whether those mechanisms acted uniformly over time, or over space.

VI SUMMARY AND CONCLUSIONS

According to the system constructed by Descartes, all changes of motion were to be explained as due to contact between matter in relative motion. Any changes resulting from such contact involved the transference of 'force' from one body to another, in such a way that the total amount of 'force' would be conserved. The measure of a body's 'force' was given by the product of its mass by its speed, taken as a scalar quantity. Exactly how 'force' gets transferred in an impact depended on whether the 'force' of one body can overcome the 'resistance' of the other.

Once Descartes had proposed his theory, some compelling arguments were formulated which showed that there are impacts in which mass times speed is not conserved, and this was confirmed by experimental evidence. This constituted a serious anomaly for the Cartesian framework. There were essentially two alternative proposals as to how the framework should be revised.

On the one hand Leibniz and his followers suggested replacing Descartes' measure of 'force' by the quantity mass times velocity squared. In support of this they developed a theory of 'living' and 'dead forces' which enabled them to explain exactly how 'force' is transferred in elastic impacts (and which also enabled them to give a satisfactory analysis of the simple machines).

The 'Newtonians' and Cartesians, on the other hand, proposed that mass times velocity, considered as a vector quantity, should be taken as the measure of the 'force' of a body in motion. This enabled them, too, to derive equations of impact. Though their views on the nature of matter were less articulated than the Leibnizians', they were not restricted to considering elastic bodies only.

Common to both the Leibnizians and their opponents was the basic structure of the original framework put forward by Descartes. For they all accepted that, whatever the measure of 'force', it had to be the case that any 'force' lost by one body in an impact would be gained by the other. This basic agreement meant, firstly, that there was a perfectly real conflict between the two positions in the *vis viva* controversy: for, in that there was agreement on the fundamental structure of the concept of 'force', all the participants in the controversy were committed to establishing which was the best amongst the alternative proposals for elaborating that structure. And, at the same time, this agreement meant that there was a stock of common premisses which could be used in arguments between the two sides.

The long persistence of the dispute presents no problem for the approach adopted here. It was due to no confusion, or lack of objectivity. It was simply that two alternative modifications of the Cartesian theory of impact were proposed when the latter was seen to be inadequate. Both these alternatives merited consideration, and time was needed for their implications and possible refinements to be explored and evaluated.

Whether there would eventually have been an agreed conclusion to the debate must remain an unanswered question. For, as we have seen, the *vis viva* controversy closed, not with the victory of one side, but with a fundamental revision of physical thought resulting in the repudiation of both.

X

LEIBNIZ'S LAST CONTROVERSY WITH THE NEWTONIANS

C. D. BROAD

IN this paper I shall give a critical account of the famous series of controversial letters which Leibniz exchanged at the end of his life with Dr. Samuel Clarke [GP vii. 352–440: A 11–125]. In this correspondence Clarke is the very able representative of Newton and the Newtonians, and Leibniz is engaged in controverting certain fundamental points in the Newtonian philosophy of nature. The central subject under discussion in these letters is the nature of Space and Time. Newton, as is well known, held a form of the Absolute Theory of Space and Time. This was because he thought that certain dynamical phenomena both enable and compel us to distinguish between absolute and relative rotation in particular and between absolute and relative acceleration in general. He held that absolute rotation and acceleration entail absolute space and time. Leibniz rejected the Absolute Theory and was one of the first persons to state the alternative Relational Theory clearly. His main grounds for rejecting the Absolute Theory were that it conflicts, in his opinion, with two general philosophical principles which he set great store by, viz. the Principle of Sufficient Reason and the Identity of Indiscernibles.

Closely connected with this central topic are certain subsidiary questions. Is the material universe limited or unlimited in extension? Is the created world limited or unlimited in duration? Are there empty regions within the material world, or is it a plenum? On all these questions the Newtonians held certain views and Leibniz was opposed to them.

Much of the controversy is conducted in theological terms. This is partly adventitious; many of the questions which are stated and discussed in theological terminology are independent of it and could easily be translated into non-theological language. But this is not true of all of them. Both Leibniz and the Newtonians were convinced theists, who took the notion of God as creator and sustainer of the world seriously, and there are many assertions about God and his operations in Newton's *Principia*. Newton had thrown out the suggestion that Absolute Space might be the *sensorium* of God, i.e. roughly speaking the medium in

From *Theoria*, vol. 12 (1946), pp. 143–68. Reprinted, with some omission, by permission of the editor.

and through which God perceives created things. Leibniz attacks this bitterly and somewhat tediously as leading to consequences which are theologically unacceptable. But it develops into the more general and interesting question: 'How does God perceive material things; how do men perceive them; and how are the two modes of perception interrelated?' On these questions Leibniz held highly original and rather paradoxical views which Clarke could not accept. Again, to any theist the question: 'How are Space and Time related to God?' is of fundamental importance; and it is plain that, whatever the answer may be, it will be very different according as the Absolute or the Relational theory is presupposed.

Two other central questions in the correspondence are the Newtonian Theory of Attraction and what I shall describe by an intentionally vague expression as the 'Conservation or Non-Conservation of Active Force'. Newton's theory of gravitation as a not further explicable property of matter seemed to Leibniz radically unscientific; it was for him a betrayal of the hardly and recently won principle that all genuine explanation of natural phenomena must be in mechanical terms, and a reversion to the purely verbal explanations of the medieval scholastic philosophers. On the second question the Newtonians held that the created universe is automatically running down; whilst Leibniz, on metaphysical grounds, had formulated and asserted what we should now call the 'Conservation of Vis Viva', and thought that this disproved the Newtonian contention. The discussion of both these subjects led straightway to the theological topic of the nature of miracles, i.e. the distinction between the natural and super-natural action of God on the created world. Leibniz said that the only way to make sense of the Newtonian theory of attraction would be to suppose that, when one material particle is moving in the neighbourhood of another, God diverts the former from the straight line which it would otherwise traverse with uniform velocity in accordance with the Law of Inertia. This, he says, is to introduce a continual miracle into the ordinary course of nature. He also said that it is discreditable to the skill of God as maker of the world-machine to suppose that he needs every now and then to clean it and wind it up miraculously.

I think that this should suffice to give a general idea of the contents of the correspondence. I shall now state the Newtonian view of Space and Time, as it gradually emerges in Clarke's letters under the stimulus of Leibniz's criticisms. I suspect that it was much vaguer in many respects when it left Newton's hands than it became when Clarke had to defend it against a critic of Leibniz's ability.

(1) The first and most fundamental point is that Space is logically prior to matter, and Time is logically prior to events or processes. There

could not have been matter unless there had been Space for it to occupy and to rest or move in and Time for it to endure through. There could not have been events or processes unless there had been Time in which they have their dates and their durations. But there would have been Space, in precisely the same literal categorical sense, even if there had never been any matter; and there would have been Time, in precisely the same literal and categorical sense, even if there had never been any events or processes.

(2) We must distinguish between the space occupied by a body at any moment or for any period and the volume of that body; for the body could occupy different spaces at different times without changing its volume. The volume of a body is a property of it, but the space which it occupies at any time is not. Limited spaces are not properties of limited bodies, even if they happen to be occupied by such; they are just parts of the one unlimited Space in which these limited substances exist. Even if it were the case that the whole of infinite Space were continuously occupied by matter, still Space would not be a property of that infinite body. The infinite mass of matter would still merely be *in* Space as finite bodies are in it.

It is plain that Clarke takes a similar view, *mutatis mutandis*, about Time and events or processes in Time; though I think that he ought to have paid more attention to the fact that it is meaningless to suppose that an event or process should shift its position in Time as a body can shift its position in Space without change of volume or shape.

(3) Strictly speaking Space is indivisible. One can indeed talk of parts of Space, i.e. different regions actually or in imagination marked out by containing certain material objects or by being traced in pencil or ink. But the parts of Space are in principle inseparable. Two adjoined regions of Space are inseparable, not merely in the sense that there is no force in nature which could overcome their mutual adhesion. This would be the case with two adjoined parts of an old-fashioned extended solid atom. But two adjoined regions of Space are inseparable in the logical sense that it is *meaningless* to talk of any region coming to occupy a different position, and it is therefore *meaningless* to suggest that two regions which are adjoined might be separated. In the same way Space is in principle continuous. It is a contingent question whether there are or are not holes in matter; it is nonsensical to suggest that there might be holes in Space. Similar remarks apply, *mutatis mutandis*, to Time.

(4) Space is actually, and not just potentially, infinite. Of course neither Clarke nor Leibniz ever entertained the notion that the geometry of nature might be non-Euclidean and that straight lines might return

into themselves like the great-circles on a sphere. The same is true of Time; it had no beginning and will have no end.

(5) The points of Space and the moments of Time are not perceptible; only the things and events which occupy Space and Time can be perceived. But, since Time is quite independent of the events and processes which happen to occupy it, it is intelligible to suggest that the universe might have been created at an earlier or a later moment than that at which it was in fact created. Again, since Space is quite independent of the things and events which happen to occupy it, both the following suggestions are intelligible on the supposition that the material universe is of finite extent. (i) That without any difference in its internal structure it might *have been* created in a different region of Space. (ii) That it might *be* moved as a whole by God from one part of Space to another, or be given an absolute rotation about any direction of Space. If this rectilinear motion of the universe were accelerated or decelerated, or if the universe were subjected to an absolute rotation, these absolute motions would betray themselves by observable forces within the world. Otherwise they would remain unobservable.

(6) Absolute motion involves absolute Space and absolute Time; and the existence of absolute motion and its distinction from relative motion is evidenced by the existence of centrifugal forces, by the flattening of the earth at the poles, and so on. Clarke points out two consequences of the theory that all motion is relative which are certainly most paradoxical and which seem to him enough to refute the theory. One is that, if a body happened to be the only one that existed, it would be meaningless to suggest that it could either be at rest or in motion whether translatory or rotational. The other is that, if all the matter outside a rotating body, such as the earth, were annihilated, it would at once become meaningless to say that it was rotating; and therefore presumably all the observable effects which are attributed to the rotation of the earth would cease to happen.

(7) A region of Space or a stretch of time has an absolute magnitude, viz. volume in the one case and duration in the other. Different regions can be compared in respect of their volumes, and different stretches in respect of their duration.

(8) The last topic which must be discussed here is Clarke's account of what might be called the 'ontological status' of Absolute Space and Time. The following are the main points. (i) They are not substances, but attributes. (ii) They are attributes, not of any created substance, but of God himself. Absolute Space is that attribute of God which theologians call 'Immensity'; Absolute Time is that attribute of God which they call 'Eternity'. Clarke says, somewhat rashly in my opinion, that

no meaning can be attached to 'immensity' except space without bounds, and no meaning can be attached to 'eternity' except time without beginning or end. (iii) Absolute Space and Time are said to be, not only attributes of God, but also immediate and necessary consequences of his existence. Since they are attributes which follow necessarily from the existence of a Being whose existence is necessary, their ontological status is much more assured than that of any material thing or event. For the existence of the latter is contingent, depending as it does on the will of God to create it. (iv) God does not 'exist in' Space and Time in the sense in which created things and events do so. For Space and Time are logically prior to created things and events, and, if a certain region of Space happens to be occupied for a certain stretch of time by a certain thing or process, that is simply because God chose to create such a thing or process at a certain place and date. Obviously God is not 'in' Space and Time, which are his own attributes, in this special way. Nevertheless God is immediately present throughout the whole of unending time to every part of unbounded space. By this omnipresence he is continually aware of all created things and he acts upon them, but they do not react upon him.

I pass now to Leibniz's criticisms on the Newtonian theory of Space and Time and to the alternative Relational Theory of them which he upheld in its stead. I shall begin with an account of his two principles of Sufficient Reason and the Identity of Indiscernibles.

Leibniz distinguished sharply between necessary and contingent truths. A truth is necessary if and only if all the apparent alternatives to it are impossible because self-contradictory. Thus e.g. the proposition that the square-root of 2 is irrational is a necessary truth. For the supposition that there is a fraction m/n, in its lowest terms, such that $m^2=2n^2$ can be shown to be self-contradictory. A truth is contingent if and only if there are real alternatives to it which, though in fact false, are logically possible because internally consistent. Thus, e.g. it is a contingent singular truth that Julius Caesar decided to cross the Rubicon on a certain occasion, and it is a contingent general truth that the sine of the angle of incidence bears a constant ratio to the sine of the angle of refraction for light of a given wavelength travelling from a certain medium to a certain other.

It is clear that the Principle of Non-Contradiction is the guarantee of necessary truths, and it is equally clear that it is not the guarantee of contingent truths. Now Leibniz held that in the case of any contingent truth, there is always a sufficient reason why that proposition is true and why the logically possible alternatives to it are false. He also held that the ultimate reason for the truth of any true contingent proposition is always of the same kind. If we trace this doctrine backwards in the letters to Clarke, we find that it rests on the following two interconnected principles. (i) Every choice is determined by motives. (ii) Any being who is capable of choosing always chooses that alternative which seems to him at the time to be the most good or the least bad of those open to him. In comparing alternatives from this point of view he will consider, not only the intrinsic qualities of each, but also its relations to contemporary and past events and its future consequences. He will choose that one which seems to him to be most good or least bad on the whole when all these factors are taken into account.

Now these general principles of choice apply to God as well as to created intelligent beings such as men or angels. But there are certain important differences between God and any created being in this matter. God is fully aware of all the possible alternatives, and can see all the relationships and foresee all the consequences of each. But a created being is always limited in the extent of his knowledge and is always liable to have mistaken beliefs about matters of fact. Moreover what seems best on the whole to God is always what is really best on the whole. But a creature is always liable to be biased by passion or impulse, so that what seems best to him may not really be so even if he makes no mistakes or omissions about matters of fact.

Now the ultimate reason for the truth of any true contingent proposition is this. God foresaw that a world in which this proposition would be true would on the whole contain more good or less evil than any possible alternative world in which it would be false. He therefore chose to create a world in which this proposition would be true, and to leave uncreated all the equally possible worlds in which this proposition would be false and one or other of the possible alternatives to it would have been true. What I have just been explaining is, I think, what Leibniz meant by the *Principle of Sufficient Reason*.

We come now to the other Principle, viz. the *Identity of Indiscernibles*. McTaggart used to say, rightly in my opinion, that a better name for the principle would be the *Dissimilarity of the Diverse*. Leibniz held that we can know for certain that there are not, never have been, and never will be two things in nature which are exactly alike. If there is numerical diversity, there is certainly some kind and degree of qualitative dissimilarity. He undoubtedly meant this much by the Identity of Indiscernibles. What is uncertain is whether he held that the very supposition that there might be two things exactly alike is self-contradictory and meaningless; or whether he held that, although it is not logically impossible that there should be two such things, we can be quite sure that God would not create them. As Clarke pointed out, Leibniz seems now to say the one thing and now the other. In his Fourth Letter, e.g. he says that 'to suppose two indiscernible things is to suppose the *same* thing under two names' [GP vii. 372: A 37]. This certainly suggests that he held that the supposition, if taken literally, is self-contradictory and meaningless. But elsewhere in this Letter, and still more explicitly in the Fifth, he seems to take the other view. For instance, in the Fifth Letter he says that he does *not* maintain that it is absolutely impossible to suppose that there are two bodies which are indiscernible from each other, but only that it would be *contrary to God's wisdom* to create two such bodies and therefore we can be certain that there are not two such.

I think that there are two things to be said about this apparent inconsistency. (i) Plainly there is a sense in which it is possible to make and to argue correctly and intelligibly from a supposition which is, in another sense, impossible. That is precisely what happens, e.g. when one proves by a *reductio ad absurdum* that there cannot be a rational fraction in its lowest terms whose square is equal to 2. (ii) Leibniz might merely be making a concession, for the sake of argument, to his opponent. His position might, perhaps, be expressed as follows: 'I can see that the supposition that there are two things exactly alike is self-contradictory; but, even if you will not grant me this, I can show from the Principle of Sufficient Reason that God never would create two such things and therefore that the supposition will always be false'.

We can now pass from the statement of Leibniz's two philosophical principles to the use which he makes of them in attacking the Newtonian doctrine of Absolute Space and Absolute Time. We will consider first his attempt to prove from the Principle of Sufficient Reason that there are not, never have been, and never will be two precisely similar material particles. The argument may be put as follows.

Suppose, if possible, that there are two coexisting material particles *A* and *B*, exactly alike in all their qualities and dispositional properties. They would have to be at different places. Suppose that *A* is at *P* and *B* at *Q*. For the present purpose it does not matter whether we assume the absolute or the relational theory of Space. If *P* and *Q* are points of Absolute Space there could be no possible reason for preferring to put *A* at *P* and *B* at *Q* rather than *B* at *P* and *A* at *Q*. But a similar consequence follows on the relational theory. In that case the point *P* is defined by certain spatial relations to a certain set of material particles chosen as a system of reference, and the point *Q* is defined by certain other spatial relations to the same set of material particles. Now, if the two particles *A* and *B* are precisely alike in all their qualities and dispositional properties, there can be no possible reason for preferring to put *A* into the former set of relations and *B* into the latter rather than doing the opposite with them. If, then, God were to create two such particles, he would (i) be bound to put them in different places, and yet (ii) would have no reason for choosing between the two alternatives which would arise by imagining the two particles transposed. Since God never acts without a sufficient reason, we can conclude that he never will create two precisely similar coexisting particles and therefore that there never will be two such particles.

The importance of this conclusion for the present purpose is the following. Leibniz used the Principle of Sufficient Reason as the basis of one of his main arguments against the theory of Absolute Space and Time. Suppose that the Absolute Theory of Space were true and that the material universe is of finite extent. Then it is intelligible to suggest that, without any difference in the mutual relations of various parts, the material universe as a whole might have been created by God in this, that, or another region of Absolute Space. But there could be no reason for preferring to create it in one region rather than in another. Therefore God would be faced with either (i) the alternative of not creating a material universe at all, or (ii) creating it in one or another of a number of alternative places between which he would have no possible ground for deciding. Since the material universe does in fact exist, we know that God has in fact created it. Since it is contrary to the nature of an intelligent being to make an unmotived choice, we can be sure that God was not really faced with the alternatives which would have confronted him if the Absolute Theory of Space had been true. Now, if the Relational Theory were true, these so-called alternative ways of placing the world would not be genuine possibilities; for there could be no space prior to the existence of matter. On that theory God creates space in creating and arranging matter. So, Leibniz concludes, we can reject the Absolute Theory and accept the Relational Theory of Space.

A very similar argument can be used against Absolute Time. On the Absolute Theory it is intelligible to suggest that God might have created the world, with exactly the same contents and exactly the same subsequent history, at an earlier or a later moment of absolute time than that at which he in fact created it. Yet he could have no possible reason for preferring one moment to another at which to start the created world. The argument then proceeds as before. On the Relational Theory of time these so-called alternatives do not exist; for time begins with the first event.

Now Clarke had answered by pointing out that God would be in precisely the same kind of difficulty on the Relational Theory if he created two exactly similar particles. And he assumed that Leibniz would admit that there might be, and in fact are, precisely similar particles, e.g. various atoms of the same substance. As we have seen, Leibniz's reaction was to accept Clarke's argument and to conclude that God would not create two precisely similar particles and therefore that the supposition that there are such particles may be rejected.

The logical position at this point is the following. Leibniz has tried to refute the Absolute Theory and support the Relational Theory by showing that a certain situation, which would conflict with the Principle of Sufficient Reason, *would* arise if the former theory were true and *could not* arise if the latter were true. Clarke counters this by saying that, if there are material particles which are precisely alike, a similar conflict with the Principle of Sufficient Reason will arise even on the Relational Theory; and concludes that Leibniz's argument cannot be decisive in favour of the latter. Leibniz counters this by accepting all Clarke's premisses except that there are precisely similar material particles, and concludes that God will never create such particles and that therefore there never will be such.

Clarke is not satisfied with this answer. He points out that a person might know that it would be better to actualize *one or other* of two alternatives A and A′ than to actualize *neither* of them, whilst at the same time he may see that it is a matter of complete indifference whether it should be A or A′ that is realized. On Leibniz's principle a person in this position will realize *neither*, simply because he has no reason to prefer one to the other, although he has a very good reason for preferring to realize *one or other* of them to realizing neither. Clarke says that in such a case of indifference a free agent chooses a certain one of the indifferent alternatives by a 'mere act of will' [GP vii. 359: A 20]. Leibniz answers that, if this were possible, which it is not, such motiveless choice would be indistinguishable from pure objective chance. I might remark that a man in this kind of situation would probably decide to associate the head of a coin with one of the alternatives and the tail with the other and to spin the coin and choose that alternative which was associated with the side that should fall uppermost. But this expedient would not be open to God; for he would know beforehand how the coin would fall, and so he would already be deciding on a certain alternative when he associated it with the face which he foresaw would fall uppermost.

I think that this part of Leibniz's argument might fairly be summarized as follows. Let us grant, for the sake of argument, that the Absolute Theory of Space and Time is in some sense an intelligible hypothesis and not just meaningless verbiage. If that theory were true the created universe could have occupied, without being in any way different internally, a different stretch of time or a different region of space. Now there would have been no possible reason for preferring to put it in one stretch of time or one region of space rather than another. Therefore God, who never makes a choice without a sufficient reason, would not have created a universe at all. But, since there is a universe, we know that he has created one. Therefore we can be certain that the Absolute Theory is false if it is not meaningless.

Like Clarke I find it hard to decide whether Leibniz would have gone further and said that the Absolute Theory is just meaningless verbiage. The following remarks in his Fifth Letter are typical. The supposition of the universe as a whole being moved is (i) meaningless, since there is no space outside it; and (ii) even if it were intelligible it would be pointless for 'there would happen no change which could be observed by any person whatever' [GP vii. 396: A 63–4]. He adds the following remark: 'Mere mathematicians, who are only taken up with the conceits of imagination are apt to forge such notions, but they are destroyed by superior reasons'. In the same letter he says that real change must be *in principle* observable. Motion need not be actually observed; but there is no motion where there is no change that *could be* observed, and there is no change where none *could be* observed.

All this has a very modern ring, and might have been said by any contemporary Logical Positivist. Nevertheless I do not feel quite sure how to interpret it. It seems to me that it is fairly susceptible of either of the following two interpretations. (i) The Absolute Theory, and various questions which arise in connection with it, are *intrinsically* meaningless; and so we must accept the Relational Theory. (ii) Even though the Absolute Theory be *not intrinsically* meaningless, and though these questions be intelligible in terms of it, yet we can reject it and accept the Relational Theory because of the argument founded on the Principle of Sufficient Reason. And *in terms of the Relational Theory* these questions *are* meaningless. I am inclined to suspect that Leibniz himself held the first view, but contented himself with the second for controversial purposes.

It is now convenient to give Leibniz's positive account of what is meant by 'Space' and 'Time'. He introduces this topic in the Fourth Letter and goes into considerable detail about Space in the Fifth. He does not discuss Time in similar detail; no doubt he thought, as so many writers on these topics have done, that what holds for Space can be applied automatically to Time. This is, in my opinion, a dangerous assumption, for the unlikenesses are at least as important as the likenesses.

According to Leibniz, Space is an order of coexistences and Time is an order of sequences. This seems to me plainly inadequate; for events may be contemporary as well as successive, and we can give no account of either rest or motion unless we conceive of identity of place at different times as well as difference of place at the same time. However, Leibniz is fully aware of the latter point and deals explicitly with it in the full account of Space which he gives in the Fifth Letter. This may be summarized as follows.

Suppose that certain bodies, *X, Y, Z* . . ., etc., do not change their mutual spatial relations during a certain interval. Suppose further that, if there is a change during this interval in their spatial relations to certain other bodies, then the cause of it has not been in themselves. Then we say that the bodies *X, Y, Z* . . ., etc., have constituted a 'rigid fixed system' during the interval in question. Suppose that, at some moment within this period, a certain body *A* stood in certain spatial relations to the bodies of this system; that at a later moment within the period it ceased to stand in those relations to them; and that at some later moment within a period a certain other body *B* began to stand to those bodies in precisely similar relations to those in which *A* had formerly stood. Then we can say that '*B* had come to *occupy the same place as A* formerly occupied'. If and only if the causes of these changes of relative position have been in *A* and in *B*, we can say that *A* and *B* have 'been in motion'.

Leibniz then defines 'a place' in terms of the relation of 'occupying the same place', and he defines 'space' as the collection of all places. He makes several interesting comments on this procedure.

(1) He remarks that, in making the notion of sameness of place primary and defining 'place' in terms of it, he follows the procedure of Euclid who starts by defining the statement that *A* has *the same ratio* to *B* as *C* has to *D* and does not begin by defining 'ratio'.

(2) He remarks that, if *B* occupies the same place as *A* did, we must not say that the present relation of *B* to the system of reference is *the same* as the previous relation of *A* to that system. Two different things cannot literally stand in the same relationship. We must say that the relationships are precisely alike. He then adds the following remark. 'The mind, not contented with an agreement, looks for an identity—for something that should be truly the same; and conceives it as being extrinsic to the subject; and this is what we here call 'place' and 'space'. But this can only be an ideal thing; containing a certain *order* wherein the mind conceives the application of relations.' [GP vii. 401: A 70]

The upshot of the matter is this. Speaking in the terminology of contemporary Cambridge logicians we may say that Leibniz regards Space as a logical construction out of places, and regards a place as a logical construction out of facts about relative spatial position. And he holds that the notion of Absolute Space and absolute places is a fallacy of misplaced concreteness. The *word* 'Space' is a substantive and occurs as the grammatical subject of such sentences as 'Space is three-dimensional'. This suggests that it is, like the word 'Cambridge', the proper name of a particular existent, though one of a peculiar kind. But, according to Leibniz, this suggestion is misleading.

It will be noticed that, in defining 'sameness of place at different times', Leibniz has had to introduce the condition that the system of reference shall not have moved during the interval. It will also be noticed that he gives a causal criterion for judging whether a body or system of bodies which has changed its relative position shall be said to have moved or not. The criterion is whether the cause of the change of relative position is or is not in the body itself. He uses this criterion in order to answer Newton's empirical arguments for absolute rotation based on the existence of centrifugal forces. In reference to this argument he says that there is nothing in it that proves the reality of Absolute Space. There is a difference, even on the Relational Theory, between what he calls 'an absolute true motion of a body' and what he calls 'mere relative change of its situation with respect to another body' [GP vii. 404: A 74]. But this difference, he says, consists in whether 'the immediate cause' of the change of relative position 'is in the body itself' or not. I take it that his view is that centrifugal forces are connected with 'absolute true motions' thus defined.

It seems to me that a prima facie objection to this criterion is that, according to the First Law of Motion, the cause of an accelerated or a curvilinear motion of a body never is in that body itself. Leibniz would not have accepted this objection because he had a general metaphysical principle that all the changes in any substance are caused by its own previous states, and that the appearance of interaction between different substances is delusive. He attempts to construct a system of dynamics in accordance with that principle, but it would take us outside our present limits to discuss it.

We can now pass to another point in the controversy. Clarke in his Third Letter said that space and time are magnitudes, whilst order and situation are not, and he made this an objection to the relational theory. He reiterates this objection in his Fourth Letter and complains that Leibniz has made no attempt to answer it. Leibniz deals with the objection in his Fifth Letter. He says there that relations can have magnitude. The examples which he gives are ratios between numbers. E.g. the ratio of 28 to 7 is equal to the ratio of 16 to 4 and is greater than that of 15 to 5. Now ratios are relations, and any pair of terms of which it is intelligible to say that one is equal to, greater than, or less than another is a magnitude. He adds that the magnitudes of ratios are measured by their logarithms. I suppose that this is because, if the ratio of x to y is l and that of y to z is m and that of x to z is n, then $\log l + \log m = \log n$. Clarke answers that ratios are not magnitudes because they are not additive. I think that the point is that $x/y + y/z$ is not in general equal to x/z. He considers the reference to the additive property of logarithms irrelevant. And, in any case, he says, time and space are not of the nature of ratios. They are absolute magnitudes which have ratios among themselves.

It seems to me that the questions at issue are confused by Leibniz's reference to the example of ratios in arithmetic. Presumably the fundamental relations on the Relational Theory are (i) the relation of *distance* between two material particles, and (ii) that of *angular divergence* between the lines joining one pair of material particles and another pair. I see no objection to saying that these are magnitudes. In certain special cases, viz. if three particles x, y, and z are collinear and y is between x and z, the distance between x and z is the sum of the distances between x and y and between y and z. But in general the relationship is more complex. Similar remarks, *mutatis mutandis*, apply to angular divergence between lines. So far Leibniz seems to be in the right. On the other hand, we have also to consider area and volume; and Clarke seems to be right in calling these absolute magnitudes which have ratios among themselves. But I do not think that this would be any reason for accepting the Absolute Theory of Space and rejecting the Relational Theory, though it might show that the Relational Theory needs certain supplements.

The next point that I shall consider is the question of the finitude or infinitude of the material world in space and of whether it is a plenum or contains empty regions within it. The Newtonians held that the material world is of finite extent and that outside it there is a boundless expanse of Absolute Space. They also held that within the universe there are regions of Absolute Space which contain no matter. Leibniz denied both these propositions. According to him the material universe continuously occupies an unlimited expanse.

The details of the controversy are rather tedious, so I shall try to state briefly in my own way what I believe to be the facts of the case. (1) The only alternatives among those just mentioned which would have a meaning on the Absolute Theory (assuming that the theory is itself intelligible) and would be meaningless on the Relational Theory are the following. (i) That the universe as a whole should rotate or not rotate about an axis. (ii) That, if the universe be finite in extent, it should as a whole either have a motion of translation or be translationally at rest.

(2) On the Relational Theory it is prima facie intelligible that the universe should be either finite or infinite in extent. The former alternative would mean that, if you take the distance between any two particles P and Q as your unit, then there is a finite integer N such that the distance between any two particles in the universe is less than N times

the distance between *P* and *Q*. The latter alternative would mean that, if you take the distance between any two particles *P* and *Q* as your unit and measure in any direction from any assigned particle *O*, then, whatever finite integer *N* may be, there is always a particle in that direction at a greater distance from *O* than *N* times the distance between *P* and *Q*. (I call this prima facie intelligible, because it involves no internal contradiction. Whether this kind of actual infinity be not unintelligible in some *other* important sense is a question which I cannot discuss here.)

(3) If the universe is of finite extent, it is intelligible on the Relational Theory to say (i) that it *might have been* bigger or smaller at a given moment than it in fact was then, and (ii) that it might *become* bigger or smaller in future than it now is. For this means simply that the finite integer *N*, mentioned above in the definition of the finitude of the universe, might have been bigger or smaller than it in fact was or might become bigger or smaller than it now is.

(4) On the Relational Theory it is equally intelligible to suggest that matter is continuous or that there are holes in it. We could define an 'empty linear segment' as a pair of particles *P* and *Q* such that there was no particle between them. Having done this we should have no difficulty in principle, though there would be considerable difficulties in detail, in defining an 'empty area' and an 'empty volume'.

It seems to me then that there is no close logical connection between the controversy about Absolute and Relative Space, on the one hand, and these controversies about the finite or infinite extent of the universe and the existence or non-existence of empty spaces within it, on the other. In the end Leibniz says explicitly that he does not maintain either that God *could not* have limited the quantity of matter or that he *certainly has not* done so. He asserts only that it is *very unlikely* that a perfectly wise and benevolent creator would have done so. This is his position in the latter part of the Fifth Letter. But earlier in the same letter he uses phrases which suggest that the Relational Theory suffices to settle the question in favour of the infinity and continuity of matter. He says: 'Since space in itself is an ideal thing . . . space outside the world must needs be imaginary. . . . The case is the same with empty space within the world, which I take also to be imaginary . . .'. [GP vii. 396: A 64] Immediately after this passage he goes on to discuss the allegation that Guericke of Magdeburg had produced a vacuum in the receiver of his air-pump.

If Leibniz meant merely that, on the Relational Theory, spaces does not exist, in the sense in which the Newtonians thought it did, either outside the material universe, if that be finite, or inside the receiver of an air-pump, he was no doubt right. But, if he thought that this has any tendency to prove that the material universe cannot be finite in extent and cannot have empty holes in it, he was, as I hope I have shown, quite mistaken.

I have now stated the arguments which Leibniz used and the conclusions which he drew in his *Letters to Clarke* about the absolute and relational theories of Space and Time. But it is important to remember that this controversy is conducted at what Leibniz would regard as an intermediate level of philosophical rigour and thoroughness. It is indeed a philosophical, and not merely a physical, discussion. But in it Leibniz is granting for the sake of argument certain assumptions which he would claim to have refuted in his more elaborate and professional philosophical writings. He is granting here the reality of extended substances and of spatial relations between them, but in fact he believes himself to have shown that the notion of an extended substance involves a contradiction, and that there can be no relations between substances. According to his considered opinion, what we misperceive as an endlessly divisible extended material thing is really a collection of an infinite number of unextended mental substances, and what we misperceive as a relation between two things is really certain qualities in the things which we misperceive as interrelated. I shall end this paper by showing that, at this deeper level, Leibniz's view is in an important sense a form of the absolute theory.

In order to do this I must first explain a distinction which was originally pointed out by the Cambridge philosopher, W. E. Johnson, in his *Logic* [(Cambridge, 1921–24), Part 2, chap. 7, sect. 7]. I shall put it in my own way. In controversies about the absolute *versus* the relational theory of space and time there are two questions to be distinguished: (1) Is position a pure quality or a relational property? (2) Does position belong to material particles *directly*; or does it belong primarily to particulars of another kind, viz. points of space, and only in a derivative sense to material particles in virtue of their occupation of points of space? The first question may properly be put in the form: 'Is spatial position qualitative or relational?' The second may properly be put in the form: 'Is space adjectival or substantival in character?' Johnson pointed out, quite rightly, in my opinion, that these two questions were never clearly distinguished by protagonists in the controversy about 'absolute' *versus* 'relative' space.

We can begin by dividing possible theories into (1) Substantival, and (2) Adjectival. The essential features of all forms of the Substantival Theory are the following. There are particulars which together constitute a single complex particular, viz. Space. These and only these have spatial characteristics in the primary and underived sense. And each of them has timelessly or sempiternally all the spatial qualities and relational properties that it has. It is meaningless to talk of a point of Space, in this sense, changing its position; or of a volume of Space, in this sense, changing its size or shape. Now, besides Space and its regions or points, there are material things or particles. Each material particle at any moment occupies a certain point of Space, and each body at any moment occupies a certain region of Space. At different moments the same material particle or body may occupy the same or different points or regions of Space. The statement that a certain body has at a certain moment a certain position, shape, size, etc., is always derivative and analysable. It means that at this moment that body occupies a region of space which timelessly or sempiternally has a certain position, shape, size, etc. A body can change in respect of its spatial characteristics because (i) it can occupy different regions of Space at different times, and (ii) these regions must differ timelessly or sempiternally in position and may differ timelessly or sempiternally in shape and size.

The essential features of all forms of the Adjectival Theory are the following. The only subjects of spatial characteristics are material particles or bodies. There is not another kind of particular existent called 'Space' beside matter. The spatial characteristics which a material particle or a body has at any moment belong to it in a primary and underived sense. So there are no timeless or sempiternal spatial characteristics. A body may happen to keep the same position, shape, and size for a long time, or it may happen to change quickly and continuously in respect of some or all of these characteristics. But there can be no question of analysing such a change into a relation of occupance to a series of terms of an entirely different kind, each of which has all its spatial characteristics timelessly or sempiternally.

I think there is no doubt that the Newtonians held, and that Leibniz rejected at all levels of his thinking, the *substantival* theory of Space and Time.

We can now consider the other pair of opposites, viz. (1) Qualitative and (2) Relational, theories. We will confine ourselves here to the characteristic of spatial position, and not consider shape or size. I think that the Qualitative Theory may be put most clearly as follows. There is a certain determinable quality, which we will call 'Spatial Position'. We might compare this to the determinable Sound-quality. The determinates under it form a continuous three-dimensional manifold of qualities. These may be compared (though the analogy must not be pressed in detail) with the manifold of determinate sound-qualities which can be arranged in respect of pitch, loudness, and timbre. Any two particulars which have simultaneously two different determinate forms of the determinable quality of Spatial Position will *ipso facto* stand to each other in certain determinate relation of distance, direction, etc. This may be compared with the fact that any two sounds which have simultaneously two different determinate forms of the determinable Sound-quality will *ipso facto* stand to each other in certain relations of harmony or disharmony of relative loudness, and so on. Thus spatial relations are *founded upon* the determinate positional qualities of the related terms; just as musical relationships are founded upon the determinate sound-qualities of the notes struck.

The essential features of the Relational Theory are the following. There is no *quality* of spatial position. The fundamental positional characteristics of any terms are its *relations* of distance and direction to other terms. These relations are not founded upon qualities in the related terms, as the musical relations between notes are founded upon their determinate sound-qualities. To say that a certain particular has a certain position is simply to state its relations of distance and direction to certain other particulars of the same kind chosen arbitrarily as terms of reference.

Now it would be possible theoretically to combine either the Substantival or the Adjectival theory with either the Qualitative or the Relational theory. But in fact the usual combinations have been Substantival Qualitative and Adjectival Relational. I think there is little doubt that the Newtonians held a form of the Substantival Qualitative theory, and it is certain that Leibniz in the letters to Clarke is asserting a form of the Adjectival Relational theory.

But this is not the theory that Leibniz really held. What he really held, when he was not arguing *ad hominem* against Clarke and the Newtonians, was a form of Adjectival Qualitative theory. That this must be so is obvious in view of his general principle that what we take to be relations between terms are really qualities in the terms which we partially misperceive. But we need not confine ourselves to such general considerations; for Leibniz has told us explicitly what is the determinable quality, present in some determinate form in every monad at every moment, which is the basis of the appearance of spatial relations. It is what he calls 'Point of View'. It is true that he would not allow us to identify point of view with the quality of spatial position; but point of view is a quality, and every difference in the apparent spatial position of apparently extended objects is correlated with a real difference in the point of view of the monads which we misperceive as those extended objects.

Suppose that we were to drop the distinction between the quality of Point of View and the quality of Spatial Position, and to speak wholly in terms of the latter. Then the Adjectival Qualitative theory of spatial position could be formulated as follows. There is a determinable quality of Spatial Position, and under it there is a three-dimensional manifold of determinate positional qualities. At each moment each material particle has one and only one of these. At two different moments the same material particle may have the same or different determinate positional qualities. At any moment any two material particles will stand in a determinate relation of relative position, which is founded upon the determinate positional qualities possessed at the moment by each of them. Absolute motion of a particle consists in its having, at each of a continuous series of moments, a different one of a continuous series of positional qualities. Relative motion of one material particle with respect to another entails that at least one of them is in absolute motion; but the same relative motion could arise in connection with very different absolute motions of the two particles concerned. It seems to me that this is the kind of view of space and motion which we ought to ascribe to Leibniz when we dig beneath the position which he occupies in his controversy with Clarke.

NOTES ON THE CONTRIBUTORS

JOHN W. NASON is President Emeritus, Carleton College, Minnesota. Besides articles on Leibniz and on religion his publications include *American Higher Education in 1980* (1965), *The Future of Trusteeship* (1975), *Trustees and the Future of Foundations* (1977).

WILFRID SELLARS is Professor of Philosophy at the University of Pittsburgh. Besides many articles on the theory of knowledge, philosophy of science, and the history of philosophy, he has published *Science, Perception, and Reality* (1963), *Philosophical Perspectives* (1967), *Science and Metaphysics* (1968), *Essays in Philosophy and its History* (1974).

DENNIS FRIED has taught at the University of Kentucky and is at present at the Curtron Technical Institute, New York State. His research interests are in the history of modern philosophy, and in ethics.

HIDÉ ISHIGURO is Reader in Philosophy at University College, London. Besides *Leibniz's Theory of Logic and Language* (1972) she has published a number of articles on philosophy of mind, philosophy of logic, and metaphysics.

DAVID BLUMENFELD is McManis Professor of Moral Philosophy at Southwestern University, Texas. He has published on ethics and the history of modern philosophy.

FRED D'AGOSTINO is Research Fellow at The Australian National University. He has published on methodological individualism, philosophy of linguistics, and methodology of mathematical linguistics.

L. J. RUSSELL, who died in 1971, was Professor of Philosophy at the University of Birmingham. Besides being the author of a number of important articles on Leibniz he wrote *An Introduction to Logic* (1914), and *An Introduction to Philosophy* (1929).

MARGARET D. WILSON is Associate Professor of Philosophy at Princeton University. She has published a number of articles on seventeenth-century philosophy, and *Descartes* (1978).

DAVID PAPINEAU is an assistant lecturer in the History and Philosophy of Science at the University of Cambridge. He has published *For Science in the Social Sciences* (1978), and *Theory and Meaning* (1979).

C. D. BROAD, who died in 1971, was Knightbridge Professor of Moral Philosophy at the University of Cambridge. He published many articles and books including *Scientific Thought* (1923), *Five Types of Ethical Theory* (1930), *An Examination of McTaggart's Philosophy* (1933–8), *Lectures on Psychical Research* (1962), and *Leibniz: An Introduction* (1975).

BIBLIOGRAPHY OF FURTHER READING

Below are details of the further reading referred to in the Introduction as being especially recommended in connection with the topics and questions raised there. There are complete bibliographies of the secondary literature on Leibniz in Kurt Müller's *Leibniz-Bibliographie: Verzeichnis der Literatur über Leibniz* (Frankfurt, 1967) and at yearly intervals in the journal *Studia Leibnitiana* (1969–). I have purposely tended not to refer to books in the Introduction; but included below are a number of these which are always worth consulting in the hope that they have something to say on the topic in hand. As introductions the best are Broad's and then either of Rescher's. At a more advanced level are Russell's classic and Parkinson's superbly documented and careful work. Ishiguro's book is narrower in scope than these, and Buchdahl's has just one, though lengthy, chapter on Leibniz; but they are always interesting and useful on the topics they cover.

(1) Abraham, W. E., 'Complete concepts and Leibniz's distinction between necessary and contingent propositions', *Studia Leibnitiana*, 1 (1969).

(2) Adams, R. M., 'Theories of actuality', *Nous*, 8 (1974).

(3) — 'Leibniz's theories of contingency', *Essays on the Philosophy of Leibniz*, ed. Mark Kulstad (Houston, Texas, 1977).

(4) Beck, Lewis White, *Early German Philosophy: Kant and his predecessors* (Cambridge, Mass., 1969).

(5) Blumenfeld, David, 'Leibniz's modal proof of the possibility of God', *Studia Leibnitiana*, 4 (1972).

(6) — 'Leibniz's proof of the uniqueness of God', *Studia Leibnitiana*, 6 (1974).

(7) — 'Is the best possible world possible?', *Philosophical Review*, 84 (1975).

(8) Broad, C. D., 'Leibniz's *predicate-in-notion principle* and some of its alleged consequences', *Leibniz*, ed. Harry G. Frankfurt (New York, 1972).

(9) — *Leibniz: An Introduction* (Cambridge, 1975).

(10) Brody, Baruch, 'Leibniz's metaphysical logic', *Essays on the Philosophy of Leibniz*, ed. Mark Kulstad (Houston, Texas, 1977).

(11) Buchdahl, Gerd, *Metaphysics and the Philosophy of Science* (Oxford, 1969).

(12) Clatterbaugh, Kenneth C., *Leibniz's doctrine of individual accidents* (Wiesbaden, 1973).

(13) Copp, David, 'Leibniz's thesis that not all possibles are compossible', *Studia Leibnitiana*, 5 (1973).

(14) Curley, E. M., 'The root of contingency', *Leibniz*, ed. Harry G. Frankfurt (New York, 1972).

(15) Davis, John W., 'Leibniz and King', *Proceedings of the Second International Leibniz Congress, 1972*, (Wiesbaden, 1975), vol. iii.

(16) Dewey, John, *Early Essays and Leibniz's New Essays* (Carbonville, Ill., 1969).
(17) Earman, John, 'Perceptions and relations in the Monadology', *Studia Leibnitiana*, 9 (1977).
(18) Fitsch, Gregory, 'Analyticity and necessity in Leibniz', *Journal of the History of Philosophy*, 17 (1979).
(19) Furth, Montgomery, 'Monadology', *Leibniz*, ed. Harry G. Frankfurt (New York, 1972).
(20) Gale, George, 'Did Leibniz have a practical philosophy of science?', *Proceedings of the Second International Leibniz Congress, 1972*, (Wiesbaden, 1974), vol. ii.
(21) — 'Leibniz's dynamical metaphysics and the origins of the *vis viva* controversy', *Systematics*, 11 (1973).
(22) — 'On what God chose: Perfection and God's freedom', *Studia Leibnitiana*, 8 (1976).
(23) Gotterbarn, Donald, 'Leibniz's completion of Descartes's proof', *Studia Leibnitiana*, 8 (1976).
(24) Grimm, Robert, 'Individual concepts and contingent truths', *Studia Leibnitiana*, 2 (1970).
(25) Hacking, Ian, 'Individual substance', *Leibniz*, ed. Harry G. Frankfurt (New York, 1972).
(26) — 'The identity of indiscernibles', *Journal of Philosophy*, 72 (1975).
(27) Harris, John, 'Leibniz and Locke on innate ideas', *Locke on Human Understanding*, ed. I. C. Tipton (Oxford, 1977).
(28) Hintikka, Jaakko, 'Leibniz on plenitude, relations, and the "reign of law"', *Leibniz*, ed. Harry G. Frankfurt (New York, 1972).
(29) Hosler, John, 'Some remarks on *omne exigit existere*', *Studia Leibnitiana*, 5 (1973).
(30) Iltis, Carolyn, 'Leibniz and the *vis viva* controversy', *Isis*, 62 (1971).
(31) Ishiguro, Hidé, 'Leibniz's theory of the ideality of relations', *Leibniz*, ed. Harry G. Frankfurt (New York, 1972).
(32) — *Leibniz's Philosophy of Logic and Language* (London, 1972).
(33) — 'Pre-established harmony *versus* constant conjunction', *Proceedings of the British Academy*, 63 (1977).
(34) Jarrett, Charles E., 'Leibniz on truth and contingency', *New Essays on Rationalism and Empiricism*, ed. C. E. Jarrett, J. King-Farlow, F. J. Pelletier (Guelph, Ontario, 1978).
(35) Johnson, Oliver A., 'Human freedom in the best of all possible worlds', *Philosophical Quarterly*, 4 (1954).
(36) Kneale, W. C., 'The notion of a substance', *Procedings of the Aristotelian Society*, 40 (1939/40).
(37) Koyré, Alexandre, 'Leibniz and Newton', *Leibniz*, ed. Harry G. Frankfurt (New York, 1972).
(38) Lloyd, Genevieve, 'Leibniz on possible individuals and possible worlds', *Australian Journal of Philosophy*, 56 (1978).
(39) Lomansky, Loren E., 'Leibniz and the modal argument for God's existence', *Monist*, 54 (1970).
(40) McCullough, Laurence B., 'Leibniz on the identity of indiscernibles', *Southwestern Journal of Philosophy*, 8 (1977).
(41) McGuire, J. E., '*Labyrinthus continui*: Leibniz on substance, activity, and matter', *Motion and time, space and matter*, etc., ed. Peter K. Machamer, Robert G. Turnbull (Columbus, Ohio, 1976).

(42) Mates, Benson, 'Leibniz on possible worlds', *Leibniz*, ed. Harry G. Frankfurt (New York, 1972).
(43) Meijering, Theo T., 'On contingency in Leibniz's philosophy', *Studia Leibnitiana*, 10 (1978).
(44) Mondadori, Fabrizio, 'Reference, essentialism, and modality in Leibniz's metaphysics', *Studia Leibnitiana*, 5 (1973).
(45) Nason, John W., 'Leibniz's attack on the Cartesian doctrine of extension', *Journal of the History of Ideas*, 7 (1946).
(46) O'Connor, D. J., 'Substance and attribute', *Encyclopedia of Philosophy*, ed. Paul Edwards (London and New York, 1967).
(47) Parkinson, G. H. R., *Leibniz on Human Freedom* (Wiesbaden, 1970).
(48) — *Logic and Reality in Leibniz's Metaphysics*, (Oxford, 1965).
(49) Priestley, F. E. L., 'The Clarke–Leibniz controversy', *The Methodological Heritage of Newton*, ed. Robert E. Butts, John W. Davis (Oxford, 1970).
(50) Rescher, Nicholas, 'Contingence in the philosophy of Leibniz', *Philosophical Review*, 61 (1952).
(51) — *The Philosophy of Leibniz* (Englewood Cliffs, 1967).
(52) — *Leibniz: An Introduction to his Philosophy* (Oxford, 1979).
(53) Resnick, Lawrence, 'God and the best possible world', *American Philosophical Quarterly*, 10 (1973).
(54) Russell, Bertrand, *The Philosophy of Leibniz* (2nd ed. London, 1937).
(55) Russell, L. J., 'Leibniz's philosophy of science', *Studia Leibnitiana*, 8 (1976).
(56) — 'Leibniz', *Philosophy*, 11 (1936).
(57) — 'Leibniz', *Encyclopedia of Philosophy*, ed. Paul Edwards (London and New York 1967).
(58) Savile, Anthony, 'Leibniz's contribution to the theory of innate ideas', *Philosophy*, 47 (1972).
(50) Scarrow, David S., 'Reflections on the idealist interpretation of Leibniz's philosophy', *Proceedings of the second International Leibniz Congress, 1972* (Wiesbaden, 1973), vol. i.
(60) Spector, Marshall, 'Leibniz *versus* the Cartesians on motion and force', *Studia Leibnitiana*, 7 (1975).
(61) Stenius, Eric, 'On the system of Leibniz', *Ajatus*, 35 (1973).
(62) Tonelli, Giorgio, 'Leibniz on innate ideas and the early reactions to the publication of the Nouveaux Essais (1765)', *Journal of the History of Philosophy*, 12 (1974).
(63) Turck, Dieter, 'Leibniz's theory of the soul', *Southern Journal of Philosophy*, 12 (1974).
(64) van Fraassen, Bas, *An Introduction to the Philosophy of Time and Space* (New York, 1970).
(65) Vinci, Thomas C., 'What is the ground for the principle of the identity of indiscernibles in Leibniz's correspondence with Clarke?', *Journal of the History of Philosophy*, 12 (1974).
(66) von Leyden, Wolfgang, *Seventeenth-Century Metaphysics*, etc. (London, 1968).
(67) Wilson, Margaret D., 'On Leibniz's explication of "necessary truth"', *Leibniz*, ed. Harry G. Frankfurt (New York, 1972).
(68) Wilson, N. L., 'Individual identity, space, and time in the Leibniz–Clarke correspondence', *The Philosophy of Leibniz and the Modern World*, ed. I. Leclerc (Nashville, 1973).
(69) Woolhouse, R. S., 'Leibniz's principle of pre-determinate history', *Studia Leibnitiana*, 7 (1975).

(70) — '"The nature of an individual substance"' *Leibniz: Critical and Interpretive Essays,* ed. Michael Hooker (Minneapolis, forthcoming).

(71) Wrenn, Thomas E., 'Leibniz's theory of essences: some problems concerning their ontological status and their relation to God and the universal harmony', *Studia Leibnitiana*, 4 (1972).

INDEX OF NAMES

(not including those appearing only in the Bibliography)